"In this vivid and evocative memoir, moving from fear to hope, Ingrid Coles née Brandt tells the extraordinary story of an immigrant in New Zealand."
–*Rob Zaagman, Ambassador of the Kingdom of the Netherlands to New Zealand*

TWO SLICES OF BREAD.

A memoir by
INGRID COLES

Interned in a Japanese concentration camp — evacuated to the Netherlands, then finding peace at last... at the bottom of the world.

Written by Ingrid Coles
E: mark.coles@slingshot.co.nz
© 2018 Ingrid Coles

Published by
Wild Side Publishing
wildsidepublishing.com

This is a work of non-fiction.
The events are portrayed to the best of Ingrid Coles' memory. While all the stories in this book are true, some names and identifying details have been changed to protect the privacy of the people involved.

All rights reserved. No part of this book may be reproduced, stored in a retrieval system or transmitted in any form or by any means electronic, mechanical, photocopying, recording or otherwise without the prior written permission of the publisher.

The *MS Boissevain* photo on the back cover credit Björn Larsson, Maritime Timetable Images
www.timetableimages.com/maritime

Proofread by Lissa Weight
PinPoint Proofreading Ltd
lydiaweight@gmail.com

Cataloguing in Publication Data:
Title: Two Slices of Bread
ISBN: 978-0-473-42890-7 (pbk.)
ISBN: 978-0-473-42891-4 (ePub)
Subjects: Memoir, Autobiography, Christian, War Crimes, Japanese Concentration Camp, World War II

Other Contributors:
Brother, John Brandt. Sisters, Juliana Dominicus-Brandt and Penny Brandt. Piet Hofhuis, supplied photos of Sragi Sugar Factory, taken in 2016. The factory was still operating.
All respondents to Ingrid's advert in the Dutch War magazine, *Aanspraak* with information: Will Corput (NL), Hans van Vuuren (USA), Jeanette Brugman van de Nagel (NL), Bill Ellerbroek (NZ), Lies Hoogterp (NL), Miechiel Albricht (NL), Henk Beekhuis (NL), Rein Bertram (NL), Suze van der Kruk (NL), Hans van Leuven (AU), Reinold Disse (NZ), Piet H.F. Hofhuis (NL), Bert van Willigenburg (NL - Kalibanteng photos), Rob Escher for his help with the SEA battles in the Java Sea in early 1942, and Leo Grollé (photo liaison).

First printing 2018
International distribution Ingram Spark

CONTENTS

	Foreword	ix
	Endorsements	xi
	Acknowledgements	xiii
	Introduction	xvii
	A Short History of Indonesia and of my Close Family	xix
1	Japanese Invasion	1
2	House Arrest	15
3	POW Camps: Women & Children	25
4	Some of John's & Father's Prison-Camp Experiences	47
5	Kamp Kramat Liberation	57
6	The Bersiap, Indonesian War of Independence	63
7	Refugees	71
8	Eerbeek	79
9	De Bilt & Bilthoven	89
10	Kindergarten & Primary Schools	95
11	A wedding	105
12	Bridging School	115
13	Greener Pastures	125

CONTENTS

14	Stories & Letters	129
15	A New Primary School	147
16	Family Friends	157
17	Turning Point	165
18	Insight	175
19	High School Days, A New Experience	193
20	The Fright of My Life	203
21	The Silver Lining	211
22	Preparations	221
23	The Operation	233
24	My Journey	239
25	The Chosen Country	249
	Postscript	263
	Translation of Foreign Words	267

FOREWORD

by Rob Zaagman, Ambassador of the Kingdom of the Netherlands to New Zealand

All immigrants have their own personal stories about their life's journey which brought them to the country they now call home. These stories are worth re-telling and preserving, not only as part of the common heritage of the nation they now belong to, but also as part of the heritage and culture of their immigrant community.

Such retelling and preserving is one of the objectives of *Oranjehof the Dutch Connection*, the Dutch national museum of New Zealand. It is part of the multicultural community centre *Te Awahou Nieuwe Stroom*, which was ceremoniously opened on 18 November 2017 in the presence of several Government Ministers and a large number of members of the Dutch community of New Zealand.

First-hand stories make the past come alive in the imagination of the listener and reader. *Two Slices of Bread* is an excellent example of this. It describes and evokes not only the life of its author, Ingrid Coles *née* Brandt, but especially her relatives come to life as well, such as Ingrid's sister Juliana and her husband Rob, who emigrated to New Zealand in 1951, eight years before Ingrid herself would arrive there—to be welcomed by her sister and brother-in-law.

But before Ingrid arrived in Aotearoa, she and her family had to pass through several difficult stages: the Second World War and imprisonment in Japanese camps; the post-war violence between Indonesian nationalists and Europeans; having to adapt to the strange country which was the Netherlands.

Ingrid deals extensively with her time in the Netherlands in the decade and a half after the Second World War. This makes this memoir even more interesting and relevant to read for younger generations of Dutch Kiwis: they can get to know the Netherlands as it was during the era when their opa and oma decided to seek a new life in New Zealand.

I read certain chapters with a particular emotion. My mother and her family went through similar experiences: the war, the camp, the turmoil and fear so vividly described in Ingrid's book. Fortunately, all survived and two of my mother's five sisters immigrated to Australia. Only twice would they see my mother and the rest of the family again, who settled back in the Netherlands. Their stories are also part of the legacy Dutch immigrants have left to their community and to their new countries.

Thank you, Ingrid, for sharing your life and *Two Slices of Bread* with us!

**Rob Zaagman, Ambassador of the Kingdom
of the Netherlands to New Zealand**

WHAT PEOPLE ARE SAYING ABOUT TWO SLICES OF BREAD

"As an ex-prisoner-of-war during the Japanese occupation of the Netherland's East Indies, aged 16, in men's camps in Pekalongan and Tjimahi, Java, I can honestly say that this book describes and illustrates the hardship and horror of that period (early 1942 to August 1945), which we all endured. A story worth reading."
– *Hans van Leuven born 02/07/1926, Glen Waverley, Victoria, Australia. Retired architect*

"I read this book with pleasure and appreciate the way Ingrid writes about her experiences in Japanese Prison camps and her journey through life afterwards. Her flowing style of writing, with sensitivity, tells an interesting story which gives a genuine account at the same time. A captivating book."
– *Jaap Saathof, ex-prisoner-of-war in Java, retired orchardist, Havelock North, Hawke's Bay, New Zealand*

ACKNOWLEDGEMENTS

To my mother, Willy, thanks for raising me, through thick and thin, and to my father, Andrew, although I don't remember you, I am proud to be your daughter. I dedicate this book to both of you.

Thanks to my husband, Mark. You endured many lonely evenings, pampered me with hot drinks and snacks while I worked on the computer and pored over my story. You kept an eye on progress, and you remained gracious and loving.

To my older sisters, Juliana and Penny, you were always ready to answer my many questions about the past, regardless of how much sadness this stirred up.

My brother, John, I am especially indebted to you for the time you spent sketching pictures and writing letters about your experiences, with much detail and crucial information, about your and our family's trials before, during and after the Second World War, although it cost you so much to do so. Without you, Juliana and Penny's help, there would be no story.

Thanks also to Gloria, John's devoted wife. You endured the hardships of returning to sharing John's difficult war experiences with me. Your devotion to my brother warms my heart!

To our ten grandchildren, I wrote this story for you; you have been my inspiration from the start.

Many thanks to Bartha Hill, writer, tutor and friend. You believed in me and taught me the basics of English punctuation, spelling, writing, family history and journalism. Your encouragement over the years paid off, many thanks Bartha!

Joy Graham, computer expert and friend. You taught me to use a computer from scratch! and made writing so much simpler. I appreciate the many hours you invested, always encouraging, and urging me to keep writing my story.

Ruth Linton, proof-reader, Christian Writer competition judge and friend. You taught me to improve my English grammar and urged me to persevere with my story. I appreciate your efforts more than I can say.

Marie Anticich, proof-reader, thanks for helping me change my manuscript from a family history to an autobiography.

Lissa Weight, you are a marvel. So nice to work with you!

Ray and Janet Curle, Thanks for removing the fear of the unknown from self-publishing. Janet, you are an amazing artist.

Ingrid.

INTRODUCTION

Ingrid Coles was born in Java, Indonesia, on 28 November 1942, during the Japanese occupation of WWII. Three months after her birth, she and her family were incarcerated in prisoner-of-war camps. Her father died, aged 43, in a prison camp. Her 6-year-old brother died of starvation and pneumonia en route to Holland, when the family was evacuated during the Indonesian War of Independence. Ingrid's mother, seriously ill, survived; but without medical treatment in prison camp, her condition turned chronic. The family received a mixed welcome in their motherland, because of their Asian connection. There Ingrid's mother continued to struggle with chronic breathlessness and was often bed-ridden; all this after losing her husband, son, brother and father in close succession, and having to care for her four children on a small widow's pension, while emotionally scarred as a result of her wartime trauma.

Ingrid writes of her and her family's experiences, of Japanese POW camps, and of the violent Indonesian War of Independence which started at liberation from the Japanese in August 1945—and they were not evacuated until May 1946! Life changed drastically in the Netherlands, for Ingrid's mother, Willy, but also for Ingrid and her three siblings, who learn to cope with their mother's post-traumatic stress and their own war-time experiences.

However, Ingrid, orphaned aged 16, in 1958, has a clear idea of her future calling and emigrates to New Zealand to begin nursing training there six months later. This book traces Ingrid's background and growing-up years, revealing the secret of her successful life in her country of adoption; and how she overcomes the hurts and hurdles of the past.

A SHORT HISTORY OF INDONESIA AND MY CLOSE FAMILY

Indonesia comprises more than 17,000 islands, and has a population of approximately 260 million people, most of whom are Muslim. More than half of that number live on the island of Java. The country was formerly known as the Dutch East Indies, having been colonised by the Dutch East India Company in the 17th century. The company was dissolved in 1800, and the Netherlands government then established the Dutch East Indies as a nationalised colony.

The first regular contact between Europeans and Indonesians began in 1512, when Portuguese traders, led by Francisco Serrão, sought to monopolise the sources of nutmeg, cloves, and pepper in Malaku. Dutch and British traders followed. In 1602, the Dutch established the Dutch East India Company (VOC), and in the following decades, the Dutch gained a foothold in Batavia and Ambon. In the 17th and 18th centuries, the company became the dominant European power in the archipelago.

This colony was one of the most valuable European colonies under the Dutch Empire rule, contributing to Dutch global prominence in spice and cash crops trade in the 19th to early 20th centuries. The colonial social order was based on rigid racial and social structures, with a Dutch elite living separately from, but linked to, their native subjects. In the early 20th century, local Indonesian intellectuals began developing the concept of Indonesia as a nation state, preparing the ground for an independence movement. Japan's WWII occupation dismantled much of the Dutch colonial state and economy, and encouraged the previously suppressed Indonesian Independence movement.

My father, Andrew Brandt, was born in Holland to Dutch parents, and my mother, Wilhelmina (Willy) Roukens, was born in the Dutch East Indies to a Dutch father and a Dutch-Indonesian mother. They met in Holland, when Willy and her three siblings were boarding with their paternal aunt, Marie Roukens, in Driebergen-Rijsenburg, Holland, in 1925, when Willy studied languages and music at Utrecht University.

Willy was the eldest. She loved Indonesia, but in 1910, when she was eight, her parents divorced while on furlough in Holland. Her father, Johannes Roukens, returned to Java alone while her mother, Neeltje Hesselberg, Willy, and her siblings, left for Switzerland. Both parents subsequently remarried. As a result, in approximately 1918, when Willy was sixteen, the four children were sent to their aunt in Holland to continue their schooling.

Willy became a keen Girl Guide-leader, and her younger brother, Gerrit-Jan, a Boy Scout. One day Gerrit Jan brought his scout-leader, Andrew Brandt, home to meet Willy. Andrew soon began courting Willy, later proposing marriage to her.

Trouble began when Andrew took Willy home to meet his parents. Mama and Papa Brandt refused to accept the young couple's engagement and insisted it be broken off.

No one knows for sure why the Brandts adamantly refused to accept Andrew's fiancée, but it is likely that there were social, racial, and religious issues behind their stance. Andrew's mother had a proud heritage of blue blood, and could trace her ancestry back to Maria van Stolberg, the mother of William of Orange who ruled over Holland in the 1500s. In Holland, mixed marriages were frowned upon in well-to-do circles, although they were accepted in Indonesia. Willy looked European, with brown hair, a fair complexion, and grey eyes. She was 5 foot 6 inches tall, but her Indonesian accent and mannerisms revealed her origins. To top that, Willy's grandfather was a sea captain and Protestant—the Brandts were liberal Catholics!

Practical considerations would also have played a part. Andrew and Willy were 21 years old and both still dependent on their families for financial support while they studied. Appalled by all these differences, the Brandts refused to grant their blessing on the proposed marriage, so Andrew and Willy reluctantly parted.

The situation worsened when Aunt Marie wanted Willy to nurse her into old age. Broken-hearted by this turn of events, Willy booked her passage on a boat back to Indonesia. Her three siblings, perhaps fearing that they, too, could be in line to nurse their elderly aunt, joined Willy, and continued their studies in Java.

Andrew kept corresponding with Willy. When he heard of her sudden decision to return to Indonesia, he decided to join her, against his parents' wishes. Abandoning his studies, he accepted a job in a sugar factory in Kaliwungu, Java, and sailed to Indonesia about six months later.

The couple were reunited, marrying at Surabaya registry office on May 21, 1926. According to Dutch custom, their union was blessed by a priest at the Malang Liberal Catholic Church. A group of Scouts and Girl Guides made a guard of honour for them to walk through. Willy wore her Girl Guide-leader uniform, and Andrew his Scout-leader uniform. Andrew was 24, Willy 23.

On April 2, 1927, their union was enriched by the birth of a daughter, Juliana, in Semarang, and on June 15, 1929, by a son, John, in Jokdjakarta. Their second son, Dido, was born in July 21, 1939, in Kertosono, after Willy had a bad fall in her eighth month of pregnancy. Dido appeared normal at birth, but a specialist discovered a clot on the brain. This was operable if performed before he turned three months. Because the surgeon practised in Germany, and the Second World War had started in September 1939 in Europe, the operation was put on hold. Sadly, the blood clot pressed on Dido's nervous system. He became spastic.

Andrew and Willy had another daughter, Penny, on April 16, 1941, also in Kertosono. In May 1941, Andrew transferred to Sragi

Sugar Plantation, 26 kilometres from Pekalongan, where he was employed as bookkeeper, but also as factory chemist and supervisor.

Other plantations where he'd worked in Java were Kaliwungu, Sambawa, Wonotjator, Pandji, Lestari, and finally, Sragi. The happiest times were spent on Pandji and Lestari, where my parents again took up Scout-leading, and made many good friendships with other Scout leaders.

Life in Java was untroubled and blissful then. But our home life changed drastically when the Japanese Imperial Army bombed Pearl Harbour, Hawaii, in December 1941, invading Java two months later.

In February 1942 the Japanese, unbelievably cruel, invaded Java and, a year later, incarcerated my family for 2½ years. In August 1945, we were liberated from the Japanese. But from August 1945, we faced another threat: Indonesian nationalists began their subsequent Indonesian War of Independence, from which we needed to be evacuated in May 1946. Holland later, in 1949, formally recognised Indonesian sovereignty, when the colony was renamed Indonesia. In 1963, Western (Dutch) New Guinea became part of Indonesia.

JAPANESE INVASION OF JAVA

CHAPTER 1

"Japanese paratroopers have landed on Java's northern shores!" It was February 1942: the Japanese had invaded Java, in the Dutch East Indies, after attacking and destroying most of America's war fleet at Pearl Harbour, Hawaii, on 7 December 1941, later boldly invading the South Pacific and Dutch Indonesian islands.

In September 1939, World War II had broken out in Europe after Germany had invaded Poland, then France and Belgium, and, in May 1940, Holland. This surprised the Dutch, for Hitler had only just signed a peace agreement!

From then on communication ceased between Holland and the Dutch East Indies. It was here that my father, Andrew Brandt, worked as a bookkeeper, chemist and supervisor at Sragi Sugar factory, 26 kilometres from Pekalongan, Java. My father quickly bought himself a new and more efficient radio to keep abreast of the latest world developments. Trouble had also been brewing in the Southern Hemisphere.

Japan had invaded Korea in 1900, Manchuria in 1931, China in 1937. By 1941 Japanese war fleets silently crept through the South Pacific Seas between the Asian and American continents, searching for more land to conquer.

Surprisingly, many Europeans in the area initially viewed Japan's early advances with indifference. Their pseudo-security altered when

Japan attacked America's war fleet at Pearl Harbour. Dutch Queen, Wilhelmina, declared war on Japan, expecting her allies to help prevent an invasion of the Dutch East Indies. American, British, and Dutch forces joined the Royal Netherland's Indies Army *(KNIL)*. Yet unaware of Japan's super power, they anticipated that the destruction of Japan's war fleet would solve the problem.

However, after a few weeks' fighting, they found Japan's troops and artillery so well prepared that all hope of overpowering them faded. This was especially so, America having lost most of her war fleet stationed at Pearl Harbour, and the bulk of the Allied forces fighting Germany in the *Northern Hemisphere war*. America's only reprieve was three aircraft carriers, which had left Pearl Harbour before Japan's fatal invasion!

The Japanese attacked many Allied aircraft, sinking their ships in the South China Sea, among them Britain's then modern battleships, *Prince of Wales*, and *Repulse* (December 10, 1941), near Malaya. Japan's huge armies then infiltrated Sumatra, Celebes, Ambon, the east coast of Molucca, and British Borneo. Random Dutch *KNIL* air attacks hampered Japan's progress, but not sufficiently to compensate for the loss of Allied aircraft and warships.

Japan also threatened British Singapore, till then regarded an impregnable fortress. But with the Allies' fleet now drastically reduced, Japan took Singapore on 15 February 1942.

The *KNIL* continued to protect Java and Australia. The Allied Striking Force by then consisted only of a few Dutch warships and a remnant of British and American fleets outside the Atlantic territory.

When Japanese warships sailed into Dutch East Indies' waters, the invasion sparked an immediate state of emergency: the ill-equipped Dutch *KNIL* hurriedly prepared to defend the Dutch East Indies. With Sumatra and Java's abundant oil supplies, an uninvited *visit* from Japan became highly likely.

During the night of February 20-21, 1942, Allied air scouts and their striking force battled a huge Japanese war fleet, resulting in losses on both sides. Despite Allied efforts, the Japanese still landed on Bali. To prevent Japan from invading Java, Allied forces hoped to sink as many Japanese troopships as possible.

Japan brought many warships and two heavy cruisers into the Java Sea to protect its convoy. The Allies persisted, and, on February 27, 1942, a heavy sea battle began in the Java Sea. Fighting continued until March 12, 1942. The Japanese hit many Allied ships, among them the British cruiser, *Exeter*, and Dutch light cruisers, *De Ruyter*, and *Java*. As the ships tried to move from the battle zone, the Japanese torpedoed the Dutch ship *Kortenaer*, causing it to break in two, and tossing its marines into churning waters covered with liquid fuel. Only a few men survived.

By March 1942, the Japanese had sunk or disabled more than 54 Allied warships. Regardless of Allied efforts, Japanese paratroopers still landed on Java's northern shores. This news filtered through to Sragi Sugar estate by *tongtong*, the bush telegraph, an *emergency fast and loud beating on a hollowed-out tree trunk* by friendly Javanese men, meaning: "Danger! Watch out!"

In a matter of minutes, the message went from one end of Java to the other. But it was too late to run from the enemy. Up until then, the rugged mountain range between Sragi and the northern coastline had instilled false security. Europeans hadn't counted on Japan's many years of rugged jungle-training in Japanese-occupied China!

My father, Andrew, and mother, Wilhelmina (Willy) Roukens, then, like all other citizens of Java, helplessly watched the Japanese take Java by storm, freezing bank accounts, and banning education. The Japanese opened all prison doors, releasing violent convicts and murderers called *rampokkers* (troublemakers), who banded together, rioting, looting, and brutally killing and raping members of the public. The Japanese weren't very different themselves. Widespread chaos erupted.

To slow down Japanese land advances, the Dutch East Indies government ordered all private motor cars to be destroyed. Along with the men from Sragi Sugar Factory, Andrew, and my twelve-year-old brother, John, drove up the mountains in the family's new *Nash* and stopped at a cliff edge.

John watched in horror as Andrew pushed his pride and joy over a precipice into a ravine. Car after car hurtled down, except for one 1927 Essex Tourer. With that remaining car, the men ferried—in relays—the owners of the wrecked cars down the mountains and back to the sugar estate. Should Japanese troops approach Sragi, they planned to evacuate their women and children to the safety of the mountains with that one car.

ESCAPE?

On 8 March 1942, the *tongtong* sounded again as Javanese men passed on their message:

"Japanese paratroopers are tramping through the jungle towards Sragi!"

Four of the five sugar-factory managers hurriedly evacuated the women and children—in relays—in their remaining car! In preparation for this event, the managers had stocked with food and equipment an unused building on a secluded vanilla estate in the mountains. Andrew stayed behind at the sugar factory to keep up the sugar production, and protect the mill against *rampokkers*.

About 11am, after the women and children had been dropped off in the mountains, the five men made their way back to Sragi in the Essex Tourer. But at 3pm, the car reappeared in a cloud of dust, with a shredded tyre and steaming radiator. Screeching to a halt, with the driver tooting wildly, the other three men jumped from the car.

"Japanese paratroopers are heading *this* way!" they yelled. "Quick! Gather food, medicines, and clothing! Hurry! Walk up the mountains! Now!"

Having heard the latest news, the men had quickly devised a new, unorthodox escape-plan for the women and children. After setting the car on fire, they joined the women, who hurriedly gathered their children and belongings to begin walking the torturous track. Willy, surrounded by her children, Juliana, John, Dido, and Penny, protested.

"I can't walk!"

"But the Japanese are half an hour away... " the men argued.

"Mother has asthma, and two-year-old Dido is too heavy to be carried all that way," Juliana reminded the men, explaining that Dido had become an invalid after birth. The men quickly arranged a *tandu* (sedan) for them, carried by two Chinese coolies. Everyone else began the wet and cold trek, ill-equipped in their footwear. Over the slippery and dangerously narrow and steep mountain terrain they trekked, cliffs on one side and deep ravines on the other. Spending the night in hastily prepared shelters, they resumed their trek after a breakfast of *ketan* (sticky rice with coconut milk) provided by kind Indonesians. Juliana and John took turns carrying eleven-month-old Penny.

One night, the exhausted women and children rested at a friendly *kampong* (Javanese village), where Javanese men and women provided food and drinks. Everyone slept on woven floor mats. Mother and Dido shared a *balebale* (bamboo slab), to keep them off the dusty floor, and to enable Willy to breathe more easily.

The next day, the party resumed their walk. By late afternoon, they reached Dieng Plateau, a holiday resort. From there, they caught a bus to Wonosobo, another resort. To their dismay, Wonosobo had become a Japanese garrison. There were soldiers everywhere! The children shook with fear, and Willy, extremely worried, struggled to breathe. She couldn't phone Andrew for fear of *rampokkers* intercepting and tracing her calls, and attacking Andrew at the factory, or the women and children in the hills! *Rampokkers* already had a reputation for their atrocious deeds: a blood bath of macabre proportions, including decapitations!

As fear immobilised Willy, she gasped for breath, forcing Juliana and John to care for their younger siblings. John, disregarding his own fear, found a Dutch doctor brave enough to see Willy.

"I'll come when it's less dangerous," he said, and arrived later that day—disguised in torn native clothes and with a blackened face. Medications were tied to his waist under a *sarong*. His ministrations gave Willy some relief.

"You must leave Wonosobo as soon as possible," the doctor advised Willy, after hearing the tale of their adventure over the mountains.

Thankfully, Wonosobo's mayor arranged for everyone's accommodation with local Indonesian families; Willy and her four children received a small room with one double bed. They spent three nights there, huddled together and shaking like leaves, wondering what would happen next, as, through partly drawn curtains, they watched Japanese soldiers roam the streets.

After leaving much destruction and many macabre scenes, *rampokkers* marched towards Sragi, where Andrew—as sole European supervisor—was running the mill. Brave Indonesian factory workers intercepted the rioting mob on the outskirts of the village to speak up on Andrew's behalf.

"*Tuan* (Mr) Brandt is the only white man here and he's a good man! Leave him alone!"

Surprisingly, the *rampokkers* listened, and left. From then on, the sugar estate remained trouble-free.

Three stressful weeks later, back at Wonosobo, Willy finally managed to phone Andrew at the sugar estate. Until then, *rampokkers* and Japanese soldiers had left the women and children in peace. On Andrew's instruction, Willy found a trustworthy Indonesian taxi driver. Together with Father's Chinese friend, Mr Koo, the taxi driver agreed to transport them to Semarang over an 80km unauthorised, unsealed, and treacherous track. It was safest to travel by back roads to avoid Japanese check points and possible arrest.

The taxi driver delivered Mr Koo, Willy, and the children to an Ambonese family, who put them up for the night. The next day, the Ambonese family organised a train fare from Semarang for the Brandt family, with Mr Koo as chaperone. The train was packed with Indonesians on their way to market. Many people hung precariously from windows, and sat on carriage roofs. Others squatted by their produce and noisy livestock, caged and loose, oblivious to the stench. Suddenly, the train stopped. A bridge had been blown up—dynamited by the *KNIL* army to slow down Japanese land advances.

All passengers, livestock included, had to walk across a narrow, makeshift bamboo-bridge to the other side of the fast, but shallow river. Mr Koo helped Willy, and kind Indonesians assisted the children. Luckily, another train waited for them at the other end.

Juliana welcomed the break of freedom and fresh air. She didn't like being pushed off her seat by locals, having her hair pulled, and having animals running wild through the smelly carriage.

The train finally arrived at Sragi train station, where Andrew waited on the platform. It was the first time they'd seen him in weeks.

"How did you know we'd be on this train?" Willy asked.

"I didn't." Andrew replied. "I've met every train this week, I worried that *rampokkers* may have come your way."

When they arrived at their home, Willy found it had become a makeshift hospital for many sick and injured Chinese and Indonesians. Andrew quickly moved the patients from their bedroom into *gudangs* (storerooms).

A few weeks later, Willy discovered that she was pregnant with me.

In the meantime, the Japanese took further control of Java, and *rampokkers* continued their wild rampage.

I wish Willy and the children could escape to Australia or New Zealand, Andrew often longed. By that stage, however, travel by sea or air had become virtually impossible. Some captains responded to bribes and large sums of cash, but most refused to travel. From 1941, the South Seas were riddled with Japanese warships and aircraft.

PRISON & HOUSE ARREST

A few weeks after the mountain-track ordeal, the Japanese arrested Andrew and the four Dutch factory administrators, marching them off to an unknown destination.

Willy worried herself sick. Japanese soldiers had made their headquarters in Pekalongan, only 26km from the estate. First one soldier came, scouting round the sugar estate, and then dozens more arrived.

The Japanese encouraged eager young Indonesian men aged 17 to 25 to stay on in Sragi. The boys had joined what was known as the unbeatable Japanese marines and army, under the pretence of becoming famous once Indonesia stood on its own feet. Trained to be a ruthless special force, the Japanese called the boys *heihos* (soldiers), and *sukarelas* (volunteers).

John watched one Japanese soldier sealing the Brandt's storage rooms with taped wire, leaving an initialled lead clamp. "Don't you break this," the soldier warned when he saw John watching. The Japanese took everything of value.

Soldiers then evicted everyone from their homes, cramming Mother and her four children, along with eighteen other internationals and their children, into the *besaran* (boss' quarters), where they remained on house arrest for approximately four months.

The besaran had many rooms, but it wasn't big enough for so many people. While the women argued loudly over whom should have which room, Willy quickly ushered her children into one of the larger rooms. Some families occupied a small *gudang* (pantry) and others shared rooms, using screens. Everyone shared the kitchen, bathroom, and one toilet.

Ironically, house arrest applied to living arrangements only. The women and children could walk freely through the sugar estate, the *passar* (market), and Javanese settlements within the sugar cane plantations. But nobody could leave the factory compound except with permission from the Japanese commandant.

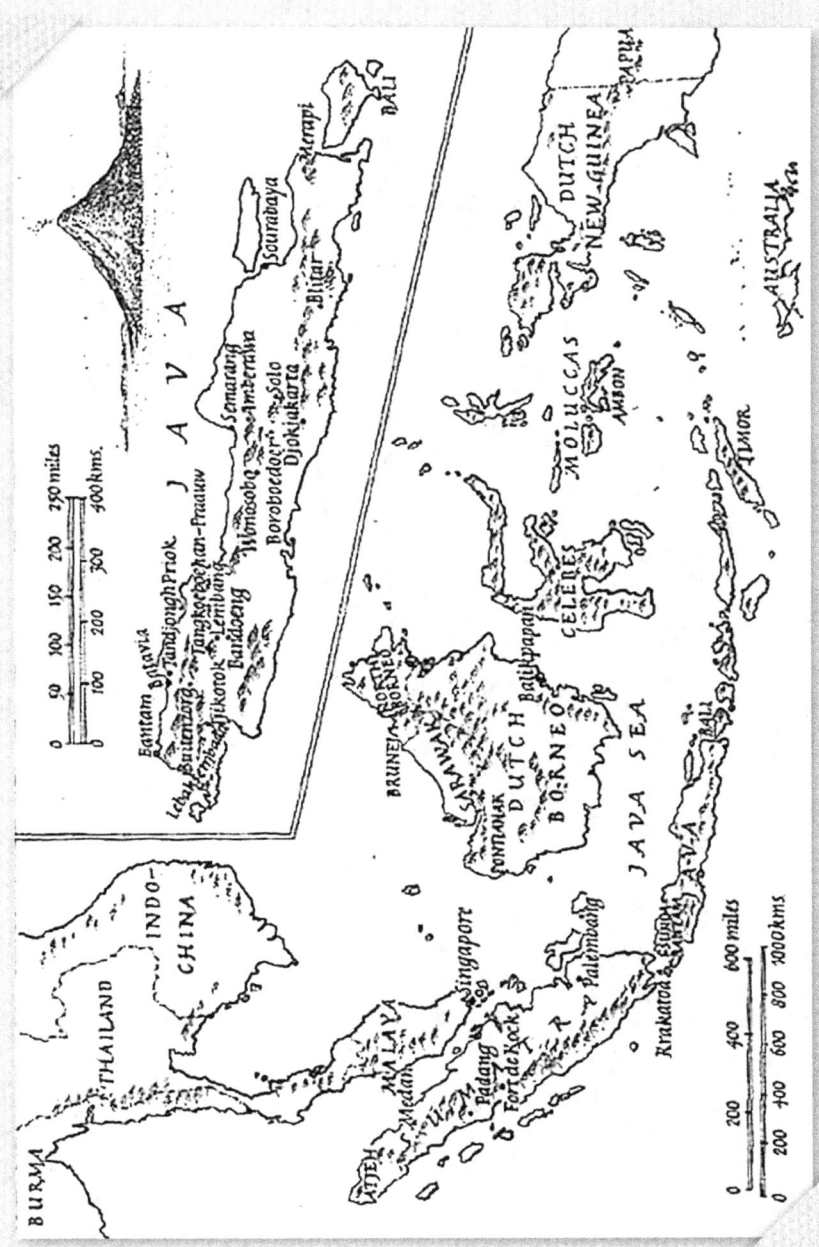

Old map of Indonesia

The map of Java, with POW camps and sugar factories

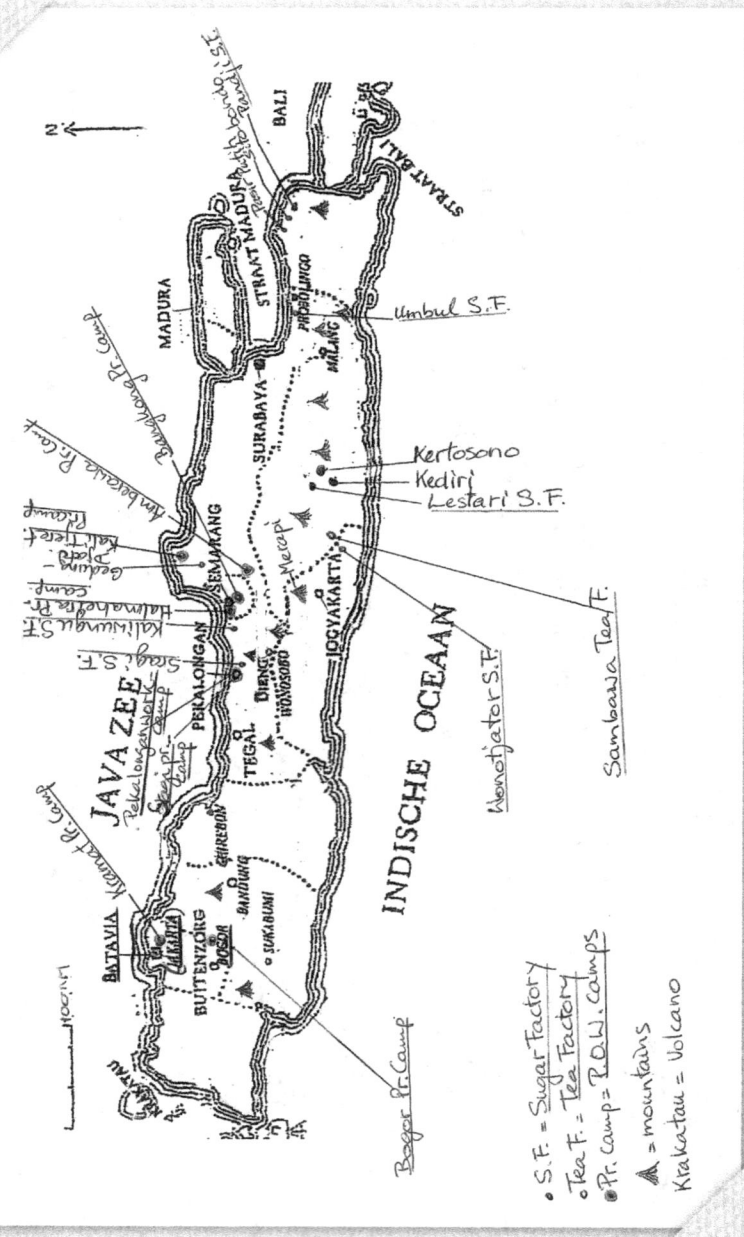

A tandu sketched by Willy Brandt

A dokar

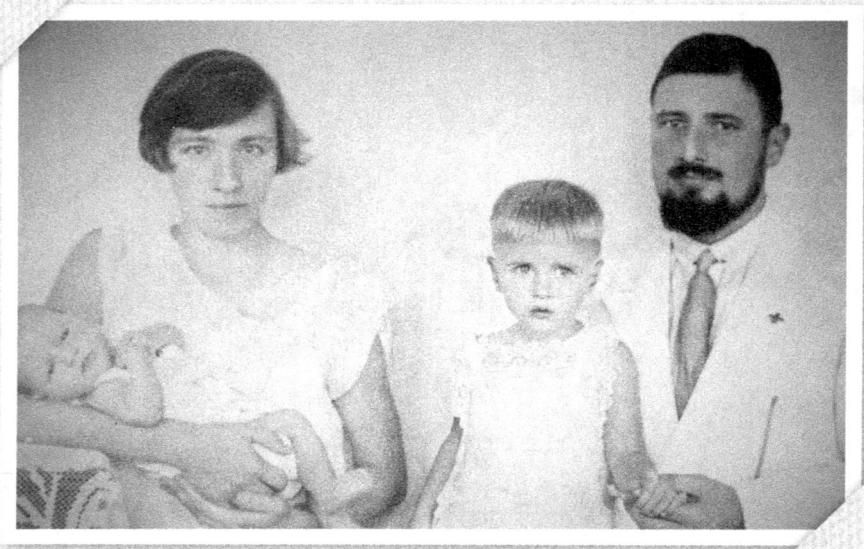

Willie, Andrew, John, Juliana, 1930s

Willie and Juliana in front of the Kaliwungu Sugar Factory, 1927

Andrew and Juliana with goat at Kaliwungu, Java, 1928

Willie and Juliana in the river, 1930s

Willy, Juliana and John, 1935

HOUSE ARREST
CHAPTER 2

The Sragi sugar estate included the *besaran*, an administration building and a society hall. There were also tennis courts, eighteen employee houses, and a passar (market) within walking distance of the refinery and surrounding *kampong* (Javanese village).

The sugar mill incorporated crushers, boilers, centrifuges, and drying floors to crystallise the sugar. The refinery was surrounded in a 50 to 60km radius, by sugar-cane plantations. Five executive staff were employed, each capable of taking sole charge of the factory, if necessary. Ten other employees supervised the work of local field workers.

Supervisors had to remain alert as they and their families could be attacked by workers for real or assumed insults or injustices. Andrew treated his employees with respect, and so for him, work usually proceeded peacefully, although his judo skills once came in handy when an intruder attacked him from behind, mistaking him for another person. When the attacker realised he had assaulted Andrew, he apologised profusely.

MIASAWA AND ISOBE

By now, Japanese soldiers had gained a bad reputation through committing dastardly deeds, savagery, murder, and rape elsewhere on the civilian population. Hoping to stamp out any form of resistance, they demanded absolute obedience from their defenceless victims, dishing out brutal acts of punishment. Thus, the arrival of two *kind* Japanese officers—Miasawa and Isobe—amazed everyone. Isobe was a gentleman in many ways, having a soft spot for children. He made a point of picking up youngsters to go fishing or swimming in Tjomal, or just letting his chauffeur drive his car and be surprised where the road led. Invariably, they'd end up somewhere pleasant, enjoying snacks and drinks, followed by ice blocks! Isobe even did this whilst they were restricted to the estate area. However, Isobe was of a much higher rank than any of the other Japanese officers on the sugar estate, and brushed their objections aside. He even visited Willy for 'friendly' chats at the *besaran*, while she and the children were kept on house arrest.

During one of those visits, Isobe told Willy that Andrew was imprisoned in the mountains behind Pekalongan. But when Willy pleaded for her husband's release, Isobe laughed.

"All Europeans are now subjects of *teno haika* (the supreme Emperor)," he replied staunchly. "We must only do what is best for him." Although Isobe was kind to children, he was a loyal servant and seemed willing to die for his Emperor—his god and ruler.

Japanese officers brought Andrew and the other four supervisors back to the estate and, under threat of harm to their families, ordered them to resume work at the sugar mill. The Javanese factory workers had made only minimal preparations for the cane-crushing season. As Andrew and the other managers had been in prison for four months, the Japanese realised that they needed their administrators' skills and expertise to ensure a good sugar harvest. Perhaps they also realised that the cramped living conditions at the *besaran* would produce poor work ethics, because suddenly the men and their families were ordered back into their own homes. They were still on house arrest and confined to the estate, but free to move around. Guards were now posted at the gates.

As well as making optimal sugar production, the managers had to teach young Japanese apprentices how to run the factory. Instead, however, they rebelled against the Japanese by secretly teaching the Japanese apprentices all the wrong methods, hoping 'they' would gradually destroy the sugar mill. The managers did this amiably so as not to attract attention, and for fear of exposing the intrigue, all staff were sworn to secrecy.

Because Andrew and Willy spoke German fluently, and Isobe was studying German, he often visited in the evenings. Their discussions usually took a spiritual slant. Isobe was a Buddhist, and he liked exchanging his views with Andrew and Willy's.

As a result, tensions rose for Andrew in the office and at home. On the surface everything seemed fine, especially to the children; however, Andrew knew otherwise.

Isobe's unfailing kindness to the children continued. He even acted as their protector when the local wedono (village-head), who hated the Dutch, came to our house and commanded Juliana:

"Give me your radio!"

"No!" she argued defiantly, not wanting to give up Andrew's brand-new radio. "This one belongs to Isobe—if you want it, you'd better see him."

When the *wedono* left, Juliana raced to Andrew's office to phone Isobe and tell him what had happened. That afternoon, Isobe visited Andrew and Willy, and laughed about Juliana's tale.

When the *wedono* visited Isobe, he played along with Juliana's story. The radio stayed.

Another evening Isobe arrived, armed with bottles of beer. Drinking one after another, he became drunk.

"Our regiment is leaving for Dutch New Guinea and the Solomon Islands tomorrow," he informed Andrew. "We're going to fight at the front. The train will pass through the estate tomorrow morning, but don't see us off!" he warned, glancing at Juliana and John.

Disobeying Isobe's instructions, a large group of children turned up at the train station the next day to farewell their Japanese friends. After all, Isobe and Miasawa had been good to them.

"Isobe! Miasawa!" they shouted, waving excitedly. But the officers' faces remained like stone, looking straight ahead as if in a trance. Later the children heard that Isobe had been killed in action.

Sragi, lane to Tjomal

Sragi Sugar Estate, one of the houses still used today

Sragi, old tennis court with Society Hall in background

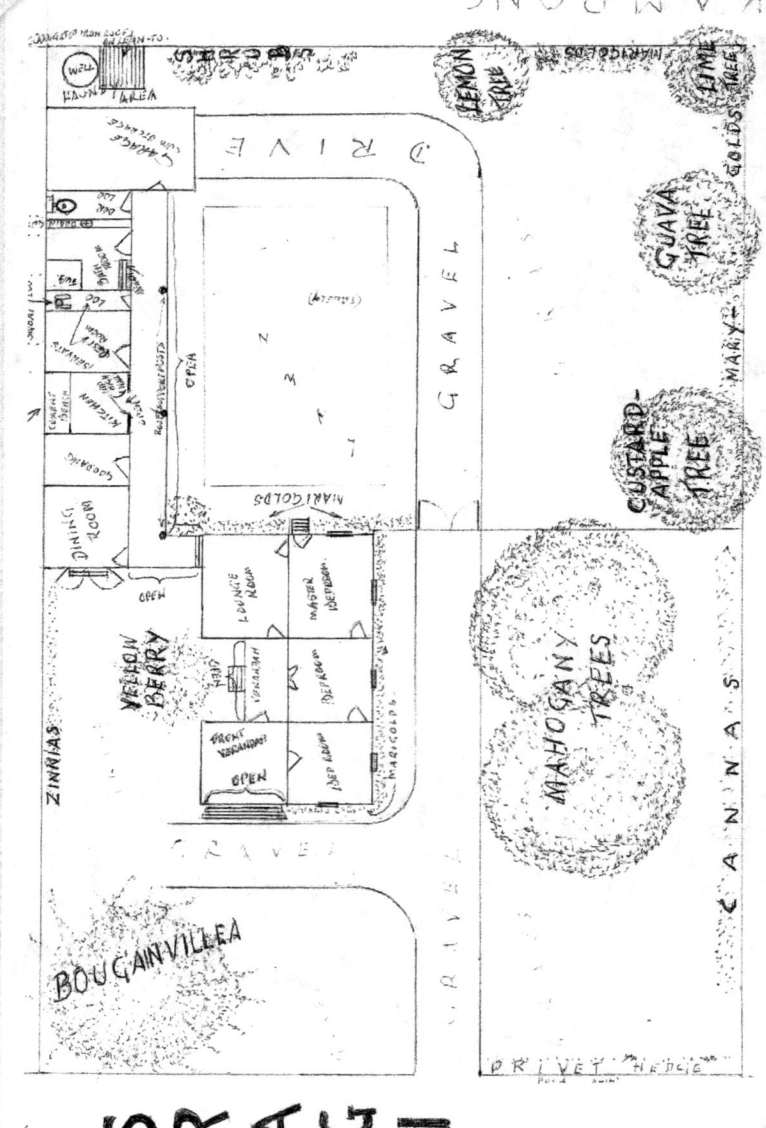

Floor plan of our house at Sragi, sketched by John Brandt

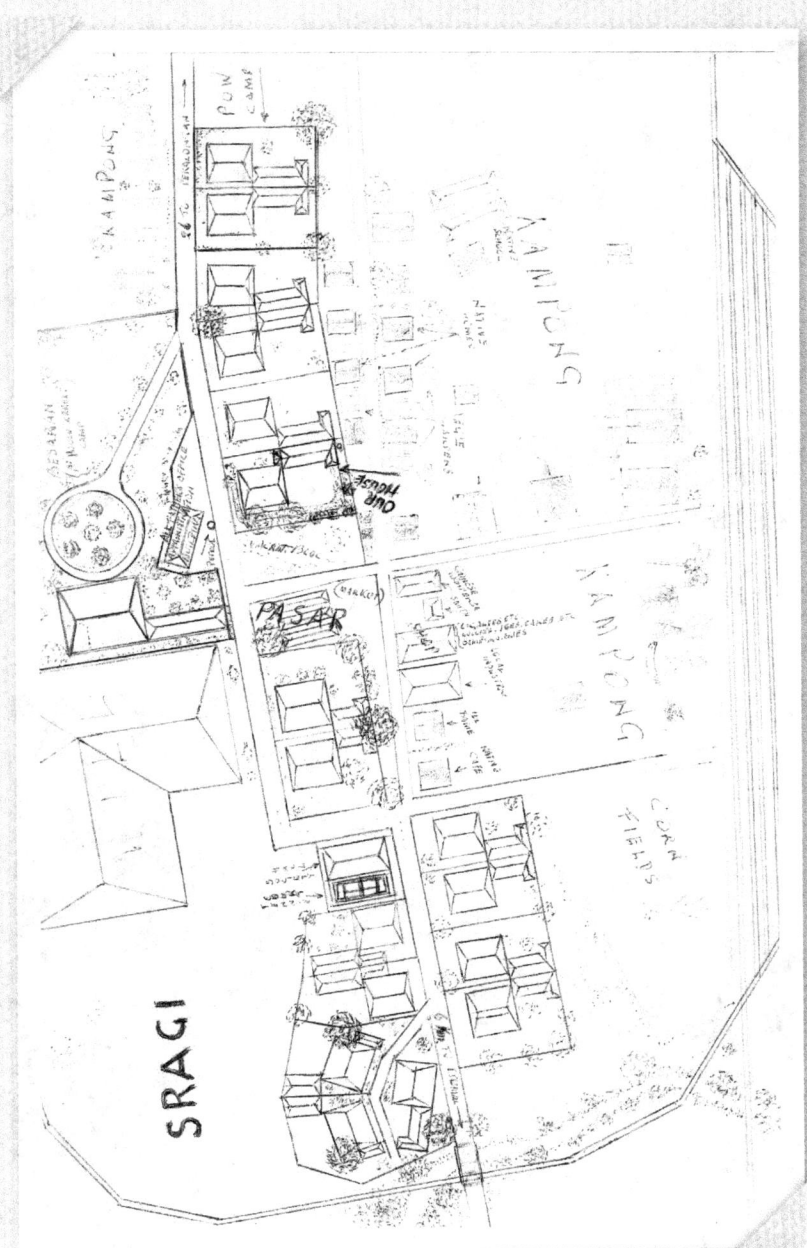

Plan of Sragi Sugar Estate, sketched by John Brandt

Sragi Sugar Factory, cog wheels still used in 2016

Sragi Sugar Factory, roller in use

Sragi Sugar Factory, reserve roller for sugar cane pressing

Sragi Sugar Factory, outside view

Sragi Sugar Factory, old steam kettles

Sragi Sugar Factory, conveyer belt

POW CAMPS – WOMEN & CHILDREN

CHAPTER 3

The children missed Isobe and Miasawa. There were no outings for them any longer and they were still under house-arrest, without privacy. The sabotage and intrigue at the factory kept Andrew busy. Willy's time for her fifth confinement came during the busy cane-crushing season. In those days, a birth occurred in hospital, or at least with a midwife in attendance. Neither was available in Sragi. Instead, Andrew had to gain permission to take Willy to a hospital, 16 kilometres from Sragi, and Willy had to endure the uncomfortable, rough track in a *dokar* driven by a *kusir* (coach driver) through vast sugar-cane plantations. When they finally arrived at the hospital, Andrew helped Willy inside. But they soon reappeared.

"No *blandas* (whites)! Only Japanese!" shouted a Japanese guard, and so they had to continue to Pekalongan, a further ten kilometres up the road. By this time, Willy's labour pains had begun in earnest. She was beside herself and almost gave birth on Pekalongan Hospital's doorstep!

A nurse rushed to her side and delivered a healthy baby girl. It was Saturday, 28 November, 1942. The next day, Andrew told Juliana, John, Dido, and Penny, that they had a new little sister, Ingrid Dorothee (me). Despite the strain and uncertainty of our future, which the children didn't know about, my birth was a happy occasion.

Willy didn't take the strain too well. She suffered terribly from a severe bout of asthma, and needed an extended stay in hospital. Rumours abounded of Europeans being attacked by out-of-control *rampokkers*, and being incarcerated by Japanese soldiers.

Andrew was happy about my birth, but he worried about our future in Java. He suspected what the Japanese would do to us, for he, and the other supervisors, by now, had discovered the harsh and brutal reputation of the Japanese. Keeping us safe from *rampokkers* was also a major concern.

To ease the stress at home, Andrew employed an extra *babu anak* (nanny) to look after Dido and Penny; and, when Willy came home still unwell, the *babu* extended her care to me, the baby.

"This is your little *adih* (baby sister)," *Babu Anak* told eighteen-month-old Penny, stroking my cheek. Ingrid was a big word for Penny to say, and so she changed *Adih* to 'Addy': I've been called Addy ever since.

DISCOVERY OF THE TREASON

"What? You defied our instructions?" a Japanese commandant fumed at the managers. Late February 1943, after approximately seven months of our confinement to the compound, and five-and-a-half months of the factory supervisors' plotting the treason, yet nursing the plant along as if nothing was wrong, the Japanese civilian apprentices realised that they were being led into sabotaging their own work. They were furious! Yet they secretly admired the unmitigated audacity of their tutors. They hadn't altogether destroyed the mechanics of the sugar mill, however, uproar followed. Then, unceremoniously, the five Dutch supervisors were demoted, and five Japanese experts took over the mill.

"Gather your families and assemble at Pekalongan headquarters in one hour!" the commandant shouted, having summoned all the employees and instructed them where to meet. There they and their families assembled before a high-ranking Japanese officer.

"You will be severely punished for disobeying orders!" the officer shouted. "All men and boys aged sixteen and over shall be imprisoned—immediately!"

"No!" Mother gasped. "Not another imprisonment for Andrew!" Then pandemonium broke out among the assembled as wives and children gathered round husbands, fathers, and their boys. Women and children, Mother, and we children included, wept. Father hugged us bravely, before he and the other men and their boys climbed onto dokars. John, aged only thirteen, remained with us, and became the man of the family. Mother, terrified, almost lost her cool. Watching in horror, she saw Father climb onto a *dokar* and disappear into the city. This was the second time Father had been imprisoned, and Mother feared for her family's safety.

How long will Andrew be away this time, leaving me to care for five children by myself? she thought. *I wish Isobe was still here...*

But after the first flood of tears, Mother put on a brave face for us children.

While soldiers escorted the men and boys to an internment camp, a Japanese officer confronted the women.

"Don't think you're getting off scot free!" he whined. "Soon women and children will also be imprisoned!"

Mother later found out that Father had been taken to an internment camp at Pekalongan's Mulo School.

We had barely returned home to Sragi when Japanese soldiers evicted all European women and children from their homes, detaining eighteen families in two of the smaller employees' houses, each with three bedrooms, at the entrance to Sragi Estate, one family per room, where possible. The rest had to share, or use tiny *gudangs* (store rooms). Around these two houses, the Japanese had built four-metre-high bamboo *gedek* fences topped with barbed wire, and posted *heiho* guards at the gates.

Rules of confinement while Isobe had been in charge, now suddenly became much stricter. Nobody was allowed to leave the compound, not even for trips to the chemist as Juliana and John had done earlier. This made it extremely difficult to remain civilised to one another. Lack of food and water, combined with the heat, flies, mosquitoes, internal camp intrigues, and difficulties with finding Dido's special dietary needs because he could not swallow and chew solid food, often brought Mother to the end of her tether.

A brutal *Kempetai* (Japanese military police) now controlled Sragi Sugar Estate from Pekalongan. His inspections always came unannounced. Everyone, fearing the worst, warned each other of his arrival. Mother quickly called Juliana and John inside, urging them to remain as quiet as mice.

By now the Indonesian people, who had assumed that the Japanese would quickly make their country an independent nation, saw their long-held dream evaporate. To compound their dismay, the Japanese treated them as defeated people.

As a result, the *heiho* guards became lenient, and kept us as prisoners inside the compound only when it suited them. They remained on friendly terms with Juliana and John, and, as long as no Japanese soldiers were watching, they allowed them to come and go from the camp compound to fetch medicines for Dido and Mother.

Once, Mother asked a *heiho* to let her and us children through the gate so we could visit Father at the internment camp at Pekalongan Mulo School. He obliged. When we arrived, Mother bravely asked a Japanese guard for permission to see Father. He refused. As a last resort, she thrust little Penny into his arms, pleading:

"Please, she wants to see her daddy..."

The kind-hearted guard disappeared inside with Penny. John remembers watching in amazement as the guard, followed by Father, with Penny in his arms, approached. Father and Mother talked for a few minutes. Father looked fit and healthy, but worried.

"They're talking about taking us to Tjimahi prison camp in Bandung," he told Mother "Oh no! So far away," she cried.

It was late February 1943. I was just three months old. That was the last time we saw him. I imagine Father kissed us all goodbye and perhaps stroked my head.

HELL HOLE

Following that experience, we endured one horror after another. First, after almost twelve months of house arrest, the Japanese took all Sragi's women and children to what we called Sragi Factory Prison Camp, an estate only 50 to 100 metres from Sragi Sugar Factory.

Fortunately, Mother had had the presence of mind to sew paper money into a bra seam beforehand. These funds proved extremely helpful when later she needed to buy medicine and food.

Kokkie Salem and our other servants helped carry our few belongings: a chest, two suitcases, and a small dresser. John held Penny; Juliana pushed Dido in his pram, and Mother, still frail, carried me.

Flanked by servants, our new camp loomed ahead. It was also surrounded by high *gedek* fencing, topped with barbed-wire; with *heihos* guarding the gates. Except for a few tall coconut trees in the distance, we couldn't see what was behind the fences. Together with Sragi's 120 women and children, we had to squeeze into two small houses. Our family of six squashed into one tiny room with another family of four!

"Servants must leave!" Japanese guards shouted.

"Why?" *Kokkie* Salem protested. "I want to stay! These people are my family…"

But a Japanese guard drove her and the other servants out. It was hard saying goodbye to *Kokkie* Salem, who had been like a friend to Mother, and a second mother to my siblings since 1928. The trauma and upheaval spiked another severe asthma attack in Mother, so Juliana and John had to care for Dido, Penny, and me.

Conditions in Sragi Factory Camp grew more and more atrocious. Even *heihos* appeared harsh and mean. Mother or Juliana often needed to see a doctor, either for Dido or Mother, to collect medication from the chemist, or to buy Dido's special food. Dido couldn't tolerate prison-camp food. It was often laced with chillies—hot! Penny and I ate it because we were hungry. But with Dido going without, he needed extra vitamins. With none of these available in camp, Mother or Juliana first had to barter with a compassionate *heiho* for permission to see the Japanese commandant. However, they learned that, even if he allowed them through the first gate, they still needed the higher camp commander's permission to leave camp.

Sometimes the guard was happy with a few cents in exchange for this privilege; but other guards expected large sums of money. So, the little cash Mother had saved dwindled fast.

Later, the commander stopped all outside shopping for Dido's food and medicine. *How am I going to manage without special food and vitamins for Dido?* Mother worried.

Luckily, local peddlers living near the prison camp heard that the Japanese starved their prisoners. The pedlars therefore sold their wares secretly over the *gedek* fences. Hungry prisoners even bartered their most valuable possessions, like gold rings and necklaces, for food. Some *heihos* turned a blind eye to this trade, but prisoners always had to stay alert. Guards could never be trusted, and Japanese soldiers were even worse.

If caught by the Japanese, peddlers and prisoners alike were severely punished, sometimes resulting in death. Once, when prisoners of war could still venture outside camp with permission, Juliana had walked through the *passar*, and seen a boy she knew from school. She called out to him, but he fled, seemingly pretending not to hear. Later, the *Kempetai* summoned Juliana and interrogated her about the boy.

"*Tia tau,*" (I don't know), she answered truthfully. But the *Kempetai* didn't believe her, no matter what she said; he beat her black and blue. He only stopped when she fainted. She woke up in another room, with a Japanese doctor standing over her.

"*Kawai so,*" (poor one) he said, while examining her swollen, blood-stained face. Another Japanese officer then entered the room, pacified Juliana with a drink of orange crush, and released her. Later, Juliana heard that the Japanese had caught and imprisoned the boy, but she never found out anything further that happened to him.

Back at Sragi Factory Camp, basic living conditions deteriorated quickly. Without a refrigerator, the milk, which had at first been available for young children, turned sour. Mother's breast milk had long since dried up, and there was no alternative, except for a little rice water Juliana scooped up for us children as she cooked the day's rice. This supplied Dido, Penny, and me with at least a few vitamins, as protein, vegetables, and fruit had long since been removed from our 'menu'. After nearly six months on this poor diet, Dido's health deteriorated. Extremely worried, and at the end of her tether again, Mother approached the Japanese commandant, carrying Dido in her arms.

"Please set me and my family free so I can buy better food and medicine for my sick little boy," she pleaded. Hoping to persuade the commandant, she added: "One of my forefathers married the Sultan of Halmaheira's daughter in 1835. That means we are of Indonesian descent, and shouldn't be interned."

Europeans with Indonesian blood were sometimes given the choice of staying either inside or outside prison camp. But the commandant refused Mother's plea. He probably didn't believe her. With their fair skin, deep blue eyes, and white-golden hair, Juliana, John, and Dido showed no signs of Indonesian blood. Instead, the commandant suggested a work camp.

"But you'll have to *work!*" he warned.

Discouraged, Mother left the office.

"I can't work with my asthma, and leave the children to fend for themselves..." she mentioned to Juliana that evening.

"I could work in your place..." Juliana suggested. So, the next day Mother and Juliana returned to the commandant's office, who agreed to the plan. Juliana was sixteen.

That very day, late 1943, Mother, Juliana, John, Dido, Penny, and I rode in a *kusir*-driven *dokar* to Pekalongan *Djalang Pandjang* (Long

Road) work camp. Both Mother and Juliana thought this would solve all our problems, especially that of Dido's fragile health. He was now four years old, and still lay feebly in his pram all day long. Provided he was propped up and supported, he could sit up and watch Penny and me playing in the lane, but he couldn't move.

As promised, living conditions at *Djalang Pandjang* (Long Road) work camp, also in Pekalongan, improved slightly compared with our previous camp. We had a whole house to ourselves, and even a *babu*. At first, Juliana's small wage provided enough money to feed us, and buy special food and medicine for Dido from the *passar* (market) and chemist. But Juliana soon discovered a sinister side to her *work*. Although she had willingly agreed to work for Dido's sake, it soon became a huge sacrifice.

At first, she laboured in a hot kitchen, plucking and preparing chickens for meals. But even the thought of touching lifeless chicken bodies turned her stomach, as she was already haunted by childhood memories of headless chickens running around the yard after *Kokkie* Salem had beheaded them in preparation for the pot.

Noticing Juliana's squeamishness, the camp chef told the camp commandant, who took pity, and gave her what appeared an easier, waitressing, job at the camp restaurant for Japanese officers.

But it was like going from the frying pan into the fire: officers, drunk on rice wine and brandy, openly propositioned waitresses, demanding unswerving obedience to their every whim. Juliana also had to serve one of the regular officers, the *Kempetai-cho* (head of Military Police). He leered at her continually. One night he became annoyed when she kept ignoring his ingratiating smile and lustful looks, and called out:

"Hey, you! I want you tonight!"

Petrified, Juliana ran to the kitchen and began cutting her wrists with a carving knife, hoping the sight of blood would deter the *Kempetai-cho*.

That instant, another Japanese officer entered the kitchen.

"What are you doing?" he asked.

"Making myself ugly," Juliana replied. "I don't want to sleep with the *Kempetai-cho*."

"That's an honour," he replied. "But I'll take care of this. You get back to work."

Returning to the restaurant he approached the *Kempetai-cho*.

"Juliana is my girl," he insisted. "Leave her alone."

Fortunately, the officer's kind act deterred the *Kempetai-cho's* leering advances. But other officers continued their lewd games, and followed girls through camp.

"Quick! Hide! A drunken officer is coming!" the girls warned one another, enabling them to camouflage themselves by clambering into trees.

Sadly, they couldn't always escape, the most distressing waitressing work taking place at Japanese private parties, away from camp and the other women's presence. Here, Japanese officers' brazen conduct escalated, often resulting in brutal rapes.

On top of her evening waitressing duties, Juliana was also forced to toil in paddy fields during the day. When she came 'home', she and John cared for us younger children because Mother was often ill in bed.

After six months at the work camp, the camp commandant addressed everyone at *tenko*:

"Pack your belongings! Today you'll be transported to a concentration camp!" he announced. "And all boys turning fourteen this year will go to a boys' camp!" he added.

It was May 1944. John turning fourteen in June, meant that he also had to leave.

"No!" Mother cried despondently. "My son is too young!"

"It's the rule," the commandant brusquely replied.

Mother wept as John was taken away. Then she put on a brave face for us younger children. When it was our turn to leave, Juliana carried all our belongings, as well as pushing Dido in his pram, which, amazingly, the Japanese allowed us to keep. Mother carried me—eighteen-months-old. Three-year-old Penny walked, while soldiers, constantly shouting abuse, herded us on towards a train station where a train with roughly boarded-up windows waited.

Other soldiers yelled more abuse while they pushed and shoved us into the dark interior. Mother and Juliana, holding us tightly, quickly squeezed into the last two spaces on some wooden seats, nursing us three children on their laps. Other women and children had to stand the whole interminable journey.

Thankfully, Mother had saved a little money to buy from a pedlar, a portion of rice wrapped in a banana leaf. Carefully dividing it into five, she kept a tiny bit for herself, and a few grains for us little ones later. She was near exhaustion, and so Juliana—although worn out herself—took care of us children. Many others fainted or collapsed in the stuffy, vile-smelling train carriages.

Two days later, the train stopped. "Out!" shouted a guard.

"Where are we?" Penny asked.

"Bogor," some Indonesians on the roadside answered.

BOGOR

"Thank God that's over," Mother exclaimed. But the jubilation quickly soured when guards herded us onto the station platform, into open-decked trucks, and then drove us to Bogor prison camp. There, a Dutch interpreter translated the camp commandant's message, and explained our housing and camp procedure.

"You must attend *tenko* parade every morning and evening," she said. "If you don't you'll be severely punished."

She was right. Punishments proved so barbaric, they even traumatised and dazed onlookers, reluctant to watch as the guards lashed and abused even weak and emaciated women.

Camp conditions depended on commandants-in-charge, and they changed without warning. Food rations could be short one day but, after a new commandant's arrival, more food reductions, unreasonable new rules, cruel beatings, and torture often followed. Our house leader then directed us to our accommodation. Together with many others, we had to share a house that had belonged to other Dutch people. Some of their pictures and photos still hung on the walls, and their furniture seemed as they left it, evidently having been forced to move out at short notice.

At first, we received three small meals a day. Then breakfast suddenly came off the menu. There was never enough, especially to sustain hard-working field-workers!

A team of supervised prisoners dished up the food into our pots or pans.

"No container, no food," was the rule.

Filth, dirty water, and lack of soap, vitamins, and medicine, lowered everyone's immunity. As a result, tropical ulcers, beriberi, and dysentery developed into serious ailments. Mother's asthma and bronchitis were aggravated, leading to chronic bronchitis, then pneumonia, and later emphysema. Women with painful tropical leg ulcers had to continue working, even in muddy paddy-fields! The Japanese didn't consider these an illness.

Compared to other camps, however, living conditions at Bogor were passable, although the sharing of bedrooms, kitchen, one bathroom, and toilet, soon caused tempers to flare.

After about six months at Camp Bogor, everyone stood to attention.

"This camp is too good for you women!" the commandant yelled. "You're leaving in five minutes. Pack now!"

Juliana brought what she could carry, although we didn't own much by then. All Dido had to wear were bloomer-shorts the straps of which Mother had extended. Penny had her undies, and I, a cloth nappy. Mother and Juliana shared one dress and a pair of shorts, taking turns to wear a bra and bloomers.

We were herded onto freight-trucks like cattle, and forced onto another train with boarded-up windows, bound for yet another unknown destination. Once on the train, we couldn't see out through the board-covered windows, and nobody could see in. The few wooden benches lining the walls filled up quickly, and, with so many people crammed into the carriages, there was standing room only. There were no toilets, no water to wash or change our clothes, and we all had dysentery! An indescribable stench permeated the carriage. After an horrendous two-day ride, we arrived at Batavia railway station. Juliana found a tap, rinsed our soiled garments, and put them back on us—still wet. Thanks to the heat, they dried quickly while soldiers herded us along.

KRAMAT POW CAMP

"Women and children!" a Dutch woman interpreted for the commandant, on arrival at our new camp. "Welcome to Kramat POW camp. Find a space in your allocated house and see your house leader about mattresses!"

Our *house* was full of screaming women, who fought over every tiny space. Mattresses lay side by side on the floor, and there seemed no room for us. Mother, not wanting to live with sparring women and wait in long queues for a bathroom with blocked toilets and smelly, overflowing drains, remembered the layout of similar houses, and ushered us outside to an empty stable. Although rough and basic, the stable was all ours! We even had an outside well to serve as a bathroom!

Mother and Juliana had their *mandi* (Indonesian shower) by the well after dark, we children during the day. Before the war, to *mandi*, we normally used a *gadjung* (a special pot), to scoop up water, then soaped ourselves, emptying the *gadjung* full of water over ourselves to rinse off the soap. But we didn't have soap in camp. All Juliana and Mother could do was to rub our skin extra hard to remove the ingrained dirt and sweat.

Our house leader found a crib for Dido to sleep in, a *balebale* with a thin mattress for Mother, and a light, double mattress on the bare, dirt floor, for Juliana, Penny, and me to share. It was good having our own space, but Camp Kramat was a horrible place. Many women tried to escape, then got caught, and received severe beatings.

If they weren't found right away—and the Japanese counted everyone twice or more daily—the whole camp was punished and received no food for as long as it took to find the culprits. Rations were always short, and we were always hungry. In desperation, some prisoners smuggled food into camp, or brazenly asked the commandant for more. This infuriated him and resulted in beatings so horrific that death often ensued. These experiences left lasting emotional damage, also on those forced to watch, and everybody had to be present, little children too.

Worse still, everyone—even small children like me—witnessed those brutal punishments during specially arranged *tenko* parades. *Tenko* parades involved, without exception, compulsory, extra deep-bowing to the sun. This was particularly important to the Japanese, because the sun signified their emperor, who was like a god to them. Singing of the Japanese anthem, and deep-bowing to their flag at the command of the officer was also required.

Prisoners had to do exactly what the commandant said. If he shouted *"Kerei!"* we had to bow and remain bowed until he shouted *"Norei!"* or *"Jotskei!"* Then we could straighten up and finally leave. Routine *tenkos* were always scheduled for sunrise and sunset. However, special *tenkos* took place when someone had escaped, or, to the commandant's way of thinking, needed a good reprimand.

But remaining deeply bowed for extended periods of time in the hot tropical sun—as the Japanese commandant demanded, took its toll on the old and very young. One had to bow from the waist downwards, with a straight back, until the head was almost parallel with the waist. It started with the house-leader's *tenko* announcement.

"Quick everyone!" she urged, running from room to room. "*Tenko* is on in ten minutes. Hurry!"

Mother and Juliana then hastily gathered Penny and me from outside, where we'd been playing with other children since sunrise.

"Faster!" Juliana urged Penny and me, holding my hand tightly as she walked next to Mother, pushing Dido in his pram. I had a will of my own, wanting to be independent, to walk alone and explore. But there was no time for that.

"Come on!" Juliana whispered again. "We're going to be late, and you know what that means…"

I didn't understand, nor did I want to go. At previous *tenkos*, angry Japanese soldiers awaiting us in the open field always shouted and waved their bayonets and knives in the air. That was enough for me. The shouting and screaming frightened me. The men's drawn swords glistened in the sun and looked frighteningly sharp. The sight made me snuggle in close to Mother or Juliana who covered my eyes with a skirt or hand, but they couldn't drown out the screams. If one was late for *tenko,* you were shot dead! A young boy arrived late for *tenko* one day, but narrowly escaped being shot, because he ran and slipped in between several rows of other prisoners, just as tenko started and he found a space to stand. He escaped being shot, but received a hefty blow to his neck with a shotgun from the guard. His neck still gives him trouble.

Unscheduled *tenkos*, often in the middle of the night, meant that the scene would be nasty. Screams reverberated throughout camp, of soldiers yelling commands and threatening or abusing women with swords and bayonets. This sent shudders up my spine.

Who escaped? What happened? we all wondered, dreading those parades. Nasty *tenkos* always involved violence, often so severe that the punished person collapsed, or even died. Together, we had to assemble in an open space in camp and stand in line, ready to be counted by the guards, who already stood there shouting and hurrying us on, while waving and pointing their bayonets at us.

The guards were always counting prisoners, and counting was difficult in Japanese. They often lost count, and then started again… and again—while prisoners stood bowed, in the blistering hot tropical sun, and with empty tummies. No wonder I hated *tenko*! Tensions at *tenko* increased when Sonnei, a vicious Japanese commandant in charge of all POW camps in Batavia, arrived unexpectedly to inspect prisoners. Once he vented his fury on Mother when Penny didn't bow correctly.

"Teach your child to bow!" he shouted, while he thrashed Mother, already weak and unsteady on her feet.

"Mother," called Penny. "Are you feeling all right?" The beating so upset Penny that from then on, she bowed extra deep to *all* soldiers—Japanese, Indonesian, and later British and Dutch—and for safety's sake also *saluted them!*

We heard a rumour that Sonnei had beaten a six-year-old boy to death…

SURVIVAL OF THE FITTEST

The violence and starvation petrified me, fearing Mother or Juliana might die, and leave us children alone. Yet Mother and Juliana never complained in front of us.

"Chew each mouthful twenty times," Mother urged, when we received our meagre rations. "It will make the food last longer."

When we received it, one small cup of white rice and watery leaf-soup had to sustain us all day. There was *never* meat, eggs, or fish. Food rations changed after every new commandant's arrival, along with more unreasonable rules, beatings, torture, executions, and further food reductions. Shrinking rations often resulted in total abstinence, sometimes for two to three days. The commanders-in-charge delighted in punishing the *whole* camp when one prisoner broke camp rules, either through theft, food bartering, escape attempts, or were found guilty of other, ridiculous charges.

To ward off hunger pangs, Mother and Juliana sipped hot water, pretending it was soup. Children with aching tummies, just cried. The little food we received lacked nourishment, and, over time, this played havoc with our physical and emotional well-being. Many in camp died. Dido lost so much weight he couldn't move. Always hungry, Penny and I kept crying, and begging for more food. Mother and Juliana then often shared their own meagre portions.

Hoping to find more food for us, Juliana volunteered for additional kitchen duties. She got the job, but no food. She sometimes found the odd scrap in the rubbish-bin and had to hide it to prevent it from being forcibly taken from her. Trying to supplement our meagre diet, she grew vegetables in a communal garden behind the stable, but this proved in vain, as the crop *walked* overnight.

Hearing of our hunger, kind Indonesians threw fruit over the double *gedek* fences. But, as tempting as those morsels were, Mother warned us to leave them alone. Anyone picking them up was usually robbed by others, or shot by the Japanese guards. From their lookout tower, heavily armed sentry guards could see both sides of the barbed-wire-topped *gedek* fencing. They quickly caught and tortured perpetrators, and many died—even the kind Indonesians.

One day, Juliana was extremely hungry and bargained with a *heiho* for food. In exchange for her watch, he gave her a handful of cooked rice. Squatting behind a bush, she ate hurriedly. As she chewed, she noticed a pair of boots beside her. Fearing trouble, she looked up and saw the Japanese commandant staring at her.

"Hungry, are you?" he asked gruffly.

"Y-e-e-s…" Juliana stammered back.

"Eat!" he ordered and walked on.

Juliana couldn't believe her ears. Other women had been beaten mercilessly for similar 'crimes' by the guards.

CAMP HOSPITAL

Like all other prisoners (except the very ill, such as Mother, and us children), Juliana had worked in Bogor and Kramat POW camps as an unpaid servant. One day, the commandant ordered her to report for duty at the camp hospital, instead of the kitchen. The hospital ward was staffed by a doctor, two registered nurses, and several untrained nurse-aides. They had no equipment, no medicines, not even bandages; they made their own from rags. They could only alleviate patients' suffering as best they could, and make them as comfortable as possible by simple means, looking on helplessly as most patients deteriorated before their eyes and died. The Japanese didn't even provide nourishing food for the seriously ill, or basic antiseptics or sanitation. Consequently, Juliana caught hepatitis from a patient, became very ill, and was also admitted to hospital. It was a miracle she recovered without medication.

By contrast to the prisoners, the Japanese ate well, and even held elaborate parties. Early in 1945, further food restrictions were imposed, many days without food. Some women and children died. Mother came close.

"I'm going to die," she whispered to Penny, as hospital staff carried her away on a stretcher.

"No Mother! Don't!" Penny pleaded.

"No children allowed!" the nurse said gruffly, and shut the hospital door in Penny's face. Penny returned each day.

"Mother! Mother!" she called by every window, hoping to catch a glimpse of Mother or hear her voice to show she was alive, but Penny never saw or heard Mother.

"Who will look after us if Mother dies?" Penny worried. She was now four years old. Perhaps Mother did hear Penny, because, although not totally recovered, she surprised us months later when she walked back into our stable. She repeated that scenario three times. How she pulled through each of those crises was a miracle. At every admission, the doctor called Juliana to say goodbye.

"Your mother won't last the night," he said. Medically, Mother's body had worn out, but Mother had other ideas. Without her strong willpower to stay alive for us children, I don't know what would have happened to our family.

SEGREGATION

Camp Kramat incorporated three fenced-off areas. Ours lay wedged in the middle between the other two. One housed more women and children, the other a group of nuns. Why the nuns were separated was a mystery. Our section was fenced off because some members of our families had been *paid* at work camps.

Many of the women in the other area sneered at girls who had worked for the enemy, accusing them of collaborating with the Japanese. They assumed that all girls had voluntarily chosen to work in what they thought were enviable conditions, and that the work had been for a favoured few. Even today, as Juliana thinks back to those times, she still feels the old shame and embarrassment welling up, although she had no say in the matter. There was no escape, no matter how hard she tried. She couldn't back out of the job!

Juliana, who had offered to work instead of Mother, did so to enable Mother to buy food for Dido, Penny, and me. Sadly, she drew the short straw. The women from the other area didn't understand that most girls had been *forced* to work for the Japanese whether they liked it or not, that many had even been taken by force—against their will—from prison camps, and been *used* and *abused*. For those who at first went voluntarily, it proved too late to realise what they had got themselves into, and couldn't flee their new 'prison'.

The Japanese knew their actions had been illegal, and had contravened the Geneva Convention. They understood implicitly that, if news of those actions spread to the West, they would be court-martialled. Thus, fearing that the abused girls would disclose their horrific experiences to the West, the Japanese separated our families from other prisoners of war.

Sadly, the 'work camp' girls suffered doubly: abuse from the other women who knew no better *and* from the Japanese. Some of the girls felt so hurt that they came to the segregating wall between them and the nuns for counselling, trying to find peace of mind.

NO LUXURIES

Soap and disinfectants in camp had long since run out. Flies and vermin thrived in open latrines. Mosquitoes bred with vengeance and spread malaria like wildfire—and nobody had mosquito nets nor quinine to treat it. Cuts and grazes became infected, spread, and quickly turned into tropical ulcers. Exacerbated by our starvation diet, those ulcers never healed.

Juliana's ulcers began at Camp Bogor. In Camp Kramat, the doctor scraped out the pus and applied some out-of-date sulphur powder. When that ran out, Juliana and Mother treated theirs with salt-water compresses, which would have been far from sterile. It was only after the war, back in Holland in 1946, when proper hygiene and nutritious food became available, that their leg-ulcers healed.

The filth also attracted cockroaches, *tokeh* (geckos) and *tjiktjaks* (wall lizards) which woke us at night. "*Tokeh! Tokeh!*" they called.

To address the growing rat numbers, one woman caught and roasted them on a little fire. To her, any protein was better than none. Feeling sorry for me one day, she shared a rat leg with me.

"Have some *muisje* (mouse)," she said, and, oblivious to what it was, I ate.

Dido, on the other hand, had a nasty experience with a rat. Waking us all in the middle of the night in pitch dark with his screams, and the Japanese always ordering 'no lights on at night', Juliana had to break that rule to discover a rat gnawing at Dido's foot, and blood spurting everywhere!

Penny's memories of Camp Kramat and *tenko* parade still haunt her today. There wasn't one good memory. With Mother in hospital or too ill to watch over us, and Juliana committed to kitchen or hospital duties, Penny had to grow up quickly. Being the next eldest and able, and only aged four, she had to keep an eye on Dido and me. It was dark when Juliana left our stable at 3:30 a.m. to light the kitchen fires. Penny and I woke at dawn, long after she'd gone. Dido sat contentedly propped up on a pillow in his pram, but I wanted to play and ran off further down the lane. I didn't listen to Penny. What four-year-old can control a stubborn toddler?

When Juliana returned from her duties she was exhausted and desperately needed to rest, but *tenko* would be on at daybreak and so

I had to be found. If anyone of us was missing from *tenko*, all 'hell could break loose' with the Japanese. As well as caring for Mother and us children, Juliana had far greater problems than we could imagine; her fear of Japanese soldiers must have been enormous.

But camp life wasn't easy for Penny either. She may have suspected some aspects of Juliana's fears and problems, but keeping me under control was no job for a four-year-old. Although she took looking after me seriously, my stubborn resistance often got her into big trouble with Juliana. It was during those times that Dido seemed Penny's only ally, an escape from reality. She then stroked Dido's face, watched the corners of his mouth twist upwards into a beautiful smile, and heard him chuckle.

Dido had that effect on many people. His eyes seemed to smile and dance with glee. Those extraordinary dark blue eyes mesmerised the whole family, even some Japanese soldiers. When food had been withheld for many days, we children cried from hunger. Big tears rolled down Dido's cheeks when a couple of young Japanese soldiers approached our stable and stopped to talk one day.

"Why are your children crying?" they asked Mother.

"They're hungry," Mother responded, indignantly.

Tears formed in the boys' eyes and they later returned with a few rations from their own table. If they'd been found helping a European, they could have been executed.

HYGIENE

Every evening Juliana kept giving Dido, Penny, and me our *mandi* by the well. But washing clothes was an unpleasant and backbreaking job, especially soiled nappies. There was no washing machine, no scrubbing brush or soap. Juliana had to hand-rub and rinse even soiled nappies, before hanging them on a makeshift clothes line to bleach in the hot sun.

There was no toothpaste, and our toothbrushes had long since worn out. Mother and Juliana cleaned their teeth and ours with their fingers, dipping them in salt and then rinsing and gargling with water. Their teeth went rotten. The only solution was extraction.

Toilet arrangements were another challenge. Apart from the open-drain latrines, the house we were part of had only one *kamar ketjil* (toilet). The drain was always blocked and smelled dreadful. With sixty people in one house, it was no wonder; and because there was no plumber, it was never repaired. Mother wouldn't allow any of us to use the open latrines. We children used a pot, Mother and Juliana an open drain behind the stable.

Apart from minding Dido and me, Penny also had a spying job. While she played in the lane with her small friends, she had to watch for Japanese officers approaching our stable. This was to give Juliana a chance to escape, because drunken officers often harassed young girls. As soon as an officer approached, Penny raced to the stable to warn Juliana or Mother so Juliana could climb a tree, and hide.

SOME OF JOHN'S AND FATHER'S CAMP EXPERIENCES

CHAPTER 4

Boys' prison camps? John's first prison camp, Halmaheira, for women and children, near Semarang, was passable. Ironically, his second, a *boys'* camp in Bangkong, also near Semarang, was his worst! One of the Korean guards, a sadist known as 'hockey stick', treated him and other boys abominably. To cope with the senseless cruelty, John totally shut off his feelings and thoughts. Although it was a struggle to stay sane, he tried to make the best of it all. However, to elaborate on that time, between August 1944 and February 1945, still revives many distressing memories for John.

The Japanese, and particularly the Korean guard, hated Europeans, and delighted in demoralising the boys. Boy prisoners at Camp Bangkong were forced to do hard, manual fieldwork from early morning to dusk in the blazing sun—and on a near-empty stomach! If that wasn't enough, they then had to meet for head-counts, endure and watch punishments at *tenko* parades: dastardly tortures, undeserved beatings, rapes, and ghoulish murders. Most of the punishments were for escape attempts and petty crimes like stealing food or eating crops while working. In one POW camp, little girls greeted a Japanese soldier, calling innocently: "Hello Jap," and as a result their mothers were forced to kneel on the hot tarmac for hours. If they swayed, they were repeatedly kicked upright… until they fell down dead.

John was on the receiving end of similar brutalities; memories too painful for him to share. Consequently, he feared the enemy's every move, but not wanting to give them the satisfaction of knowing his terror, he tried hard not to show it.

A typical workday at Bangkong boys' camp began at dawn. Breakfast consisted of a ladle of watery tapioca starch-meal that seemed to keep the worms at bay for ten minutes only. Lunch was a dry nugget of hard tapioca bread the size of three matchboxes with a butter-tin of black tea; dinner, a cup of rice with revolting vegetable hash, *never* any protein. At night, the mosquitoes buzzed round John's ears, relentlessly trying to extract blood from any place they could. Nobody had the luxury of mosquito nets or sheets to cover themselves.

Camp days began with early morning rising, a quick cold *mandi* without the longed-for soap that had long since run out, then breakfast and washing-up of spoon and plate. Following that, the boys had a short time for toilet and a wash. Then it was *tenko* parade immediately prior to marching together from the compound for fieldwork in the blazing sun.

If he could evade the guards' view while in the field, John found it especially thrilling to sneak away, pick some young vegetable plants, and surreptitiously gobble them up there and then, despite the plants having been dowsed daily with freshly brewed manure! He just brushed them off before quickly devouring them. One couldn't afford to get caught: punishment for this 'crime' was a torturous couple of hours kneeling with a bamboo pole behind the knees in the blazing sun! The consequences of that punishment were diabolically painful; agony lasted well after the ordeal.

The punishment of the 'crime' resulted in the prisoner's bent knees being tied to the bamboo pole and a series of other sharpened bamboo spikes all around him sticking up from the ground, pointing directly at his waist only centimetres away. This meant that the boy endured the pain of the bamboo stick behind his knees, but also the sharp bamboo sticks, should he come in contact with them if he tired.

The sharpened sticks prevented him from sitting down or changing position. Two hours of this torture in the hot sun without water, was unbearable, and against the Geneva convention for treating prisoners of war, especially young boys! There were other cruelties John had suffered which left him with lasting physical and psychological injuries, however, he hates to recount these, for retelling amounts to reliving the ordeals: they are too distressing to discuss. The next story came directly from John, especially for me.

A CHANCE MEETING

Late in December 1944, John returned from fieldwork and the customary *tenko* parade, and hurried to the toilets. En route, he passed several newcomers, and thought he recognised a familiar face, but dismissed the idea. John passed the newcomers again on his way out, and the man with the familiar face grabbed him.

"I've seen you before," he said. "What's your name?"

"John Brandt," John answered.

The man stepped back, slapping his hand over his mouth.

"Good God!" he gasped, his voice breaking. "I'm your father!"

There and then John and Andrew embraced. Both their physiques now skeletons covered with skin, they didn't recognise each other! And it was only twenty months previously that they had said goodbye…

The harshness of life in the POW camp, heavy manual work from early morning till late afternoon, appalling experiences of brutal torture, starvation, dysentery, malaria, and death, had left their mark on both, and particularly on Andrew. He was ill and visibly wasting away from tuberculosis. Forced labour, torture, and denial of medical care had taken their toll.

The Japanese had discovered that Andrew was fluent in high, low, and middle Javanese, Madurese, Sudanese, Malay, Dutch, English, French, German, Danish, and even a little Japanese, demanding that he spy for them.

But Andrew refused to cooperate, and so the Japanese placed him in isolation for many days—without food or water—in a tin shed in the scorching heat. When finally released, he was incoherent. Desperately hungry, he scoured the area for food and found a few wild mushrooms. Without questioning whether or not they were poisonous, he ate them there and then, raw. They caused severe diarrhoea, but, like all Japanese prisoners of war, he received no medical treatment. Pneumonia set in, and his condition worsened.

While in that febrile state, Andrew had been transported from Camp Tjimahi (near Bandung) to Camp Ambarawa and then to Camp Bangkong (both near Semarang). Squalid transit arrangements, prolonged starvation, and lack of medical care exacerbated his condition, and eventually tuberculosis set in. Disease had already ravaged his body and, on arrival at Camp Bangkong, his condition deteriorated further. Andrew was admitted to the camp's two-roomed *hospital*—a morgue, where patients died.

John volunteered to work the detested 'graveyard shift' (10pm to 6am), so he could spend time with his father. Other prisoners hated that shift, handling corpses, so the Japanese camp commandant granted John's request instantly.

Contagious diseases terrified the Japanese, causing them to keep their distance. There was no doctor and no medicine, only untrained nurse-aids like John. Thus, during lulls in John's shiftwork, he and Andrew could talk undisturbed and without fear of being overheard. Andrew needed to get several things off his chest, things he'd never shared with anyone previously, painful as they may have been to him. Hearing these things caused John to understand our father better than he had before. He felt that Andrew had suffered on a greater scale than we had, because Andrew felt *responsible* for *our* suffering!

Knowing he was dying, Andrew had urged John to ask Willy for forgiveness—why, is anyone's guess. He also asked John to pass on the information he shared with him during their last few weeks together. John, however, having had plenty of time to digest all Father had shared with him, found the conversations so painful that he decided to keep the essentials to himself. He couldn't see why it was necessary to upset Mother with stories of Father's suffering, after her own horrendous camp experiences.

Andrew died on 5 February 1945, five weeks after his reunion with John, and five months before liberation from the Japanese. Whatever Andrew shared with John remains a mystery, but John's silence and tact proved to be wise in the long run, especially for Willy. John must have sensed she was physically and mentally exhausted, unable to cope with more negative news.

MORE ABOUT JOHN

To escape the cruelty of the Korean guard in Camp Bangkong, and as timber-cutters were required to supply other camps with firewood, John volunteered for a timber-cutter's job at Camp Kali Tjeret, a camp in the mountains, north of Gedung Djati, also near Semarang. A church building, crammed with about forty straw mattresses served as prisoners' quarters, a small outhouse as their bathroom, but there was never enough water! A deep trench with bamboo poles straddled across, served as a latrine, and as usual, a four-metre-high gedek fence surrounded the complex.

Compared to the prisoners' quarters with only bare essentials, the Japanese commander and his *heihos* lived in luxury in the 'manse'.

The boys' mattresses literally 'crawled' with bedbugs. If he had time, John carefully checked his allotted thirty inches of space before sleep. It was absolute bliss to get five minutes' rest from the insects before his fellow prisoners arrived and the bedbugs would jump from their mattresses to his. With the continuous biting and resultant itch, sleep from then on was hell, and morning light a blessing.

Speaking fluent Javanese, John quickly established a good rapport with one of the Indonesian guards when he became one of the 'water detail'. This job required two boys, two five-gallon kerosene drums joined by strong fencing wire affixed to them, and a stout bamboo pole to carry the drums on. They walked two kilometres from the marshalling place in the forest to a locally revered and spot-lessly tended *holy* spring. Being allowed to dip their empty kerosene drums in the spring, the boys carried water back to the marshalling place, emptied their drums into a large container and lit a fire under it. Back and forth they went to the spring until the water reached the required level in the large container. When the water boiled, the guard blew a loud whistle to alert the axe-men and their assistants to collect their butter-tins of tea and have a rest for half-an-hour; those were the good times among the bad.

John clearly recalls the morning of August 26, 1945. After breakfast, a strange concoction of baked beans and corn, and *tenko* parade, the camp commander announced dejectedly:

"The war has ended."

Pandemonium broke out amongst the prisoners. John felt elated. Then an emptiness took over.

Why had all this misery been necessary? he asked himself.

Melancholy followed relief, then a strong urge for revenge. The Japanese Commander and several *heihos* escaped; others weren't so lucky. Prisoners, so incensed by Japanese brutality, administered an *eye for an eye*, there and then. John, however, soon discovered that taking revenge caused mixed feelings of inadequacy, shame, and guilt. Although he found it difficult to do—for his own sanity, he discovered that forgiveness was the only answer.

Before the announcement of liberation, John had noticed a change in the camp *heihos*' attitude, but couldn't quite fathom what was going on. The Japanese flag, a red ball on a white background, had always flown high above camp until then, but, over the last few days, he'd heard singing and noticed unfamiliar flags of equal horizontal bands of red and white.

The Japanese commandant's short speech at liberation solved the flag mystery. Suddenly John understood. Earlier he'd heard *heiho* guards quietly debating the possibility of independence, as suggested by their leaders. The horizontal red-and-white flags represented the then regionally fragmented, but politically united infant nation of Indonesia, wishing to be liberated from Dutch rule. Regardless of liberation from the Japanese and the war in the East, much suspicion, hatred of whites and their perceived intentions, now raged in the minds of Indonesians. To them, all Europeans, regardless of nationality, became probable enemies of Indonesia's drive for *merdeka* (freedom).

"The war ended much earlier than we were told," John and his fellow prisoners heard later. "It finished on August 15!"

"What?" they fumed. "And the Japanese kept up their use and abuse of us *after* liberation!"

Unbeknown to prisoners, Allied leading world nations had tried negotiating peace with Japan from July 17 to August 2, 1945, at the *Potsdam Peace Agreement*, however, Japan refused.

Assisted by sympathetic Indonesians, John and his fellow prisoners at Kali Tjeret began the journey back to Camp Bangkong. Little did they know there was a *Bersiap* (Civil War of Independence) in progress into which they soon blundered headlong. They found it preferable to return to Bangkong, and so they sneaked around via a semi-deserted prison camp in Amberawa that had received a heavy mortar attack during the night. Not knowing where to find safety, they remained there. This proved to be a good decision. No breakfast that morning—the kitchen, toilet, and bathroom had been destroyed! Escorted by sharp-eyed *Ghurkas* and their rifle-fire protection near Bangkong, the boys continued their journey to Semarang by train and trucks. Many of their erstwhile prisoners of war had gone elsewhere.

John established friendly relations with several Indonesians across the road from Bangkong, and learned that one of them was the Ambonese taxi-driver who had transported Mother, Juliana, John, Dido, and Penny back from Wonosobo to Semarang in early 1942! This made John think of the rest of us, and wonder where we might be. The Japanese had not passed on the postcards from Mother. Searching through the Red Cross lists of survivors, he found Mother's name in Camp Kramat, Batavia.

*Bangkong POW boys camp, Semarang, John's camp
—and where Andrew died.*

*Kalibanteng, Honourfield Cemetery entrance.
Photo credit Kalibanteng photos: Bert van Willigenburg, NL.*

Kalibanteng Honourfield Cemetery with bronze boys statue in front and remembrance crosses in background, My father's cross of remembrance is amongst those many crosses in the background.

Kalibanteng Honourfield Cemetry with Boy's statue in honour of all boys who died and survived Japanese Boys POW camps.

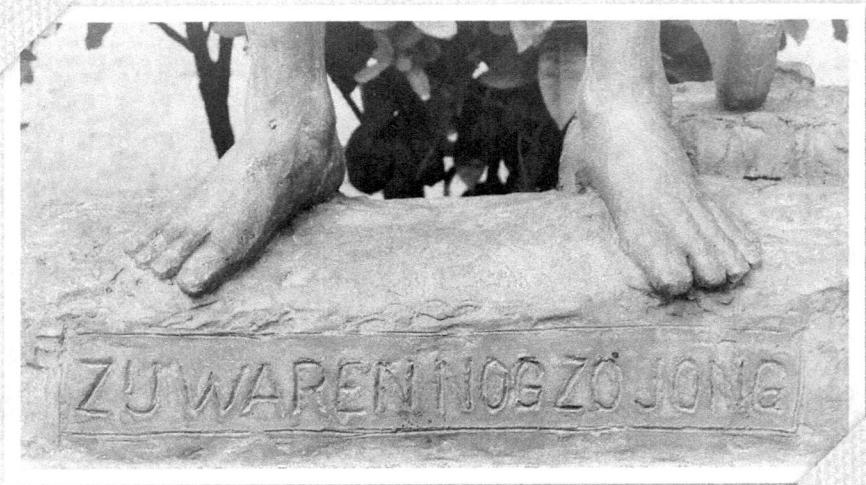

Kalibanteng Honourfield Cemetery, the feet of the bronze statue with the inscription, 'They were still so young'.

Boys statue at Kalibanteng Honourfield Cemetery

CAMP KRAMAT LIBERATION

CHAPTER 5

On August 23, 1945, while Dido lay in his pram, and Mother, Juliana, Penny, and I stood in line, waiting as usual for the order to bow, at camp Kramat's *tenko* parade, the commandant announced dolefully:

"The war is over. You don't need to bow any longer. You can leave camp if you wish, but be careful, the Indonesians are restless."

Mother and Juliana didn't believe him.

"It's a trick," Mother muttered. "Didn't they make similar announcements before and shot people in the back as they walked out the gates?"

We suddenly received nutritious food, meat, eggs, oil, fruit, vegetables, sugar, soy beans and extra rice, which we hadn't received for years. Where did it all come from? We ate it gratefully, of course, but it was easy to eat too much and overload our stomachs after the many years on a starvation diet.

Mother was still suspicious: "They must be up to something," she whispered. "I bet they want the Allied troops to think we've been treated humanely all these years..."

However, the Allies couldn't be fooled when they drove into camp two weeks later. Emaciated bodies, beriberi bellies, and tropical sores told their own stories.

Apparently, many Red Cross parcels had been sent to us in camp, but we never received them.

"Your food parcels went to Japanese U-boat troops," British soldiers told Juliana. "And your commandant conveniently forgot to tell you the war ended on the 15th August, soon after the bombing of Hiroshima and Nagasaki."

Thankfully, those soldiers remained in camp as our protectors against *rampokkers*.

Some Japanese soldiers also remained to protect us—this time the roles being reversed, and they as prisoners-of-war, but well-treated by the Allies.

British soldiers brought us many goods we hadn't seen for years: cloth, needles, thread, soap, toothpaste, make-up, bread, butter, condensed milk, cigarettes, chocolates, biscuits, cakes, even sweets! Mother immediately began sewing clothes for us, by hand.

"Are you for real?" Juliana asked the British soldiers. "Is the war really over?"

"Yes," they chuckled, grinning from ear to ear. "We've come to liberate you."

Prison-camp atmosphere changed overnight. British soldiers asked Juliana and other girls out to dances, the theatre, and movies. Finally, Mother and Juliana believed that the war was over.

The commandant had been right about the Indonesians being restless. Although some Indonesians were kind and helpful to Europeans, many weren't. Violent civil unrest in Batavia's streets forced us to remain in camp three to four weeks longer while Indonesian mobs brutally killed and raped Europeans, also those with mixed Indonesian blood.

But British soldiers brought smiles back to our faces. Penny's smile, however, was temporarily wiped off.

"Come for a ride," young soldiers urged her and her playmates one day. Lifting the children onto the back of an army truck, the soldiers treated them to a joy-ride. Suddenly the truck lurched to a halt as it hit a rock on the potholed road. Penny lost her balance and fell onto the tailgate. Blood spurted everywhere and her two front teeth fell on the deck.

The soldiers didn't know what to do about Penny's teeth, but they cheered her up with hugs and sweets. Sadly, Penny's new teeth took a long time to grow, and for years, photographers told her: "Shut your mouth! Don't smile!"

Following liberation, the Red Cross did their best to reunite all families. Sometimes, however, they bore bad news. Tens of thousands of civilians had died in Indonesian prison camps, and without qualified nursing staff, names often got muddled. With the Red Cross receiving the wrong information, announcements were occasionally incorrect.

While still at Camp Kramat, Willy received a letter from the Red Cross informing her of Andrew and John's deaths; but she and Juliana wouldn't believe it. The Japanese had frequently told women that their husbands or sons had died when they hadn't. So, when Willy and Juliana heard about Andrew and John, they prayed that a mistake had been made.

Sure enough, John proved to be alive! After liberation, and his release from camp Bangkong, the Red Cross helped him find Mother, Juliana, Dido, Penny, and me at Camp Kramat. Having hitched a ride with a friend's mother, he met Juliana in camp, but didn't recognise her.

"Where is *Mevrouw* (Mrs) Brandt?" he asked her.

Juliana looked hard at his face.

"Hey!" she said, "it's me! Juliana!"

Both had matured beyond their years; Juliana, then 18, and John 16, had come of age and changed.

Juliana wept as John told her of Father's death. John consoled her, as they walked together to our stable to find Mother.

"Andrew!" Mother called, excitedly as they approached.

"No, Mother," replied John, sadly. "I'm John. Father died."

Now sixteen, John resembled Father much more than when the

Japanese had separated us, when John was only thirteen. More than two years in prison camp by himself, witnessing and suffering horrific cruelties, he had matured beyond his years.

"But that can't be," Mother remarked stunned. "The Red Cross informed us you're dead…"

Mother would have dreamed of Father's homecoming for years. Perhaps she planned for them to make a new start and never again visit the mistakes of the past. Alas, the moment she had pined for shattered her dreams and hopes for the future. John still becomes emotional thinking of it today. Mother was lost. Her man would not come home.

John felt that Mother had no need for further upsets, so he simply told her about Father's last few weeks in Camp Bankong, and of the short time they'd had together.

"Father loved you, and asked for your forgiveness," John said.

Mother looked worn out. She'd hoped for a miracle. Father's death finally sank in. For a few minutes, she was grief-stricken, then she composed herself for the sake of us children.

Mother must have guessed what Father had talked about, and forgiven him there and then. Later, during the years when I grew up, she never mentioned anything nasty about him to me. All she shared about him was good and uplifting. It made me want to be like him. Mother missed Father enormously; I often caught her in tears, thinking of him. It was obvious to me that she had never stopped loving him. I even asked her why she didn't marry again and have more children. The thought made her shudder.

"I married your father for life," she said, quietly.

"Don't shake your head. It might fall off!" Mother said to John, perhaps to alleviate the serious mood of the moment. John resembled a walking skeleton.

The reality of the years ahead, with five children to bring up alone in her ailing state of health, must have been a terrifying vision. From then on, John stayed with us at Camp Kramat. Juliana appreciated his presence and help with Dido, Penny, and me, as Mother was still too ill to care for us.

FATHER'S EMPLOYER

Not long after John's release from prison camp, Mr Mahler, head of Sragi Sugar Factory, visited Mother at Camp Kramat. He'd spent the war years in the same POW camps as Father, and was also transported to Camp Bangkong, where Father died. Mr Mahler confirmed John's story about Father's death, especially the lead-up to it, going into detail about his refusal to collaborate with the Japanese, which resulted in their taking revenge.

Heroism is little consolation for loss, however. Mother was distraught; Juliana dazed by the news; Dido, Penny, and I didn't understand. I was almost two years old, and could not have remembered Father, since I was only three months old when the Japanese imprisoned him.

After liberation, life inside Camp Kramat became a little more bearable, but outside, in Batavia's streets, it was far from tranquil. Ear-splitting uproar, shooting and shouting, filled the streets. Thankfully, our British protectors made us feel more secure inside the camp compound. Soldiers kept spoiling us with food parcels and sweet treats, condensed milk and... soap! Penny and I gathered around those young boys like ants to a honey pot.

One of them, Johnnie Shepherd, became a good friend to Juliana, and our whole family. He often visited our stable, taking Juliana to the theatre, cinema, and dances.

Juliana, aged 19, 1946

Juliana, passport photo, aged 19, 1946

THE BERSIAP, INDONESIAN WAR OF INDEPENDENCE

CHAPTER 6

Boom Crack! Bang!

"Another bomb!" Penny cried, clinging to Mother's legs. Gunshots reverberated, shaking the house day and night, as British and Dutch soldiers fought armed Indonesian rebels in Batavia's streets.

When our Japanese *protectors* prepared to return to Japan, Camp Kramat had to be disbanded. Batavia's authorities allocated us a house in Brantas Straat, shared with another family. They used the ground floor, we the upper. Unless British soldiers accompanied us, Penny and I remained indoors or played on the balcony, as violent, bloody battles suddenly erupted.

"Merdeka!" Indonesian crowds screamed as they thronged the streets, shouting liberation slogans.

Caught among them one day, John's all-over tan and quick thinking saved his life. Copying the crowd, he too waved his fist in the air as if he meant it, shouting: *"Merdeka!"* The rioters must have taken him seriously and let him pass. Grandfather Roukens wasn't so lucky. They murdered him gruesomely on his way home from POW camp in 1945.

Mother scraped together enough money to hire a *babu* who shopped, cooked, and cared for us children. Indonesians weren't at risk outside, only Europeans. She overcame the continual power cuts by cooking on an *arang* (charcoal fire) on the floor in the kitchen. In her spare time, she played with Penny.

"*Kepiting* (shrimp)," she called her. Penny was small and light as a feather.

Water arrived daily in freight trucks, delivered and guarded by *Ghurkhas* who were part of the British Army. Public transport had ceased. Although risky, Juliana walked to work unless passing soldiers went her way and made room for her in their military Jeeps.

Low-flying planes and bombs exploded continually, particularly at night. They frightened us children. Flashes of light, followed by ear-splitting explosions, caused nightmares for years to come. Yet, when soldier Johnnie arrived, we felt safe. He, in his army uniform, spelt security.

Johnnie called Mother, Ma, Dido, Dido-Wido, Penny, Penny-Wenny and me, Addy-Waddy. He always had chocolate or toffees in his pockets for us! Arriving in a military jeep to pick up Juliana, he sometimes also took Penny and me to the club for treats.

Mother couldn't come; she was sick, pretending to be happy sewing winter clothes, in preparation for Holland, where we would soon be going.

"What are those?" Penny asked.

"Pyjamas," Mother said. "For Holland. It's so cold there, that water freezes, and hail and snow fall from the sky."

Penny roared with laughter, trying on the pyjamas. They seemed so strange.

Because of the rampant violence and mistrust, schools in Java remained closed. They couldn't function under those war conditions. John, however, had to catch up on three years' lost studies. Thus, in November 1945, aged sixteen, he boarded the *SS Bloemfontein* at Batavia's Tandjong Priok Harbour, with hundreds of other student refugees, to attend school in Holland.

As he stood on the ship's deck and took a last look at Java, he felt numb. Then, as the ship sailed, a lump lodged in his throat, and tears filled his eyes. Impulsively, he waved at the mountainous land of his birth, to Father, Mother, his family, his life. Deep emotions welled up inside him, emotions that still bring tears to his eyes when he thinks of that painful moment.

Will Indonesia ever rise from the ashes and return to normal? he wondered. Leaving Java was one loss; coping with his experiences of the past five years, another. It had all happened so fast, without time to reflect. Father's death... the gentle, patient man John loved was gone forever—John would never hear his voice and comforting talks again...

How will Mother cope alone in her frail condition? he pondered. *What kind of life will be in store for the rest of our family now?*

THE JOURNEY

John's voyage proved to be very different from any he'd experienced before; his first solo sailing, and aged only 16.

The ship had five decks: A, B, C, D, and E. His, E deck, was in the bowels of the ship, the aft deck—or hold. The only way to reach E deck was through a small room, designed to keep the weather out, and down several narrow flights of stairs, directly adjacent to the last stern cargo-hatch. Just below that deck, the ship's machinery and engine room's propellers and motors roared and steamed. During the war, the ship had been converted into a troopship for the war effort. Later, it was used for returning refugees to their Motherland, Holland. But it carried far more people than it was designed for.

There was no lounge. Refugees could only shelter in the stifling hot, cramped bunks below deck or outside on A deck, where it was cold and windy. All the ship's spare spaces were filled with countless makeshift bunk structures five high, with hardly room to spare. John's bunk was the highest, affording him barely room enough to sit up. The ship's engines below his E deck droned continually; the propellers' whirring and creaking making the bunkhouse hot and sticky. The weather, favourable the first half of the trip, allowed John to spend time in the fresh air on A deck. But three extremely trying days of rough, high seas and heavy rain got the better of him.

Seasickness overcame many passengers. By nightfall, the whine of the propellers dipping in and out of turbulent water just below his bunk, and the shuddering of the ship, combined with the constant sound of his now violently retching hold-mates, and the odour of vomit, became too much for him.

I must get out of here but where can I go? he thought, even more thankful for his top bunk, safe from his neighbour's vomit showers. But he still had to watch the slippery floor. Those unaffected by seasickness, were meant to clean up after the sick. John, however, felt beyond that.

The first night of the storm he spent holding a smelly dishcloth over his nose. Then the stench became too much. Rough weather or not, at 4 a.m., he made a beeline for fresh air on A deck. Worn-out through lack of sleep, and reluctant to return below, he crept under a vacant lifeboat's canvas cover, and slept for two days, undisturbed! It was cramped and hard, but heaven by comparison with the smell in the hold. When the wind died down, however, and the seas calmed, others unceremoniously evicted him from his hide-out, and made him help clean up.

The bathrooms were filthy, like those in men's prison camps. The men's area was on one side of a partition; the women's on the other. Both toilets sported the same arrangement: a large space with fifteen toilet-bowls side by side facing one way, and another fifteen immediately behind, facing the opposite way. No walls. No screens.

After two days without food, John's stomach regained its equilibrium and his appetite returned. Having an aversion to meat, John helped set tables and polished brass door handles in return for vegetarian meals. One of the kitchen staff took a liking to him and delivered a billycan of steaming hot coffee each morning while he still lay in his bunk. Not wanting to drink it all by himself, he shared it with his bunk neighbours. In the afternoon, he and a group of friends played cards or talked on the stern cargo-hatch-cover. Most claimed a section of the decks as their personal territory, and vigorously encouraged others to respect that arrangement.

When the ship entered the Suez Canal, John and other refugees took a trip to Attica in Egypt, where they received shoes and warm clothing for Holland's upcoming cold climate. Coming from the tropics, nobody possessed winter clothing. One person took their measurements, another dumped the nearest-size clothes into their arms—no time or chance for choice! Consequently, garments often ended up two or three sizes larger, perhaps a blessing.

Following their hot outing, several boys, John included, dived off the upper deck into the harbour for a refreshing dip beside the ship. They'd only been in the water five minutes when someone shouted, "Shark!"

Instantly ship's personnel threw cargo nets over the ship's side. Loudspeakers reverberated, ordering John and his mates to climb up the netting. They obeyed smartly, not keen to share the water with sharks. However, climbing up was harder than expected!

Back on board, the First Officer gave them a stiff lecture,

"Without passports," he reminded them, "you can't leave ship, and swimming is like deserting ship."

"I'll let you off this time," said the captain. "But such pranks won't be tolerated again!"

The weather, warm throughout the Suez Canal and Mediterranean Sea, turned nasty after the Straits of Gibraltar. John silently blessed Mother's foresight in sewing and packing his winter pyjamas and a lieutenant's discarded woollen battle dress. Those, plus the recently acquired winter clothes, all donned simultaneously, helped him endure the shivering passage through the English Channel. For thirty-six hours, he wore all the clothes he had!

HOLLAND

At last they reached Amsterdam. Feeling cold and miserable, John joined a queue to board one of many buses waiting on the wharf to transport refugees as near as possible to their assigned destinations.

There's mine, he thought, and jumped on. *Huizen, where Grandfather and Grandmother live.*

After his arrival at the village, and a short walk through tree-lined lanes, Valkeveenselaan came into view. Grandfather and Grandmother Brandt welcomed John with open arms. Not having changed his clothes for a week, he must have smelled, for they immediately arranged a bath and supplied him with clean, warm clothes. They looked shocked when he re-emerged wearing only 'one' layer instead of all his garments. He was skin-on-bone.

Grandfather and Grandmother lived in a wing of a double-storey gate house on the estate *Saint Michael,* belonging to the Liberal Catholic church. The large property had many extra buildings, including a church, where Grandfather ministered.

John stayed with our grandparents several months to recuperate before moving to Bilthoven to attend Kees Boeke High School. Along with other teenagers, he boarded with the Vinkenborg family.

Unrest brewed, however. One boarder continually insulted and trashed Indonesians.

"The Dutch Government doesn't recognise Dutch Indonesians as Dutch citizens," he claimed. The boy's parents obviously knew about the Dutch government's attitude regarding this issue, for John soon received a letter from the government stating: 'People who are born in Indonesia, who have lived there more than ten years, are regarded as Indonesian nationals who will be granted asylum in the Netherlands until the Indonesian problem is resolved. However, the Dutch government will not be held responsible for their welfare in the interim.'

That attitude created much insecurity for Dutch East Indies' citizens, John included. Although many spoke Indonesian and Dutch, most were Dutch or Dutch/Indonesian. Indonesian nationals had rejected them, and now so did the Netherlands! If they returned to Indonesia, where the Bersiap was in full swing, they would all be massacred!

Grandfather interceded on John's behalf and resolved the matter for him, but it remained a long-standing concern for others.

In the meantime, the Dutch boy continued his taunting. John suffered in silence but, finally the abuse became too much. He lost his cool and lashed out. The Vinkenborg couple backed John and sent the boy home. John inherited the boy's bed. Good friendships were forged with the remaining boys in the room.

Kees Boeke High School, in 1946, consisted of two villas on Soestdijkseweg North, Bilthoven. Separated by approximately 100 metres, one villa stood near the train station, the other on the corner of van Dijklaan and Soestdijkseweg. Both villas housed five to eight students in each room. A new, circular school structure was being built nearby, on Frans Halslaan.

John attended lectures in both villas, studying hard, catching up on four lost years of schooling. Considering his emotional state, and what he'd been through during the war, he did extremely well. Thankfully, Grandfather kept an eye on him.

It must have been a busy time for Grandfather and Grandmother, who lost two sons during the war, and now worried about the rest of us still in the midst of a gruesome Indonesian Civil War.

REFUGEES

CHAPTER 7

"Pack your bags and prepare to evacuate Batavia in two days!"
Back in Java, Batavia had become a boiling pot of unrest. Brutality on the streets escalated as the Bersiap came to a head, leaving all Europeans endangered, also those with mixed blood, together with Indonesian sympathisers of the Dutch. British and Dutch troops did their best to keep order, but couldn't guarantee our safety. Attacks on the innocent became more macabre as time progressed. Violent and ghoulish scenes contrasted with Java's pre-war serenity. Thus, when news of our British protectors' impending retreat to England reached our ears, our hearts trembled.

Until then, the urge to survive had kept Mother and Juliana functioning, but only just. Juliana kept working at the Traffic and Waterworks office in Batavia as Mother needed her income. Handouts were still unheard of.

Then on 2 May 1946, the Red Cross sent a message to all Dutch citizens at Juliana's work:

"Be prepared to evacuate from Java on 4 May. The *MS Boissevain* will evacuate you to your Motherland, the Netherlands!"

Juliana resigned from work there and then and rushed home to pack for our six-week trip. With Mother still ill, everyday responsibilities rested on Juliana, as they had throughout our two-and-a-half years in prison camp, and the eight months of the *Bersiap*. Packing, however, was easy. Between the five of us we owned nothing more than one kit-bag of clothes!

When we departed from Tanjong Priok Harbour, an ambulance transported Mother and Dido, both emaciated and feeble, directly to the ship's sickbay. Juliana, Penny, and I rode on a British military truck, escorted by an extra few fully armed British and Japanese soldiers in front and behind. Soldiers helped us on and off the truck's high deck. Japanese soldiers were now polite and helpful, but I still didn't trust them.

Our ship, the *MS Boissevain,* also carried far more passengers than it was designed for. Without enough cabins and bunks to cater for everyone, hammocks hung side by side far below deck in the cargo hold, where Juliana, Penny, and I, together with other women and children, were expected to eat and sleep. But sleeping proved impossible. I only needed to stir before falling out of my hammock! Juliana tried holding me in hers, but that kept us both awake. Even when we did sleep for a while, we still fell out.

To complicate matters, without air-conditioning or fresh air, the heat in the hold became so unbearable it drove us and many others up on deck to sleep under the stars. People lay everywhere! Juliana found us a small space next to the crew deck, where sleeping was much nicer and safer. Some of the crew, feeling sorry for Penny and me, handed us pieces of fruit, which we heartily devoured. We lived, ate and slept there for about three-and-a-half weeks.

Mother and Dido, in the ship's sickbay, slept in wooden bunks, Mother high up, Dido in a bunk with sides to stop him falling out. Owing to a shortage of nurses, Juliana helped with their care. She also looked after Penny and me. Still affected by her own camp experiences, however, she almost snapped. Penny and I thus often entertained ourselves, wandering round the ship alone.

With camp food shortages still fresh in our minds, the ship's galley had a strange attraction. Lost for something to do, we often ventured down the steep stairway to the galley, where we stood by the kitchen door until the chef or kitchen staff noticed us. After long conversations with them, they developed a soft spot for us, and always ensured that we walked away with a tasty morsel! Feeling they'd become our friends, we returned daily.

The steep stairs to the galley, however, could be slippery, and Penny tumbled down and hurt herself. The delicious aroma wafting up the stairs, however, couldn't keep us away. The ship's cooks inspected Penny's grazed knees and bruises with sympathetic eyes, and placed more snacks into her hands to soothe her pain and crushed spirit.

Because we were alone, Penny, being 18 months older, had to keep an eye on me, but I, a strong-willed three-year-old, did as I pleased, and totally ignored her. Without a playground or entertainment, I climbed the railing overlooking the ocean one day, balancing precariously without a care in the world. Penny, however, became alarmed.

"Addy! Come down!" Penny called. "You'll fall into the sea!"

Maybe I didn't hear, I certainly didn't obey her orders, and without adults to help, Penny ran up the stairs to sickbay to tell Mother. Juliana finally got me down. I repeated that scenario more than once.

Regardless of our daunting experiences, Penny and I kept exploring the ship and one day visited Mother and Dido in sick-bay.

"Father came down from heaven during the night and took Dido back with him," she said, as we sailed through the Indian Ocean near Colombo, Ceylon (Sri Lanka). Dido had contracted double pneumonia, and in his emaciated state couldn't fight the infection.

"It's a blessing," said the doctor. "As an invalid he would have had a dim future."

Still, we all grieved. Penny loved Dido, and missed her cuddles with him. He'd been her only solace at times, especially in prison camp.

The day after Dido's death, the captain asked Mother what she wanted done with Dido's body and whether she wanted a telegram sent to notify relatives in Holland. Mother, in her distraught state, didn't know what she was saying and suggested a ship's burial. But the captain found a small space in the freezer and decided to store Dido's body there until arrival in the Netherlands. He then sent a telegram to Grandfather Brandt, notifying him of Dido's death.

The ship continued its journey through the Indian Ocean, then the Red Sea and Suez Canal, where it sailed very slowly. It was pleasantly warm. Just as John had done, Juliana, Penny, and I also picked up warm clothing and blankets from Attica, the then small Egyptian location near the northern end of the Suez Canal.

Mother, too sick to accompany us, remained in sickbay. Sailors ferried us to shore in a rowboat. We then walked to a huge shed where Juliana chose clothes from a *mountain* of winter garments. She had to hurry.

People swarmed like bees around the pile of clothes. We couldn't try anything on. Had we done so, the best clothes would have disappeared. Instead, Juliana quickly held the garments up against us to ensure a roomy fit. For herself and Mother, she selected woollen coats and shoes: taking similar sizes made choosing easier.

After that adventure, we again walked to the canal where sailors rowed us back to ship. The boat then sailed on to Port Said, where Arabs in small boats sold leather handbags and carpets. They didn't believe Juliana had no money!

The warm Mediterranean Sea enabled us to keep sleeping under the stars. South of Spain, however, the weather changed drastically, forcing us below deck, where we battled with the hammocks once again. This time we appreciated the warmth of the hold.

In the Bay of Biscay, near France, extra-cold north winds whipped up; and Penny and I, never having experienced cold weather before, caught the measles. That made Juliana busier than ever, nursing us day and night in the hold and caring for Mother in sickbay.

Juliana shared her predicament with two kind *N.E.F.I.S.* officers (Dutch East Indies Forces Intelligence Service), who kindly offered her their cabin with two beds for the rest of the journey while they moved to the men's hold. Penny and I top-and-tailed on the bottom bunk, and Juliana slept on the top, on blissfully soft mattresses covered with *blankets* and *sheets!* I hadn't experienced that luxury in my life. The cabin was ours for a week, until we arrived in Holland. While Penny and I recuperated, time passed quickly.

"What's Holland like?" we asked Juliana. "Will there be snow?"

"No," Juliana answered. "It's supposed to be summer."

When the ship neared Holland's coast, dark clouds loomed overhead; and as the ship approached Amsterdam, Penny and I ran to sickbay to tell Mother.

"Mother! Mother!" we called excitedly. "We're in Holland!"

"Yes... I know. The nurse told me," Mother said, embracing us as we climbed up onto her bunk. She then told us she was going to Naarden Hospital, close to Grandfather and Grandmother's home.

"Grandfather is meeting you, so be good."

"Hospital?" we gasped, our thoughts turning to past realities in camp. "Are you going to die?"

The word 'hospital' spelt death to us. Dido's recent death and Mother's near-death experiences in Camp Kramat had impacted us. Just then, Juliana arrived and we had to leave.

"Bye, Mother!" we called tearfully, neither of us wanting to leave. It was 6 June, 1946. Penny was five years old. and I, three.

Juliana, having packed our few belongings again, took us by the hand to walk down the gangplank. An old gentleman called out.

"Grandfather!" Juliana exclaimed, and hurried to embrace and kiss him.

"This is Grandfather," said Juliana, turning to Penny and me.

He was a kind-looking old man, smiling broadly. Grandfather knelt to hug us, one at a time.

"It's good to see you both, at last. I've yearned for this moment so long... though not under these circumstances," he added, almost under his breath as tears welled up in his eyes. Then he composed himself.

"Now, who is Penny and who is Addy?"

"I'm Penny," Penny answered, "and this is Addy."

"Come here and give me another hug, both of you," Grandfather said, opening his arms wide again.

"Where's your mother?" he asked Juliana.

"She's going to Naarden Hospital, by ambulance," Juliana whispered. "Her lungs are in bad shape. The doctor doesn't give her much hope for recovery."

Mother, severely malnourished, on top of her asthma and emotionally unstable state, without medical treatment for her lung condition, had developed pneumonia and emphysema in camp. Her body had worn out long ago, yet her spirit battled on for us children. That fighting spirit caused her to strive with her illness yet again, just as she had in camp, when no one else would have cared for and protected her children. Perhaps Penny's anxious voice in Kramat prison camp still echoed in her ears as untrained nursing staff had carried Mother away to camp hospital. Our future was her main concern. She, or a nurse must have prayed, for in her condition, God was her only hope.

Juliana felt numb, exhausted, and emotionally depleted, almost unable to care for us any longer, still haunted by her horrific experiences during her tender teenage years. She hated thinking about those, yet certain things brought the memories rushing back. The reality of finally being safe had not totally sunk in.

What will the future hold for us now? she wondered. *Without Father to support me, Mother still gravely ill, Penny and Addy mere youngsters, and our grandparents at an age where they can't simply take over, will these responsibilities fall on me again?*

The future didn't bear thinking about...

The MS Boissevain: departed with 1,899 passengers from Batavia Harbour (Tandjong Priok Harbour) on 4 May 1946 and arrived in Amsterdam on 30 May 1946

EERBEEK

CHAPTER 8

"I'm cold," I cried, clutching Juliana's hand.

"Walk quickly, and we'll soon be on the warm tram," Grandfather encouraged, as he led the way to a waiting carriage and helped us aboard. Juliana hugged me. She'd been like a second mum to me the last three-and-a-half years when Mother had often been too ill to care for us younger children.

"We'll be home soon," Grandfather's voice interrupted my thoughts as he pulled the tram cord above the window, signalling to the driver we wanted to get off at the next stop. The road home was still an unsealed lane, Valkeveenselaan. Geese and ducks waddled freely round our feet as we walked to Grandfather's home within the St Michael's Church complex, in Huizen.

"Where is your house, Grandfather?" Penny asked.

Grandfather pointed to the end of the lane. "Ours is hidden among the trees."

"Juliana, Penny and Addy!" Grandmother greeted, hugging and kissing us warmly on the doorstep of a two-storey house, while Grandfather beamed behind us.

Grandfather, a 'Liberal Catholic Bishop and preacher,' was well known. Apart from ministering to the small congregation of Saint Michael's Church, his outreach also involved other areas in Holland and Belgium.

The church building, modern for its day, had been designed by our Uncle Lex van de Zoo de Jong, Father's brother-in-law. Penny and I, however, were far more interested in what was important in life—food! We soon befriended Bertus, the butler, in the kitchen. He was a father-like man, whom we liked instantly. We found him by following the tempting aromas wafting from the kitchen. There, this kind man greeted us, handing us treats we hadn't tasted before. Bertus sat Penny on his knee, holding long conversations, while I looked on. Grandmother, however, found out, and wasn't amused!

"Don't you ever go to the kitchen again," she warned us. She believed employers shouldn't mix with the working class.

That wasn't Grandmother's only grievance. She also frowned upon Penny's only possession, a chipped tin mug from prison camp, which Penny carried round like a much-loved toy. To Penny's dismay, Grandmother threw it out as if it were rubbish!

Two days following our arrival, Juliana, already run down, caught the English measles, while Penny and I were still recovering from our bout. As if that wasn't enough, Juliana also nursed a nasty boil under her armpit, and the only person able to care for us was Grandmother.

My Jules has far too many responsibilities, thought Grandfather, concerned about Grandmother's well-being. Their General Practitioner was also our great-uncle, Ko Wouters. Ko had married Grandfather's sister, Aunt Daisy. The kindly GP worried about our health, and made many house calls. He drove his 1926 Packard more than 80 kilometres from his home in Velp to Huizen, on the then slow and rough, unsealed roads.

It may have been on the doctor's recommendation that Grandfather arranged for Penny and me to meet a young couple.

"Penny and Addy, meet Mr and Mrs Brukker."

"Uncle Jel and Aunt Corrie," the man interrupted kindly.

They seemed a likeable couple, doing their utmost to make Penny and me feel at ease. Unable to say her name, I called the woman 'Bobby' instead, and from then on everybody called her by that name.

TWO SLICES OF BREAD

Uncle Jel and Bobby adored children. They were kind and gentle. Uncle Jel joked and made us laugh. Towards the end of their visit, Grandfather hurriedly arranged for Penny and me to be christened. Uncle Jel and Bobby became our godparents. Unbeknown to Penny and me then, they also took on guardianship of us in case Mother should die, which was highly likely at the time.

When Uncle Jel and Bobby began packing their suitcases to go home, they asked, "Would you like to stay with us in our home in Eerbeek and wait there for your mother to get well?"

Penny, giving the question some more thought, asked:
"But do you have bread for us to eat?"
"Oh, yes," said Bobby.
"And sweetcorn and chickens too," Uncle Jel added.
"But do you have beds for us to sleep in?"
"In a nice little room near ours," Bobby reassured.

We didn't need any persuasion after that, and soon we were sitting on the shiny, wooden seats in the train to Eerbeek. Time flew as Uncle Jel spun one funny story after another. Bobby described their home, the garden, and the friendly neighbourhood children. When the train finally stopped, we couldn't wait to see everything for ourselves!

Uncle Jel and Aunt Bobby's home was only a short walk from the train station, on a sand path. There we found a swing hanging from a big branch, and took turns on it.

"Hang on tight!" Uncle Jel called as I soared through the air. Halfway up, I lost my grip, slipped off the seat and fell on the ground. In an instant Uncle Jel crouched beside me.

"Sorry," he said, holding me tight. "I must have pushed too hard." Then he rubbed my sore knees, and kissed and hugged me.

Shaken, but none the worse for wear, I melted in his embrace, unable to believe that a stranger could be so kind; so different from the harsh Japanese soldiers I'd known in my short life.

"Let's search for eggs in the garden," Uncle Jel suggested, diverting my attention.

"Eggs?" we asked. "In your garden?"

"Follow me."

We couldn't believe our eyes when we found warm eggs in little dust hollows.

"This must be Paradise!" we called excitedly.

As Uncle Jel took us into the house with our bounty, he told us more about his chickens.

"Do you know my chickens can read?" he said with a twinkle in his eyes.

"No! Chickens can't read!" Penny said disbelieving.

"Mine can. I'll show you after dinner."

While Bobby set the table and prepared lunch, Uncle Jel took us upstairs to a little bedroom where he unpacked our small bag.

"Let's wash your dirty hands and dusty feet," said Uncle Jel while filling an old-fashioned porcelain washbasin with water, and lifting us one at the time onto the edge of the bowl.

"That tickles!" I laughed, as he scrubbed my toes.

We admired the room, and jumped excitedly on the soft mattresses. Then we returned downstairs to the set table, ready to eat. Uncle Jel thanked God for the food and our safe arrival in Eerbeek. He also prayed for Mother and Juliana's recovery. Bobby cut up our bread topped with cheese *and* jam into small *koetjes* and *kalfjes* (cows and calves). I couldn't believe we were allowed to eat so much food!

"Have another slice," Uncle Jel said.

"*Two* slices of bread?" I asked, never having been allowed that many before.

"You're hungry, aren't you?" Uncle Jel joked. "Would you like another egg too?"

Unable to contain my excitement, I eagerly tapped the shell, preparing to tuck into my second egg, only to find an empty shell. Tears welled up in my eyes, and Uncle Jel quickly handed me a proper boiled egg. *From then on, lightly boiled eggs became my favourite. Uncle Jel played the same trick on us and we kept falling for it. Later we also* tricked him, and roared with laughter when we 'thought' he had also fallen victim.

When we finished eating, Uncle Jel again thanked God for the meal. Penny and I usually left the table to run outside and play. Because one of the chickens was always looking for food around our feet, we named her *Rakoes* (greedy).

"Now, let me show you how my chickens read," Uncle Jel said, walking outside after he'd helped Bobby clear the table. He spread maize kernels on the ground, placed a sheet of newspaper on top and before long, the chickens flocked onto the paper, cocking their heads as they looked down at the print in search of the maize kernels.

"Look at that!" Uncle Jel called. "They're reading the newspaper! Aren't they clever?"

Another time, Uncle Jel told another story about his chickens.

"Did you know chickens also pray and thank God for their food and water before they eat and drink?"

"How?" we asked.

"Watch them carefully," Uncle Jel said. "See how they look up to heaven before swallowing? It's their way of saying 'thanks' to God."

Uncle Jel also worked as a chemist in a laboratory on their property. The building was partly underground. A large tree concealed the doorway, and unless you knew it was there, you could easily miss it.

On Sundays, Uncle Jel had yet another job. He cycled to a little church down the road, where he changed into a long, white robe, with a purple sash. Most Sundays he was already preaching when Bobby, Penny and I arrived, having walked to church. So excited to see Uncle Jel, Penny and I ran into his outstretched arms at the pulpit! Uncle Jel never scolded us for interrupting the sermon. Instead he scooped us up in his arms, and told the congregation what we'd been up to that week. They always laughed. Bobby then took her place at the organ, and played hymns. She never missed a Sunday.

The rest of the week, we followed Bobby around the garden to gather vegetables, freshly-laid-eggs, and delightfully scented sweetpea flowers from the vegetable garden in the backyard. Our hosts' home bordered on a railway line, and Bobby, knowing exactly when each train would pass, dropped whatever she was doing to take us outside to wave. We were so excited to see total strangers wave back!

Sometimes, when we were still in the garden, Bobby pumped the handle of a big, old-fashioned water-pump, to fill the chickens' water bowl, and we washed our hands under the stream of crystal-clear water.

Uncle Jel and Bobby never shouted or argued. Giving us their undivided attention, and showing their love, they slowly worked on removing the fears that had gripped us in prison camp, and with the *Bersiap*. To instil confidence in us, Bobby often took us to a field with tiny daisies, where the three of us sat down, and she plaited daisy-chains for our hair. Those garlands made us feel like princesses; we never tired of them.

Each night before bed, both Uncle Jel and Bobby bathed us—again in the big washbasin in our room—paying special attention to our dusty feet. I had ticklish toes, so I wriggled and giggled as Bobby scrubbed, and made bath-time fun. Dressed in our pyjamas, we then inspected our prized sweet-wrapper collection, pinned up on the wall. With post-war sweets still a luxury, we treasured even the wrappers! After tucking us in, Uncle Jel and Bobby told stories, prayed, and sang songs. I remember one song that made me feel safe.

In Dutch:	**In English:**
s Avonds als ik slapen ga,	In the evening when I go to sleep,
Daar komen veertien engeltjes aan,	Fourteen angels come to me,
Twee aan m'n hoofden end,	Two at my bed head,
Twee aan m'n voeten end,	Two at my feet,
Twee aan m'n linker zij,	Two on my left side,
Twee aan m'n rechter zij,	Two on my right side,
Twee die me dekken,	Two to tuck me in,

> Twee die me wekken, Two who'll wake me,
> Twee die me wijzen Two who'll guide me
> naar 't hemel's paradijsen. To heaven's paradise.

Then we prayed for Mother and Juliana.

Unfortunately, Penny and I were also far from well. We took a long time to recover from the measles, and our great-uncle Ko, the doctor, made many house calls, visiting all the way from Velp.

On reflection, Uncle Jel and Bobby sensed our ingrained fears, and reassured us with their love, giving us security. Although I didn't realise it at the time, their faith in God changed the way I viewed the world, slowly preparing me for life in general, including the ability to cope with the knocks I would still face in the years ahead. As I grew older, still lacking full self-confidence, I saw glimpses of it growing through them as they had sowed the seeds for recovery. People like Uncle Jel and Bobby tended my spiritual garden. Their input is hugely memorable, even today. Later, others helped me on the road to that security we all need. It helped me answer the question 'who really cares for me?' or 'who will choose me, despite all the drama and pain of life?'

My biggest fear at that time was that Mother might not come out of hospital alive and that I'd never see her again. Although Bobby and Uncle Jel helped me trust God to take care of and heal her, I missed Mother terribly, often crying myself to sleep at night as I longed to be with her.

Mother still lay in Naarden Sanatorium, recuperating from psychological and physical illness. Doctors had expected her to die; and although Penny and I weren't told this, I feared it would happen. When Juliana regained her health, she regularly visited Mother, and I gather our grandparents did, too.

Because of the distance between Naarden and Eerbeek, and Mother's poor condition, Penny and I hadn't seen her since our separation at the wharf in Amsterdam. Then one day, Uncle Jel and Bobby woke us early.

"Your mother is coming out of hospital," Bobby said. "Quick, let's get dressed so we can catch the train and see her."

I couldn't get my clothes on fast enough. To hear that Mother was well again, was an answer to prayer.

Parting from Uncle Jel and Bobby was sad, although the true reality of it didn't sink in until later. They would have made great parents, but just as blood is thicker than water, I couldn't have lived with them long-term, knowing that Mother was still alive.

We didn't see Uncle Jel and Bobby much after that. Eerbeek was a long way from our new home in de Bilt. Instead, we treasured the good memories in our hearts. Sadly, something else prevented them from seeing us.

Someone told Mother about Uncle Jel and Bobby's wish to adopt us in the event of her death. This caused Mother extreme anxiety, fearing the Brandt family might take Penny and me away from her. Her state of post-traumatic stress likely led her to the decision to shun all help, even financial, from the family. Years later, I learned that she also refused to allow Uncle Jel and Bobby to visit. It saddens me how Mother treated them. If they'd been allowed to, they could have enriched Mother's life as well as ours.

Holland, 1946, Penny and Addy soon after arrival

Eerbeek, Penny and Addy, daisy chains, 1946

Bobby with Rakoes

DE BILT AND BILTHOVEN

CHAPTER 9

I *can't wait to see Mother again, I thought, wriggling on the train seat. Why is this train so slow?*

Little did I know that Uncle Jel and Bobby only *pretended* to share my excitement. Years later, I heard our departure hurt them deeply. Penny and I missed them both. I especially missed Bobby.

It may have been providence, however, as only three years later, Uncle Jel died. Bobby moved to St. Michael's in Huizen and played the church organ every Sunday.

Many changes took place in both my life and Penny's. Our government-allocated rental in De Bilt, was the nearest they could find to *Kees Boeke High School* which John attended in Bilthoven. The rental dwelling was so tiny that there was no room for John. He had to continue boarding! Mother, Juliana, Penny, and I had to share the two-roomed house with two other women. They used one room, we the other. We shared the kitchen and toilet. There was no lounge or dining room, nor a bathroom nor laundry. We washed ourselves in the kitchen sink, washing clothes in a bucket.

The house was one of many in a long row, with small front and back gardens. Our back garden overlooked a paddock with horses, which Penny and I fed clumps of grass to until Penny received a nasty bite. Mother wouldn't allow us to feed the horses from then on. She worried about our safety and health. She really needed friends to talk to, but that was difficult when illness confined her to bed. We had no telephone. If Mother needed the doctor urgently, Juliana had to use the neighbour's. It took three more years, even with a doctor's recommendation, for us to get one!

Holland's bitterly cold and windy weather caused Mother's frequent relapses of bronchitis or pneumonia. This, complicated by her now-chronic emphysema and asthma, made her cough and gasp for breath even more, especially at night. With the four of us sleeping in the same room, none of us slept soundly.

Juliana needed eight hours' sleep: she attended evening classes at the Bridging High School in Utrecht, and studied during the day. She, too, had to catch up on *war-lost study years.*

"Go and see the Administrator of Housing about another house for us," Mother urged Juliana. "We need a larger home... John should also be living with us."

But that was easier said than done.

"Thousands of people need houses," the clerk brushed Juliana off. "Be thankful you have a roof over your head."

"You don't understand," Juliana insisted. "Come and see what my mother has to put up with..."

She kept hounding the man, until he visited our home one day after work.

"This is appalling!" he mumbled, visibly shocked by our living conditions. "I'll work something out as soon as I can."

A week later, the clerk greeted Juliana with a smile.

"I have a four-bedroom villa for your family in Bilthoven. But you'll have to share it with a widow..."

"Fantastic!" Juliana exclaimed, almost hugging the clerk. "With that many rooms, I can have a room to myself, and my brother can move in and help care for my mother and little sisters!"

Our new address would be Prins Hendriklaan 4A, Bilthoven, perfectly situated for John, and near school. The house looked impressive. Trouble loomed, however, as John discovered.

"I'm helping demolish a house in Prins Hendriklaan," said Jacques, one of John's friends in class. "SS collaborators are moving in and we're ransacking the place in retaliation. Want to help?"

"Oh," John answered, casually. "We're moving to that street. What number are you working at?"

"4A."

"*What?*" John exploded. "That's *our* number! We're not collaborators! Who told you those lies?"

"The widow who lives there…" Jacques mumbled apologetically.

Horrified at his mistake, Jacques ensured that he and his mates reinstated the house as much as possible before we moved in, though some things had been wrecked beyond repair. Thankfully, the widow who initiated the rumours, moved out. Juliana couldn't believe we had a whole house to ourselves! John could easily move in now.

Penny and I loved having John around, especially when he put us to bed. The best part came after his tucking-in and kissing routine, when he walked out of the bedroom, into the passage and closed the door. Returning instantly, he closed the door onto his neck, pulling silly faces. Then he wriggled his neck from side to side, like a snake, keeping his head straight while repeatedly opening and closing the door onto his neck and making more funny faces. When he'd finished his *act*, we fell asleep, exhausted from laughing!

Juliana, now attending evening classes at *Schoevers Typing School* in Utrecht, did the housework, cooked dinner, nursed Mother, and, together with John, cared for Penny and me. John prepared breakfast and relieved Juliana from some chores after school so she could also study. Both had lots of homework.

When aged twenty, Juliana qualified in shorthand and typing, and applied for a secretarial job at Het Gemeentehuis (de Bilt's City Council), round the corner from us. Being chosen out of 48 applicants, said something about her maturity and communication skills.

Before work and school, however, she and John had many tasks to complete. Mother needed a bed bath, and Penny and I had to be taken to school and kindergarten. John prepared breakfast—porridge boiled with milk—afloat with *skin*, which I hated, but was forced to eat!

I still see myself sitting at the table, staring at my untouched porridge—by then stone cold. When I could, I often crept up to the cold, Etna coal fire in summer, and emptied my plateful into it! Thankfully, nobody ever found out, because Mother, Juliana and John would have gone berserk. With prison camp and starvation still fresh in their minds, they never threw out food! I, however, couldn't see why they didn't understand my aversion to milk skin. When I was old enough to be taken notice of, I refused to eat porridge cooked with milk. Years later I made it myself, stirring it continually, so no skin formed.

At first Juliana and John took us to school and kindergarten on their bikes, Penny on John's front bar, and I on Juliana's carrier. My feet often got caught in the spokes and hurt badly, but any mention of visits to Juliana's friends made me get back on the carrier smartly.

John took Penny snow-sledding in Bilthoven North. Penny and I loved swimming at Natuurbad with both Juliana and John. To keep us safe, they wound old patched and blown-up inner-bike-tubes around our waists. That way, Juliana and John could also swim, instead of keeping an eye on us continually. We couldn't swim yet, and I watched in awe as they dived from the highest diving-board into the deepest pool. They, too, needed diversion from stress. Each had their own needs and Mother, possibly owing to her post-traumatic stress and breathlessness, was demanding, and hard to live with.

Adding to the consternation, the ransacking of our home's plumbing and basins left us with cold water only. In summer, Penny and I gladly took our weekly *mandis* outside on the walled-in back porch in a free-standing tin tub. John heated the water in a pot on the kitchen element. In winter, we stood a bucket filled with warm water *inside* the upstairs bath tub (minus the hot tap) for a weekly *mandi*, washing our faces and feet with cold water morning and night in a hand-basin. Later, a small gas water-heater was installed over the kitchen sink. Much later, an electric boiler was plumbed in the bathroom with its own tap over the bath, but to economise on hot water we continued using the *mandi* or bucket method.

Mother ensured that we economised, and, compared with wartime Java, living conditions improved considerably. But Holland still suffered the after-effects of war and consequent shortages, especially food and power. Basic foods such as bread, cheese, milk, margarine, and potatoes could be bought, although not freely. Meat, eggs, coffee, tea, sugar, and butter were scarce, and only obtainable with coupons, which were rationed.

Mother couldn't afford the latter. She constantly reminded us of prison camp shortages and made us eat everything on our plates. This bizarre perspective, regardless of appetite, was hard to break!

I still remember walking home from Bilthoven's train-station, all the street lights suddenly flickering and then turning off. In pitch dark, we walked home, unable to see a hand before our eyes. I was so glad to hold Juliana's or Mother's hand…

UNREST AT HOME

Even as a small child, I realised something was wrong in our family; that the war had had a strange and frightening effect on us. It had been peaceful at Uncle Jel and Bobby's home, where there was much love. It was different at our home. Shouting was a regular occurrence. It seemed that the Japanese way of dealing with friction in POW camp had rubbed off on Mother. Although family life could be sweet and loving one minute, all hell would break loose the next! Sometimes I feared for our safety, but also for Mother's and Juliana's who sometimes fought. I loved them both. Thankfully, Penny's and my tears and screams disarmed them.

Later, when Juliana and John had left home, and Mother directed her outbursts at Penny and me, I learnt to shut off my feelings. Although Mother's words stung, I didn't believe she meant to harm us, and excused her fits of temper. At the first sign of flare-ups, I ran to my room and locked the door. Yet I also wanted to be close, and later pretended nothing had happened. I couldn't understand why she acted so violently, exploding like a bomb. Yet, regardless of her shortcomings, home with Mother, often sick in bed, was still my haven, a place to run to from trouble.

Prins Hendriklaan 4A, Bilthoven,
era 1947-1958

De Bilt, 1947
Penny and Addy

KINDERGARTEN & PRIMARY SCHOOLS

CHAPTER 10

"Hurry Ad!" John urged. "Time for school."

Penny and I started attending Kees Boeke Primary School and Kindergarten during 1947, in the same villa where John had had his lessons a year earlier, on Soestdijkseweg North. Penny's class was upstairs, mine downstairs.

At first Juliana and John lifted us on their bikes. When John changed schools to the *Overbruggings HBS* (Bridging High school) in Utrecht, we caught the bus.

"Always stay together and wait on the bench for the bus," Mother instructed five-year-old Penny. "Get off at Gezichtslaan, walk straight to school, and hold Addy's hand so she doesn't run onto the busy road."

One morning, the temperature dropped well below freezing. Icicles hung from wire fences, bare branches, and leaves. A cold wind bit into our faces, whipping our clothes about, while rock-solid dirt footpaths vibrated, and hurt our feet.

"I want to go home," I cried. "My feet are ice-cold!" But Penny wouldn't hear of it.

"It'll be warm on the bus," she coaxed, firmly holding my hand.

We made it to the bus stop, but I continued crying. Suddenly, a young man and young woman cycled towards us. They put their bikes to one side, and knelt down.

"What's the matter?" the woman asked, in the sweetest voice I'd ever heard.

"My feet," I sniffed, "are sore."

"Would you like me to rub them for you?" she asked.

I nodded, and watched in wonder, as she removed my shoes and massaged my feet. They gradually warmed, as she rubbed them and reassured me. When the bus approached, she quickly put my shoes back on. The man and woman then helped us get onto the bus. We waved as to old friends.

All that winter, they returned daily to the bus-stop, to rub my feet. When spring came and the weather warmed, we never saw them again.

Could they have been angels sent by God? I often wondered.

THE DUTCH ROYAL FAMILY

Bilthoven was only six kilometres from *Paleis* Soestdijk, the Dutch Royal Palace, where the then Dutch Queen, Wilhelmina, lived with her daughter, Princess Juliana, her son-in-law, Prince Bernhard, and granddaughters, Princesses Beatrix, Irene, Margriet, and Marijke. In 1947, the three eldest girls also attended Kees Boeke School, Beatrix, and Irene in classes below John's; Margriet was in my kindergarten class. Their younger sister, Marijke, now known as Christina, was still a toddler.

Princess Margriet planned to celebrate her fifth birthday party on 19 January 1948. All pupils in Penny's and my classes were invited. I'd never attended a party before, so when the day arrived for us to be picked up, I stood excitedly in line in front of the school, ready to board a bus. Penny's class had already taken their seats when our class clambered aboard, and I too started climbing the step.

"Stop! You're not going," a teacher said gruffly, holding me back. Then she pushed another girl forward, a girl I'd never seen before. The bus departed, leaving me alone on the driveway until Juliana arrived on her bike to collect me. Someone had phoned her at work. Following the party, Penny handed me a concertina paper toy attached to two small sticks. It eased the hurt, but I wondered why I'd been excluded from the party.

Family outings were rare because of Mother's ill health and her lack of money, but in summer she caught fewer chills, so we sometimes ventured out on our bikes. Although she still wasn't well, I enjoyed those times together, and think Mother did too. But if we walked or biked too fast, or if the wind blew, she struggled to breathe and had to sit down to recover before continuing. I hated seeing her breathless. Yet Mother was determined to continue.

One family outing I recall was Queen Wilhelmina's birthday on 31 August, in Utrecht. In 1948, after reigning for 58 years, Wilhelmina abdicated in favour of Princess Juliana. Utrecht hosted a big celebration with a fair, helium balloons, and monkey string-puppets. Brass bands marched and played national anthems in the streets.

Queen Wilhelmina had reigned longer than any other Dutch monarch. From then on, *Koninginnendag* (Queen's birthday), was celebrated on 30 April, Queen Juliana's birthday.

I'll never forget the tune to the song 'Oranje Boven' (Honour the House of Orange). Part of the *Koninginnendag* celebration was dressing up in our best clothes, pinning orange ribbon-brooches on our coats, and wearing orange ribbons in our short-haired pony tails. Orange signified allegiance to the House of Orange, Holland's royal family. The Dutch flag, red, white, and blue, horizontally striped, flapped from poles on almost every house.

My favourite attraction was a man holding a huge bunch of colourful helium-filled balloons.

"Please Mother," Penny and I begged. "Please, please can we have a balloon?"

But Mother wouldn't give in, and continued walking to the fair with us in tow. She hated children to nag!

Although disappointed at remaining empty-handed, our eyes feasted on *escaped* balloons bobbing up and down in the sky. With many other things to see, John rewarded us with a big candy cane that we kept sucking all day. Mother dragged us round the stalls and shops to see the wares. She didn't buy much, and nothing for us.

"Money doesn't grow on trees," she always reminded. "My widow's pension isn't nearly enough for the five of us, even with Juliana's salary."

I decided this was because we had no father. I vowed to study hard and have a job to fall back on should my husband ever die when I grew up.

I liked looking at shop fronts, especially a toy shop near the market. Above the entrance a teddy bear blew bubbles which floated all the way down the street. I could have watched those bubbles all day! Although I enjoyed the outing, all that walking hurt my legs. John sometimes carried me. Mother didn't have energy for that.

On our way back to the bus, Mother softened, and bought Penny and me a balloon each, maybe because we hadn't nagged.

"Oh, thank you, Mother!" we cried, as the man tied the string onto our wrists so the balloons wouldn't float away.

At home, Juliana cut the balloons off our wrists to let them drift up to the ceiling. We talked about brass bands excitedly, about when they would one day march through our street too, and how we, together with our friends, would march after them. Then John put us to bed.

MELLE

"Oh no! Melle is crying again!" Mother groaned. "What's the matter now?"

I pretended not to hear. It was difficult sharing our house with two extra people, especially as we all needed to use the kitchen and bathroom.

Mother attempted to earn extra money by taking in Agatha and Melle as boarders.

I loved Melle's company. We played together all the time. However, differences in child-rearing methods, and extra pressure on the gas and electricity bills, caused upsets.

"I wish they'd cooperate!" Mother grumbled.

I wish I had the kitchen to myself, Juliana thought secretly.

I was five and Melle younger, when Melle and Agatha arrived. We explored the neighbourhood, and enjoyed our escapades away from the bickering adults.

"Look! Berries!" I exclaimed one day, as we played on a vacant lot near home.

"Let's eat some," Melle agreed. They tasted sweet, but left a sour taste in our mouths.

"Oooh! I feel sick!" I cried.

"Me too," grizzled Melle, and we raced home, vomiting on the way.

Our sickness started yet another argument.

"Addy should know better," Agatha accused. "She's five!"

Mother and Juliana staunchly defended me. After a huge uproar, Agatha marched out with Melle in her arms, never to return.

Seeing Melle go upset me, but the rest of the family felt relieved.

Neighbourhood friends soon filled the empty gap Melle had left. I found every excuse to get out of the house, a distraction first from the chores Mother found for me to do, and later from the stress of Mother's unexpected, volatile outbursts. I could have played outside all day if given half the chance.

"Addy! Penny!" the children shouted from the street to draw us out.

At first, that was a trigger for Mother to allow us outside, sometimes even letting us off finishing our chores! Later we weren't so lucky. Chores came first.

MONTESSORI PRIMARY

After a year at Kees Boeke Primary and Kindergarten, Penny and I moved to Montessori Primary on Rembrandt *Plein*. Father's brother, Uncle Marijn, was the headmaster. However, Montessori Primary's lack of funds and buildings meant Penny and I had to attend lessons at the Van Dijck School. As soon as Juliana and John said goodbye, and Penny went to her class, I panicked. To make matters worse, Van Dijck School pupils bullied Montessori school children.

They called us names, pushed, and shoved us, pulled our hair, grabbed our hats and mittens, and threw them far away. I dreaded school, being in the playground, and going home.

"Leave those little girls alone!" Maarten Vos, an older Van Dijck School pupil, called to the bullies, as Penny and I walked to the bus one day. Maarten was tall and strong. When the bullies saw him with us, they scattered.

Maarten took a shine to us, devising ways of keeping us safe. He escorted Penny and me to and from the bus stop, and protected us in the playground. Later, when we attended Montessori Primary, he kept up his vigil. Meeting us at the bus stop each morning, he escorted us to our school. Then he returned to his school. When his lessons finished, he escorted us from our school gate to the bus stop again.

Poor health prevented my regular attendance, and Holland's cold and wet climate didn't help. Consequently, school progress suffered and, altogether, I lost almost three years' schooling to illness.

My sporadic attendance didn't help, especially when I was left to my own devices, still unable to read. Playtime was the only school activity I enjoyed. All children received *cold* milk to drink at morning play. I, however, had to drink mine warmed.

The teacher, thinking having mine warmed might improve my condition, made me drink it hot. She took me into a kitchenette behind the classroom and showed me what to do.

"Take the pot off the element when it boils," she instructed, having poured the milk into a pot. Then she left me to pour the hot milk into a cup while she taught the rest of class. Thick skin formed on the hot milk, so once alone, I poured it down the sink. When she returned and saw the empty pot, she assumed I'd drunk the milk. She had never asked me how I preferred it.

BULLIES AT HOME

In 1949, for my seventh birthday, and first party, Mother allowed Penny and me to invite two friends each to celebrate, perhaps to cheer us up. It was fun until my two so-called friends from Montessori Primary wanted to exclude me from the games. Mother and Penny straightened them out, but they hounded me at school at playtime from then on. As my health deteriorated further, I spent fewer days at school and more in bed. Still unable to read, I had nothing to do. We had no television, and the radio was downstairs. Mother brought up my meals and medicines, but then she left me alone.

If someone helped me downstairs to the living/dining room divan, Mother's presence and visitors cheered me up. I lacked energy to come down on my own, and became weaker as time progressed. With a high fever, I couldn't even make it to the bathroom.

I yearned for Penny's return from school, when she would read from my favourite books, Hans Christian Anderson, and Grimms' Fairy Tales. But Penny had to help Mother and do her homework.

As far back as I can remember, Penny was my best friend, always protecting me. I was shy and fearful of strangers; Penny was confident and loved making friends. Yet we had a common bond, were always together, caring for and understanding each other, sometimes without even saying a word. She was very forgiving too. Soon after our arrival in Bilthoven, we met some children on our street.

"Can we play with you?" Penny asked.

"Where are you from?" one of the boys asked.

"Indonesia," Penny answered.

Suddenly they pushed us into their holly hedge. It hurt, and I never returned. However, Penny did, and even played with one of the boys. She had a remarkable talent for turning enemies into friends.

There was a lot more to Penny than people realised. She looked tiny but in character she was a giant and — generous. Each year, on 5 December, Aunt Tine and Grandmother's half-sister, Aunt Marietje, gave us chocolate 'letters' for *Sinterklaas*. Penny preferred milk chocolate, and kept her letters long after I'd finished mine. Then she shared hers with me! I was in for a real treat when she gave me her 'whole' *dark* chocolate letters.

Penny acted as my bodyguard and comforter. If we hadn't had such a good bond between us, with interludes of fun and distraction during the continual stress and tension we faced with Mother, I'm not sure how we would have coped. We often ran all over the house chasing each other, laughing, and joking. We also wrestled, hoping to make ourselves strong, as defense against the violent men roaming Bilthoven and Zeist's quiet streets, spoken of during radio broadcasts. Regardless of the many scary ordeals we faced, Penny always gave me courage.

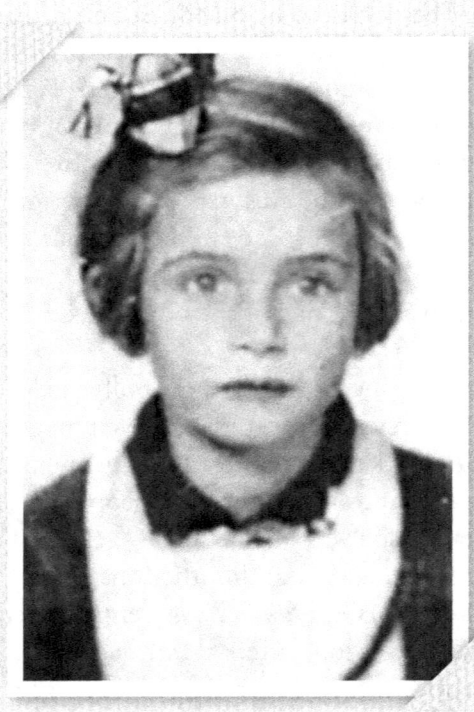

Penny, 1947

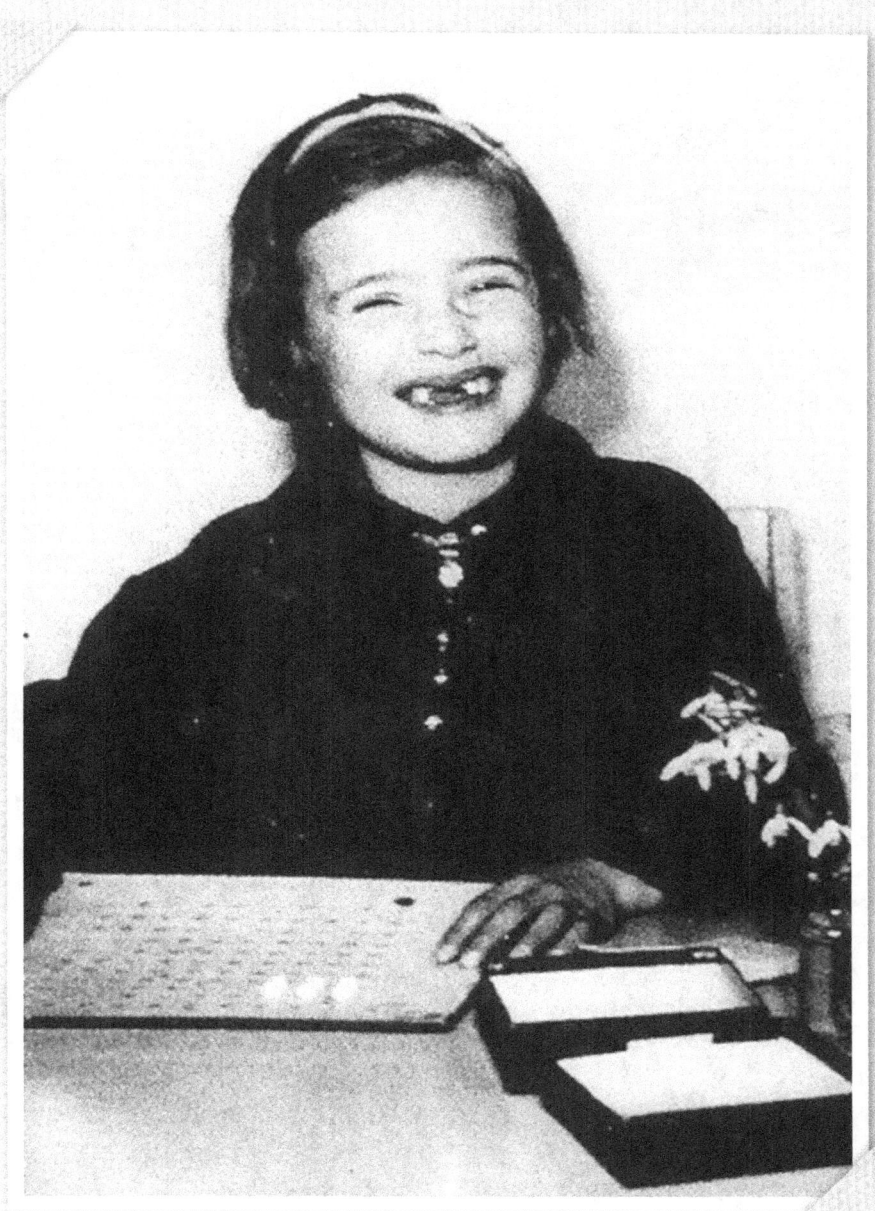

Penny in class, 1947

Penny with Lapjes the cat, 1949-'50

A WEDDING

CHAPTER 11

"Hello," a young soldier greeted Penny and me with a charming grin. Meeting our future brother-in-law seemed like a fairy tale. It was 8 June, 1948. Penny, aged seven, and I, five, were playing outside on the street with our neighbourhood friends, when a military truck approached. Racing to the footpath to let the truck pass, I wondered why it detoured through *our* quiet street when the wider Soestdijkseweg was so close. But before I could fathom the mystery, the truck slowed down and a young soldier jumped off, slinging a canvas kit-bag over his shoulder, and walked towards us.

"Do you know where Juliana Brandt lives?" he asked.

Juliana? I thought, stunned that this soldier knew her name.

"She's our *sister*," we said proudly.

"Then you must be Penny and Addy," he replied, grinning from ear to ear. "Would you take me to her, please?"

"What's your name?" Penny asked forthrightly.

"Rob Dominicus," the soldier answered. "I knew Juliana in Indonesia." Penny led him to the back door, through the kitchen and into our passage with me following close behind.

"Juliana!" Penny called. "There's a soldier to see you... from Indonesia!"

I shut the door and turned to see Juliana and Rob embrace each other, tears trickling down their faces. I froze.

Why are they crying? I wondered. Very soon Mother joined them, also crying. More hugs and kisses followed.

"Go outside and play!" Mother told Penny and me, waving her hand toward the door. Normally I'd have given anything to play outside, but not this time. After all, Dutch and British soldiers had always been my heroes. I wanted to see more of *this* soldier—in *our* house! Mother, however, was adamant that we leave Juliana and Rob alone.

Juliana and Rob's friendship had begun on 1 August, 1941, in Java, when Juliana, aged 14, and John, 12, returned from a bike ride around Lestari sugar estate.

"Look! Visitors!" John called, as they cycled into the driveway.

"Oh no!" Juliana cried, hunching down over her handlebars, hiding from the guests' view.

Mother was talking with two boys on the verandah. One of them, Roel, attended Juliana's school, and had a crush on her. The feeling, however, wasn't mutual. She didn't know the other boy.

Pretending not to have noticed them, Juliana hid in her bedroom, hoping they'd leave before she came out. The boys, however, didn't plan on departing so soon. As they'd cycled nearly 100km over the mountains from Malang to Lestari, Mother invited them to lunch.

Consequently, Juliana had to join the family, and face the boys after all.

"Juliana, this is Rob Dominicus," Father introduced. "You know Roel from school, don't you?"

"Yes," she answered coolly, not wanting to encourage the boy. Not knowing Rob, she also ignored him.

Roel had attended the 1937 Scout Jamboree, and showed Father his photo album recording the event. Juliana felt sure that Roel was trying to get a foot in the door where she was concerned, by impressing Father and Mother, knowing them to be keen Scout-leaders.

Meanwhile, Rob, aged nineteen, sat opposite Juliana, vying for her attention with all his might. He winked one of his typical both-eyes-winks, and smiled broadly, gradually breaking her icy glare. She increased her interest in Rob, and they became firm friends. Rob was attending Teachers' Training College at the time.

As they talked long into the evening, Father invited the boys to stay overnight, cycling in country areas not being safe. Streets lacked lights; and tigers and panthers roamed the hills after dark. Instead, Father found a tent, which the boys pitched on the lawn. One night stretched to two. Everyone enjoyed themselves, especially Juliana and Rob. The boys then cycled back over the mountains; and Rob and Juliana promised to write. Two weeks later, Rob's first letter arrived. Rob and Juliana's relationship blossomed by mail from then on.

On December 7, 1941, after the Imperial Japanese Airforce bombed Pearl Harbour, Hawaii, the KNIL (Royal Netherlands Indonesian Army) conscripted Rob into their army. He disliked Teachers' Training College, so was pleased with the change. His father, a teacher, and school inspector in Java, had coerced him into teaching. Rob's family had lived in Java all his life; his mother was born there, his father originated from Zeeland, Holland.

In 1942, after the Japanese had invaded Java, Rob and his platoon were captured in Batavia. The Japanese planned to transport the whole platoon by ship to Sumatra and Thailand, but Rob, along with about twenty others, contracted serious dysentery. The Japanese, not wanting the whole platoon to be infected, leaving them without workers, shipped the sick boys to Singapore Hospital, in isolation. Rob's illness became a blessing in disguise, as the American navy, unaware that the Japanese ship was loaded with Allied POW soldiers, torpedoed it. The only survivors were those sent to Singapore Hospital!

Following their recovery, the Japanese transported the remaining boys, including Rob, to Thailand, in primitive steel railway wagons—blisteringly hot during the day, and bitterly cold at night—with nothing to wear except shorts.

Once in Thailand, they walked about 100 kilometres a day carrying huge cast-iron cooking pots on their heads, following a leech-infested river, using it to wash themselves as best they could. Along the way, they camped at POW camps.

At the Burma Railway, they found many dead bodies. Each day, more prisoners died, and Rob and his mates had to bury them. Repulsed by it all, Rob volunteered when the Japanese needed truck drivers for transporting food to other camps, and he got the job.

The only doctor in the region, "Weary" Edgar Dunlop, persuaded all drivers to smuggle medicines in their rice cargo, for distribution to needy camps. Rough jungle crossings caused extreme delays. Excursions which normally would have taken half a day, took four days. It was so humid that, on arrival, the rice had sprouted! All the smuggled medicines, however, arrived safely—a godsend for prisoners of war. The smuggling ring was never discovered.

When the project ended, Rob and his mates were returned to Singapore, to Changi jail. They remained there until liberation in August, 1945.

Two days after the Japanese surrender on August 15, 1945, Rob underwent a medical examination, and was declared fit for the Allied Military Police Force. His first post was Singapore's Wilhelmina Prison Camp, which he guarded against rampokkers. Later the Allies transferred him to Batavia.

Juliana desperately tried to find Rob after our liberation in Batavia, by writing to friends whose names and addresses she found advertised in a Red Cross paper.

"I just received a letter from your girlfriend," a friend remarked to Rob at Singapore Hospital. "She's looking for you."

Rob immediately wrote to Juliana, and asked her to marry him, and join him in Singapore. Mother wouldn't hear of it.

"Eighteen is too young for marriage," she said.

But Rob didn't give up. He planned to surprise us all with a visit. However, our sudden evacuation to Holland meant Juliana couldn't notify Rob. On May 6, 1946, he arrived to find our home in Batavia empty. We'd left two days earlier! Sad, but undeterred, Rob again enquired about Juliana's whereabouts through the Red Cross—this time in

Holland. He remained with the Military Police until his release in 1948.

Rob's surprise visit to Bilthoven caused quite a stir. Juliana and Rob became engaged that day, and Rob stayed with us for what seemed a very long time.

I loved having Rob in the house. He had a special way with Mother, and altered the usual tense atmosphere. He always smiled and joked. Mother was a different person when people visited, and with Rob, her mood change was exceptional. His optimism infected everyone. He didn't only spend time with Juliana, but included Mother, John, Penny, and me, and took us on enjoyable outings. Although Mother's illness often precluded her from joining us, she came once on an outing to *Keukenhof* in Lissen, in a hired Volkswagen.

Rob showered us with treats I'd never heard of: ice-cream sundaes at *Keukenhof's* café, walks through the tulip-and-daffodil-bulb gardens, and drives past many colourful tulip fields—in a *car!* Before we drove back home, we stopped at a roadside stall where Rob bought a huge lei of tulips, and draped them over the car bonnet.

"This way everyone will know where we've been," he said, and they did. Our friends greeted us excitedly on our return!

On warm days, Rob and Juliana took us swimming at *Natuurbad* in Bilthoven North, surrounded by landscaped gardens. The place even had a café. Bilthoven's other pool was *Brandenburg*, a smaller, but sparkling clean pool near our home.

With plenty to occupy us at the baths, Juliana packed a picnic, so we could stay the whole day. We swam, paddled canoes down a stream, and played on soft, green grass. Penny and I couldn't swim yet, and still wore our pink, inflated inner-bike tubes to keep us afloat, while Juliana, Rob, and John swam.

Home again, Juliana usually cooked dinner. I liked her food, but I wouldn't eat meat, hating the thought of eating wonderful animals.

"Which animals don't you like, then?" Juliana asked.

"Tigers," I said.

Next day, Juliana made rissoles for dinner.

"I don't want any," I said.
"It's tiger meat," Juliana announced.
"Oh… that's all right then," I said, and tucked in heartily!

All too soon, Rob left to study at the *Landbouw School* (Tropical Agricultural School) in Deventer. I missed him, but looked forward to his weekend and holiday returns. He already felt like one of the family. Penny and I loved playing rough games with him. Then he'd tickle us, but stopped when we'd had enough.

A RAINCOAT

On 9 March, 1949, Grandmother Brandt died unexpectedly. Grandfather grieved. He visited us afterwards, and brought Mother some of Grandmother's clothes.

It rained when he entered our hall, wearing an unusual, clear plastic raincoat. He hung it on a spare coat hook in the passage, then he and Mother conversed in the family/dining room, leaving me alone in the hall. I looked at the raincoat, the balloon-like material appealing. Penny and I often blew up pieces of broken balloons into tiny, cherry balloons, so I fetched the scissors, and cut a piece off the coat to try this!

It wouldn't blow up, and I couldn't patch the coat again! By now, I felt guilty, and dreaded Grandfather going home. When he finally came out into the passage, Mother noticed the cut and glared at me as if she knew who the culprit was. Grandfather didn't say a word. Nor did I hear anything about it from Mother later, but I learned my lesson.

Sadly, on 4 July, 1949, Grandfather also died, "Of a broken heart," Mother said. Although he missed Grandmother immensely, he really died from an aneurism. Because Grandmother and Grandfather died prior to Juliana and Rob's wedding, older relatives urged them to postpone the wedding to enable the family to grieve. When the wedding went ahead as planned on July 30, 1949, some relatives refused to attend.

To me, even the preparations for the wedding were exciting. Juliana, Rob, and John's friends visited our home and spoilt Penny and me with sweet-cigars.

Considering Mother's asthma, I'm amazed that everyone smoked in our home! In Juliana's room, cigarette butts overflowed the ashtrays.

Juliana and Rob's dentist and friend, Wiard Sprey, also became Penny's and my friend.

"Come and see me at the surgery when your teeth wiggle," he said.

After extracting the milk tooth, he'd give us a handful of sweets as a reward. Mother had no spare money for sweets, so when I felt like a sweet rush, I wriggled and wriggled a tooth until it loosened. Then Penny and I dropped in at Sprey's. He whipped the tooth out smartly, and handed over the sweets. Going with Penny meant a reward for both of us!

John's friendship with Sprey had begun when he sold him, what he later found to be illegal, Chesterfield cigarettes. He'd obtained them in 1945 from new friends on the *SS Bloemfontein*. When one of John's teachers heard of his 'smuggling' efforts, he suggested earning pocket money through honest means such as furniture repairs. This led John to diverse places and junk, with which he recreated all kinds of useful items.

For Penny's seventh birthday John made her a red scooter, or *autoped*, as we called it. He redesigned it from scraps, using an old bike handlebar, 12-inch wheels, with rubber blow-up tyres from a Vespa scooter, and fashioning the rest from odds and ends. It was unique, fantastic for its day. Other scooters didn't have inflated tyres, and consequently didn't ride as smoothly. When we stepped on it, we sailed along the quiet roads. I sometimes preferred the scooter to my bike.

A SPECIAL DAY

Finally, on July 30, 1949, Juliana and Rob's wedding day arrived. Sprey drove Juliana and Rob in his silvery-blue 1939 De Soto car, to the Council Chambers in Bilthoven for the civil wedding ceremony, and later to Utrecht, for the church blessing. Being a warm, sunny day, Mother, feeling somewhat better, also attended.

The only damper on the day for Juliana and Rob was Grandmother and Grandfather Brandt's absence, and also some of the older relatives, who were still mourning their deaths. Grandfather had hoped to conduct the church ceremony.

Penny and I were flower girls, dressed in white, with satin ribbons in our hair. All family members wore white carnations. My carnation's perfume lingered the whole day. The scent of the blooms seemed much stronger than that of today's carnations.

Afternoon tea was served at home: the formal lounge and family/dining room doors opened to make one big room.

Juliana and Rob then departed for their honeymoon, staying in Bennekom, at Uncle Ko and Aunt Daisy Wouters' rebuilt holiday home. The old thatch-roofed homestead where Father, Mother, Juliana, and John had spent their furlough in 1936, had burned down during the war, when a spark from shrapnel ignited the thatch.

After their honeymoon, Juliana and Rob moved to Deventer, where Rob continued his studies. I missed them immensely. On certain days, I felt their absence more so, and hibernated in the attic's north-side room. The only window was high up off the floor. By climbing on furniture, it became a fantastic sentry post overlooking our street, right up to Leyenseweg's junction. I often peered at people from there. At first they appeared as small dots that I hoped would materialise into Juliana and Rob. Sometimes, to my excitement, they did! Then I bounded down the stairs.

"Juliana and Rob are on their way!" I called, running out of the door and into the street to greet them. They usually returned home for weekends or short holidays.

1949, Juliana and Rob surrounded by family and friends:

Back row: *K. v.d. Woord, Ge Dominicus, Puck v.d. Ploeg, Jo Berends-Dominicus, Mira and Tanja Brandt*

Middle row: *John, Renee Vos, Mother (Willy), Hans Berenbak*

Front row: *Addy, Juliana and Rob, and Penny*

1949, Juliana, Rob and Willy
Front row: *Addy and Penny*

BRIDGING HIGH SCHOOL

CHAPTER 12

I missed Juliana and Rob, but life carried on as if my feelings didn't matter. Then in 1947, John changed high schools to Utrecht's *Overbruggings HBS*, which enabled him better to catch up on his lost schooling caused by the war events. Classes at this new school consisted of fifteen students whose ages ranged between sixteen and twenty-eight. Teachers addressed students as *Mister* and *Miss*. John breezed through first and second class; third and fourth were challenging, but *fifth*, in 1949, became a *nightmare!*

With his final exams looming in August 1949, finding the time to study was extremely difficult.

Before Juliana and Rob's wedding, family life had been passable for John. Juliana's help around the house halved the chores. John managed at school then, even gaining top marks in Class 4. Although wedding preparations had been a pleasant distraction, his assistance, and the noise of foot traffic to and from Juliana's room, interrupted John's concentration, his room being opposite hers.

After Juliana and Rob's wedding on 30 July 1949, and their departure for Deventer, John was the only responsible adult in the house for Mother to rely on. As much as he wanted to help Mother, his ability to concentrate on study was severely jeopardised.

With Mother extremely unwell, and often bedbound, the management of our household now totally rested on John. He had to shop, cook, do all the chores, nurse Mother, and care for Penny and me before and after school, *plus* try to study for his final exam!

Mother needed more personal help and there was none, other than John. He tried studying elsewhere, but that didn't work. Then he tried sleeping from 8pm to 12 midnight, in the hope of getting uninterrupted study time in the early hours of the morning, expecting everyone in the household to be asleep. This gave him more time, but not for study.

"John!" Mother would call repeatedly, knowing he was awake. "Please make me some hot coffee to ease my breathing difficulties."

John couldn't just leave Mother gasping for breath.

"Come, sit down," she urged him, on his return with the coffee. "I want to talk…"

"Mother…, I must study. My final exam is in August!"

"Just a little while… A break will clear your brain," Mother pleaded.

Other distractions interfered with his concentration during the day. Hospital stays or government-subsidised home-help were unheard of for cases like Mother's. Post-war Holland was recovering in that area too.

I clearly remember John staying in his room most of the day, and Penny and me 'tip-toeing' past his door, so he could catch up on lost sleep. I wondered what kept him going.

I didn't realise then that he'd also looked after Mother at night!

John sat his final exam in August 1949. He was devastated when he failed by just two marks in English and French. It hit him even harder when he learned that both the English and French teachers would have made exceptions in awarding him a pass, had they known the difficulties he faced at home.

Consideration like this had been given to a girl in John's class, who, because of her sisters' needs, frequently complained she couldn't cope. But John considered such complaints as whinging excuses, and, although he, too, experienced extreme difficulties at home, he never mentioned his struggles to his teachers.

"John's predicament is my fault," Mother explained, when she met the teachers. Her ill health and our resultant living conditions were glaringly obvious. Although the teachers were sympathetic, it was too late for them to do anything by then. The results had been sent to The Hague. John had no other option but to repeat another twelve months' schooling and sit the exam a year later.

His disappointment mounted when he heard that Grandfather's brother, Uncle Alf, had booked him a place at Leiden University to study medicine. John felt cheated, and succumbed to depression. Up until, then he had pushed all his past griefs into the background, and got on with life. Now he suddenly felt depleted, without purpose and hope.

He contemplated migration, but for Mother's sake, moved schools to Bilthoven's Lyceum, closer to home. Still depressed, and now an older student, 21 in 1950, in a class with much younger pupils, his mind strayed from study.

Mother worries about making ends meet on her widow's pension, he thought. *I'm twenty-one. I should be making my own way through life. Mother can well do without me eating her out of house and home.*

About this time, John befriended Bert and Koos, two kind men who needed assistance with their furniture-removal business. Helping them was a good distraction from John's problems. The job was only on a friendly, casual basis. The men gave him pocket money, all expenses paid away from home, and a pleasant time in exchange. It was a good chance to get his thoughts together, and helped reinforce his resolve to emigrate to Australia.

Unaware of John's troubles, Penny and I lapped up his attention and enjoyed his bedtime antics. To give Mother and himself some respite, he took us for a refreshing swim at *Brandenburg*, the small, sparkling clean swimming pool near home, where Penny and I later learnt to swim. Penny sat on the bar at the front of his bike, and I on the carrier.

Then Mother made an announcement.

"I'm making my notary public your legal guardian."

"What?" John objected. "I'm twenty-one, Mother! I don't need a guardian! It's fine for Penny and Addy!" I don't need a stranger telling me what I can and can't do!"

He immediately started looking for ways to neutralise this new issue. Emigration seemed the answer to all his troubles, and he forged ahead, by saving for a boat fare, and buying a ticket.

"I'm emigrating to Australia," he said to Mother. "I've bought my ticket."

"What?" Mother gasped, aghast, and visibly shaken. "Are you sure? What about your studies?"

"Yes, I'm certain," John replied, adamant about his decision. "You don't need me eating you out of house and home. I can make my own way in life."

When Mother realised nothing would change John's mind, she assisted him with all the necessary arrangements for his rapidly approaching departure. Then another problem arose. While catching up on schoolwork, John had been excused compulsory military training. Unless young men had a good excuse, the Netherlands enforced compulsory army training at age eighteen. Outright refusal to the call-up could result in a prison sentence. John, now twenty-one, and having stopped attending school, was expected to report for duty!

When the Dutch authorities heard of John's emigration plans and possible evasion of military duty, they were horrified. Unfortunately, he needed a clearance certificate from them to leave the country permanently. This took some doing. Finally, the officials decided an intending emigrant, determined to become an Australian citizen by renouncing his allegiance to Holland, wouldn't make a good soldier. John didn't care who or which department gave him clearance, so long as he received it. But waiting was frustrating.

Meanwhile, John bought himself a warm, second-hand army uniform, minus insignias, and worked on odd jobs around the country. Anticipating the issue of his clearance, he took a last look at Europe.

He hitch-hiked through Belgium and France, then to Switzerland, where he visited Great-uncle Andrew Brandt, and his wife, Aunt Helene, in Geneva. From there he travelled to Zurich to see the house at No. 6 Axelstrasse, where Mother had spent some of her youth. The house had a charming outlook over the lake. Then he hitch-hiked to Berne, back via the Saar Country, onto a pretty route to Belgium and back to Utrecht.

Finally, John rushed around seeing to last-minute formalities for his trip to Australia. 'Red tape' and unfinished papers caused him to miss his freight ship, *De Ridderkerk* at Amsterdam. It had left for Genoa!

"Please hurry the process," John urged Dutch authorities. "Genoa is my last chance to catch my boat!"

When he finally received his leaving clearance, he had just enough time to travel to Genoa. The quickest way was by Rhine Express, a non-stop train from Utrecht to Genoa through Germany, the Austrian mountains, Switzerland, and Italy. He departed at short notice from Utrecht's train station on a spring day in April 1951. Hiring a car for the occasion, he drove Mother, Penny, Renee Vos, Kees Rebel, and me to the station. Kees drove us home, and returned the car.

Penny missed John terribly. Suddenly, many of his responsibilities landed on her ten-year-old shoulders.

THE RIDDERKERK

An uneventful train trip to Genoa followed. Getting to know an older passenger at home before the ship sailed, made the trip more interesting; and making friends with a younger passenger, Wim Bruyning, in Genoa, made the voyage more fun. As a wharf strike delayed their ship, John and Wim were forced to stay an extra night in Genoa before embarking. John mixed with the cargo ship's varied crew of Dutch, English, Malayan, and Bahasa (Indonesian) origins. To gain pocket money, he washed and ironed for the eleven fellow passengers, fixed watches, and sewed on missing buttons. He even made a profit!

After Genoa, the ship was plagued with wharf strikes: a 'go slow' in Suez, four days' delay in Aden, six in Freemantle, and more in Melbourne. In Port Said (Bur Said), passengers could walk safely, but Aden (Al' Adan), could only be visited by car with a special security guide, as discontented locals vented their frustrations on tourists, especially those with white skin. To John, it was a pleasant outing, but once was enough!

Freemantle and Perth were different altogether. The first glimpse gave John a warm glow. Freemantle was a quaint old port, with old-fashioned buildings, and a circular prison that, after being decommissioned, became a 'must see' tourist attraction.

Perth was modern, with Governor's Palace, wide streets, a mixture of old and modern shop facades, attractive beaches, and King's Park on a hill across the Swan River. Owing to Freemantle's wharf strike on the third day there, the captain advised his passengers to accept a free train ticket to Sydney. Those wishing to stay in Freemantle had to pay board and lodging for the duration of the strike.

John and Wim chose to stay. John, however, ran out of money. To rectify that problem, he obtained a job at the sawmill in Midlands on a Friday as *tail-out*, a repetitious job receiving planed or sawed timber, as it came out of a machine.

Because he hadn't complained about the monotonous nature of the job, with red-gum sap and coarse sawdust flying all over him off the big circular saw, he was asked to return on Monday. Most of the previous *tail-outs* had walked off the job! John, needing the money, said he'd be back. He told the bosses his circumstances, and as it was 'payday', they gave him a week's wages in advance—on trust. So, when John felt the ship move as he woke on Monday morning, he panicked! The captain had received permission to leave the harbour under the ship's own steam. John frantically tried to phone the sawmill manager, but couldn't contact him. He felt sad leaving that friendly area, and afterwards often wondered what the people at the sawmill thought of him. In Melbourne, passengers hurriedly disembarked. Another wharf strike loomed, and those in charge wanted all passengers off the ship. Customs and immigration officers checked their papers early in the day. Baggage was inspected, and a bus waited on the quay to deliver passengers to the railway station—but they didn't get clearance until 5pm! After much confusion, John and Wim travelled that evening to Sydney on the Melbourne Express. Worn out, they fell asleep. Several hours later, they woke to a shouting guard.

"Next stop is Albury! Get ready to change trains!"

The railway tracks in the state of Victoria were wider than those in New South Wales, and the boys had to haul their luggage across the platform and tracks to the waiting train on the other side. Although that train had sleeping bunks, it took several hours before the passengers closed their eyes, only to be woken by more shouting.

"Everybody change at the Eden Monaro Junction at Goulburn!"

"Not you, boys," other passengers reassured John and Wim, almost prepared to change trains again. "This train continues to Sydney."

With sleep now out of the question, the boys resumed talking about their uncertain future in Australia. On arrival, they left their belongings at the baggage repository, and set about exploring Sydney on foot. That's when they learned about Mrs. Aitcheson's boarding house on Darley Road in Manly, a North Shore suburb at the other end of the port. After a picturesque ferry ride across the harbour, they found the well-run boarding house, where they shared a room beside the kitchen, and quickly found jobs. Wim was a fitter and turner by trade. John didn't fancy labouring in a factory, so he phoned the only person he knew, a German surgeon, Doctor Friedlander, in Roseville. He and his wife had escaped the Nazi regime in 1938, and he earned a living as General Practitioner in Sydney. One of Mother's acquaintances had recommended him for assistance, if required.

Doctor Friedlander helped John find a job at a removal firm in Cremorne. John applied himself with gusto, until the day they were to lower an upright piano down a curved flight of stairs. The house had been in the family for many years, and the piano had become a permanent fixture, after being hoisted up to the second floor before the stairs and wall had been completed.

The boss insisted that the piano, carefully secured with plenty of rope, could safely be lowered down the stairs. This all began well enough, until they reached the curve of the stairway. When the piano jammed, the boss decided to raise one end much higher, and jiggle it through the available space. This action resulted in two injured employees—one of them seriously—a wrecked piano, damaged staircase and wall, and a lawsuit against the company. John narrowly escaped injury. Fortunately, he'd changed places with one of the casualties just before the accident. He resigned from the company immediately.

His next job came by chance, as he returned from a Chinese meal in Sydney. Being vegetarian, he searched far and wide for decent meals. Curiosity got the better of him when he saw an advertisement in a window for a jackaroo on a sheep-and-cattle station in the country.

What's a jackaroo? John wondered.

After a long discussion with Wim about the station's need for a stable-hand and John's lack of experience, John phoned *Braemar* sheep and cattle station. They hired him on the spot, and provided a ticket on the night train to Bourke. Assured of further transport by semi-trailer to the 'letterbox' (an empty old fridge) of *Braemar Station*, three days later he was dropped off with the mail and various provisions.

A further 24km by car brought him to a two-bedroom shack, some 200 metres from a big rambling house where the owner and his wife lived. John being vegetarian shocked them, for their diet consisted of chops, sausages, eggs, and toast for breakfast, cold roast meat and ham sandwiches at lunch, and roast meat, pumpkin, and potatoes for dinner.

It turned out that a *jackaroo* was a general roustabout who could ride a horse, kill a beast, then cut it up into sections for human consumption and 'tucker' for three dogs. Of course, John couldn't ride a horse, and refused to kill a steer. His jobs were limited to collecting the mail, maintaining the kerosene levels and flames of the refrigerators, joining a cattle drive, fighting bush fires, helping maintain supplies in the shearing shed, and doing a weekly 250km drive round the property to check water troughs and windmill pumps. He lasted five months.

Returning to the boarding house in Manly, he took a job as tram conductor in North Sydney. After a month or two, he was promoted to *bus* conductor in Manly. While John wasn't really looking for a girlfriend, he attended a dance with his friend. Wim was a keen dancer, and had partnered the same girl several times. On the way back to the dance floor, they bumped into John, and Wim proudly introduced Gloria Weirick. Butterflies rumbled in John's stomach.

This is the girl I saw doing a belly-buster from the beach-tower-side swimming pool a few days ago, he thought. Wow!

After dating Gloria, John learnt that she'd seen him on the bus a few weeks before meeting him, and excitedly informed her parents:

"I've seen the man I'm going to marry!"

John proposed, and on 13 June 1952 he and Gloria were married at St Mark's Anglican Church in Harbord, a Sydney North Shore beach-side suburb adjacent to Manly. On April 8, 1953 they had a son, Lance. I remember feeling extremely proud to be Lance's *aunt*, and dreamed of one day meeting him in person.

(John and Gloria now live in the Blue Mountains in a retirement village. Their son, Lance, and daughter-in-law, Carol Mcleod, have two daughters, and four grandchildren).

A year after arriving in Australia in 1951, John studied structural engineering by correspondence, and worked as a structural engineer.

The sadistic cruelties inflicted by Korean and Japanese soldiers in POW camps, however, left indelible scars on John's mind. Never totally healed, they are still ripped open with every memory of those war years. At the time of writing in 2017, John is 89 years old.

The Brandt family, 1951, before John's emigration
Back row: *John and Addy*
Seated: *Mother (Willy), Penny, Juliana and Rob Dominicus*

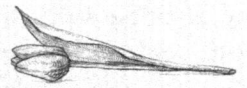

GREENER PASTURES

CHAPTER 13

After John's departure, Juliana and Rob also thought of emigrating. In June 1951, Rob finished his studies at Deventer's Tropical Agriculture School, and almost accepted a managing position on a rubber plantation in Sumatra, Indonesia. The job came with a good salary, a house, and paid passage. But when he heard that the plantation's two previous managers had been murdered, he decided against it. Next to Indonesia, he favoured Australia or New Zealand. As some of his agricultural colleagues had chosen the latter, Rob researched the possibilities there. Obtaining an entry permit was easy, but, as a married couple, they needed guaranteed accommodation.

A colleague then contacted Rob. He'd planned to leave for New Zealand with his wife and young son, but couldn't do so because of a serious illness.

"Please replace us," he urged. "It's temporary work. My employer needs someone for a year to care for her elderly husband while she's overseas. The job comes with accommodation."

That's just what we need! Rob thought.

He and Juliana, excited at the prospect of emigrating to a warmer climate with agricultural possibilities, accepted the offer instantly. After a few letters to their prospective employer, they began emigration proceedings. They had to be in New Zealand by early October 1951.

Juliana would care for the elderly gentleman while Rob could work anywhere he chose.

Rob immediately enquired with Dutch shipping companies about fares on immigrant ships. All were taken. On 24 August 1951, only five days before the ship's departure, they found two cancellations, *single* berths on an ex-troop ship, the *SS Zuiderkruis*, and accepted them so as to arrive in New Zealand on time.

Unable to transport their furniture at short notice, they packed all they could in suitcases and trunks and left the rest with family.

The ship departed on 31 August 1951. Rob hired a taxi from Bilthoven to Rotterdam Harbour. Mother, Penny, and I came for the ride. I remember standing on the wharf, Penny on Mother's right and I on her left. As Juliana and Rob walked onto the ship's gangplank, a dark cloud enveloped me.

Surrounded by many passengers, Juliana and Rob waved and cried. Tears filled my eyes; many more followed later.

Why are they leaving? I, then only eight, thought, as the boat steadily moved away from the dock. *I'll never see them again…*

New Zealand was at the other end of the world, and in those days, sea voyages were expensive.

Following their sad departure, Mother, Penny, and I caught the train back to Bilthoven. With John in Australia and Juliana and Rob now gone, life lost its sparkle. Nothing interested me anymore. All I felt was the pain of yet another loss; there had been too many in my short life, and I almost gave up hope.

Thankfully, Juliana wrote weekly letters and, sad though it was at first, her departure with Rob became the start of an unknown, greater journey for me.

At the time, however, the pain of John's, and then Juliana and Rob's emigration continued. There also seemed an oppression over our household that never lifted. Mother now lay ill in bed most days. For a while, strangers cooked and cared for Mother, and cleaned the house. For me, however, without Juliana and Rob's visits, life soured.

Although life had been difficult for some time, our close-knit family was my security. But as my outside world grew more insecure and unpredictable, with bullying at school, and unkindness from unexpected quarters, the pattern of loss and illness, combined with Mother's high expectations of Penny, aged ten and me eight, became enormous.

I tried to communicate with Juliana and Rob by scribbling note after note. Mother wrote on pre-paid aerogrammes, but as my stunted writing—in those days with ink—smudged badly, Mother made me use plain, heavy, paper and only included my 'better' letters in the odd parcel. Others lay forgotten in drawers or waste-paper baskets.

Juliana's letters helped to a point.

New Zealand, I daydreamed. *A warm and exciting country, with different surroundings and scenery to explore.*

Unbeknown to me then, Juliana's marriage to Rob had also been an escape from the increasing tensions with Mother at home. For them, marriage and emigration seemed the obvious solution.

NEW ZEALAND

On 27 September, following five weeks of uneventful sailing, Rob and Juliana arrived in Wellington. They travelled by bus to Hastings, where their employer, Mrs Cotterill, met and drove them to her home in Crosses Road, Havelock North.

Mrs Cotterill instructed Juliana on how to care for her husband while she was away. The next day she departed. On her return a year later, Juliana and Rob rented a house in rural Middle Road, and later moved to Hastings. They settled in New Zealand and befriended many Dutch immigrants and New Zealanders, making life-long friends.

Their daughter, Jennifer, was born in May, 1957. After many miscarriages, they adopted Melanie in December, 1963. Both girls married. Between them, Jennifer and Melanie now have five children and seven grandchildren.

In 1989, drawn to a warmer climate and tropical fruit cultivation, Rob and Juliana moved to Balgal Beach, Northern Queensland, and later moved to the Sunshine Coast, near Brisbane.

Sadly, Rob died in 2004. Juliana is now 91 years old, and lives in a retirement village in Sippy Downs, Queensland. Her family is the apple of her eye.

STORIES & LETTERS

CHAPTER 14

"Sit down and listen," Mother urged, following Juliana and Rob's emigration in 1951.

Melancholy still enveloped me, but Mother's tales diverted my thoughts as she brought her stories to life.

"Imagine John, a two-year-old, riding his tricycle through peak-hour-traffic in Bandung!" she said, laughing till tears filled her eyes. "Then the police whisking him up, taking him to the police station and treating him like a hero!"

Mother laughed. Apparently, John had escaped repeatedly, and each time arrived home in a police car, wearing a policeman's hat and smiling from ear to ear. It took ages for him to outgrow his wanderlust. In the end, Father tied him to the leg of a heavy dining table.

"Dido, on the other hand, was a delicate but beautiful, blue-eyed, blonde-haired baby," Mother said, pointing to a small photograph on her dresser as a tear rolled from her eye. "He seemed normal at birth, but as the weeks progressed, we suspected something was wrong. He was never able to roll over or crawl."

His problem had started when Mother fell onto her abdomen in her eighth month of pregnancy. This must have caused a brain haemorrhage, because a specialist performing tests on Dido when he was about four months old, discovered a blood clot on his brain. The clot could have been removed had this been done timeously.

There was a surgeon willing and able to operate, but he practised in Germany. Dido, however, was born July 21, 1939, and in September 1939, WWII broke out in Europe, after Germany had invaded Poland, causing unrest all over Europe. By May 1940, travel from Indonesia to Europe had become extremely dangerous.

To compound their challenge, Father looked Jewish with his jet-black hair and beard, sharp facial features, and dark complexion. During their furlough in 1936, he'd already been advised to be careful in Germany, for he could easily have been mistaken as Jewish, and been deported as many Jews were at the time. Thus, worsening world problems turned Dido's mercy dash into an impossible liability. The operation was put on hold, but the blood clot pressing on Dido's brain gradually caused his muscles and tendons to spasm and contort his little body.

Father then enquired about alternative therapy in America for children with Dido's condition. By then Japanese warships had invaded the South Pacific Seas near Java. In December 1941, Japan bombed Pearl Harbour in Hawaii, which started WWII in the Southern Hemisphere. This made sailing to America impossible. Dido's *therapy* had therefore to be put on hold again.

Mother, greatly upset about the lack of action, felt guilty that she might have caused Dido's problem through her fall. Although she searched high and low for alternative cures, she found that nothing more could be done, except for her to love Dido. However, Dido's care demanded a great deal of time and energy. *Kokkie* Salem helped Mother through those desperate months, and when Father employed an extra *babu*, the whole family could finally enjoy Dido again.

THE PANTHER

My estimation of Mother rose when she showed us her driver's licence from before the war.

Mother driving a car? I thought. *Wow!* We couldn't afford a car then, but knowing that Mother had her licence amazed me.

TWO SLICES OF BREAD

Mother told us that she had driven Juliana and John, much younger then, through the mountains one time. On their way from Malang, still four hours from home, and with dusk falling, the car suddenly swerved.

"Oh no!" Mother sighed. "Not a flat tyre! Just when it's getting dark." She stopped the car in the middle of nowhere. Checking confirmed her suspicion. As she opened the boot to change the wheel, she noticed the car lights reflecting on something.

"A panther!" she gasped, seeing its massive body, and rushing back into the car.

"Wind up the windows!" she yelled. "Close the canvas roof! Lock the doors!"

The passengers remained in the car all night, regardless of the unbearable heat. Next morning the panther had disappeared. Still too fearful to change the tyre, Mother flagged down a passing bus. Mother, Juliana, and John, then joined native passengers with their smelly and noisy piglets, caged chickens, ducks, and birds, on their way to market. Roosters broke free, then jumped on seats and passengers, flying over their heads, and missing them by centimetres. Piglets squealed and birds squawked, some escaping from their cages and depositing droppings all over the bus, while their owners ran about trying to recapture them. After what seemed an eternity, Mother, Juliana, and John arrived home.

The next day, their chauffeur left to fetch the car. Father instructed him on where to find it, and handed him the car keys, his bus fare, and extra money.

"Be careful," he warned.

"Don't worry," the chauffeur said. "I'll take my gun."

When he didn't return two days later, Mother worried.

Maybe the panther has eaten him, she thought.

Three days later, when the chauffeur drove the car up the driveway, Juliana and John ran to him.

"Did you see the panther?" they asked.

"Yes, and I shot him through the head."

Next time Mother arranged a trip over the mountains, Juliana and John refused to go unless the chauffeur drove the car.

Another time, the joke was on Mother.

While she had an afternoon nap, John occasionally caught a harmless snake, draped it over his shoulders and woke Mother to surprise her. Mother hated snakes, and reacted with revulsion. That was nothing compared with the time that Father and Mother enjoyed lunch with a friend in the dining room.

Suddenly, their friend froze and announced through clenched teeth that there was a snake on her leg. Mother advised the woman to remain quite still, so that Father could identify it. It was one of the nasties; and the three could only sit very still whilst the *djongos* devised a way of coaxing the snake out of the room. He set a saucer of milk in the doorway of the outside exit. The snake drank, and then slithered harmlessly out of the house.

MOTHER

Another of Mother's adventures happened in Switzerland, where she had lived with her mother and three siblings. Mother, her sister, Tine, and a friend, often played on open, grassy valleys. One day, they walked through an orchard where rosy apples hung invitingly from the branches. They were hungry, so they picked an apple each. Suddenly a roar echoed through the valley! The owner headed straight for them!

Clutching their dresses, they ran as fast as their legs would carry them, clambering over obstacles, and rolling down hills until the man was out of sight. Safe from one tyrant, their governess reprimanded them severely on their return home. Their 'crime'? Dirty clothes!"

Mother loved Switzerland. There she learnt to play the violin and piano. Later she taught herself to play the guitar and lute. Her teacher was impressed, but her mother wasn't. Without warning, she bundled her four children back to Holland, to attend school in Zeist. Then she deposited them on their Aunt Marie Roukens' door-step, in Driebergen-Rijsenburg, and never returned! Aunt Marie was a spinster, a sour woman, mean with love and money. When she expected visitors, she instructed the children explicitly:

"When I offer our visitors a second helping, I'll offer you one too. But you must refuse politely. Is that understood?" and they usually agreed obediently.

"No thank you," Mother's siblings answered, as arranged. But Mother, hungry, saw her chance of getting more one day.

"Yes, please," she replied boldly.

Aunt Marie glared at her, but, in front of the visitors, had to fill her plate. When the visitors had departed, however, Mother never heard the end of it!

ROWING

Grandfather Brandt had been a keen sportsman. He competed at the first Olympic Rowing Regatta in Paris in 1900, while studying at Leiden University. He and a team of students raced on the Seine in Paris. The French used children as coxswain, the Dutch, much heavier adults. The French won the first day's race, and as best losers in the double sculls, Grandfather and his teammate, Roelof Klein, were to challenge three other teams the following day. To improve their chances, the Dutch coach searched for a young boy-coxswain for the race. The French then presented Grandfather's team with one of their boys, who knew his job well, and they won the race! On his way home, Grandfather carried his prize—a big bronze statue—through Belgian customs.

"Are you Brandt or Klein?" the officer asked.

"Brandt," Grandfather replied, surprised the man knew his name.

"No customs to pay! Go through."

WHALING

Our great-grandfather, Jo Hesselberg, born in 1849 in Texel, Holland, had been a sea captain and whaler. After the death of his father in 1866, young Jo, aged seventeen, took on his father's trade, starting at the lowest rank and working his way up.

"Great-grandfather Jo was a kind and brave man," Mother reminisced, "a whaler when they still used small boats to bring harpooned whales back to shore. Wounded, they lashed their tails, often capsizing the small boats, and throwing the men overboard."

When Mother was about five years old, Great-grandfather Jo picked her up in a horse-drawn coach and took her to sailors' cafés. She could listen to his whaler's stories all night.

"They made oil for lamps with the blubber, bags from the skin, and corsets from the bone," he'd told her, as sailor's sweat and stale beer, mixed with bacon and onion smells permeated the café.

"I loved Grandfather Jo so much, I'd do anything to please him," Mother mused, "so when he set a plateful of brown beans, fatty bacon and onions before me, I ate every morsel, hoping it would stay down. However, after a speedy exit to the bathroom, that rich food came up again! It never spoiled our outings though."

GREAT-GRANDMOTHER, JEANETTE HESSELBERG

On his journey round the world, Great-grandfather Jo Hesselberg met and married a part-Indonesian girl, Jeanette Leijman-Derks. She was born in 1861 at Ternate, a small Moluccan island, formerly the centre of the powerful Sultanate of Ternate, off the west coast of Halmahera, east of Java. In the pre-colonial era, the island had been a major producer of cloves.

Although no further written information on Great-grandmother Jeanette was found, an unwritten story had been circulating about her mother, Maria Derks.

As was the common custom in Java in the 1700-1800s, one of Maria's forebears had ruled a small Moluccan island. Years before her birth, this forebear offered his daughter in marriage to a European, in response to his kind deed to her father, the Sultan. Although this story may seem far-fetched, the fact remains that both Indonesian and

Dutch blood coursed through Great-grandmother Jeanette's veins, and consequently, ours.

Great-grandmother Jeanette accompanied Great-grandfather Jo on his travels as he sailed his three-masted barques through Indonesian waters. She even gave birth to their first three children on board ship. Our Grandmother, Neeltje Hesselberg, was born in 1883 on the barque *Barendine Osira*. Later, the imminent birth of their fourth child, motivated Great-grandfather Jo and Great-grandmother Jeanette to move to Surabaya, and remain land-based.

DENMARK

Long before Grandfather Brandt was born, his ancestors lived in Copenhagen, Denmark. The oldest known was 16th century Thomas Brandt, whose forbears were thought to have come from the Baltic region. Thomas's great-grandson, Johannes Hegelund Brandt, was a wholesaler and trader. His son, Andreas Luvic Brandt, became the Danish Consul for the Netherlands, where he also represented the family firm *Ebeling and Brandt* in Amsterdam. There, in 1844, he married Deborah Petronella van Eeghen, and moved to 366 Herengracht, Amsterdam, now the Bible museum.

Grandfather Brandt's father, Andreas Hegelund Brandt (senior), bought the manor-house, *Klein Gelresteyn* in Velp, where Aunt Daisy and Uncle Ko Wouters later lived, and where Penny and I spent many memorable Easters.

THE SS POTSDAM

In 1936, Father, Mother, Juliana (9), and John (7), were returning to Java on a German passenger liner, the *SS Potsdam*, from Antwerpen, Belgium, after a six-months' furlough in Holland. Late at night, the ship sailed through the English Channel. But during the night, the passengers woke to shouts reverberating through the ship's passages.

"Fire!" yelled the crew, herding people onto the top deck and handing out life-jackets.

Assuming it to be an exercise, my family joked with other passengers. But chaos erupted when sailors lowered lifeboats into the water, and ordered women and children to get in.

Suddenly the captain's voice boomed over the intercom: "Halt! Back to your cabins, everyone!"

Mystified, but thankful, everyone returned below deck to their cabins. It so transpired that the engine-room had caught fire, and the head machinist had dashed through the flames and turned off the main oil supply. The man saved the ship and its many passengers. Sadly, he received third degree burns. Father visited him in hospital to thank him.

The engine-room was so badly damaged that the ship couldn't sail on, and tugboats towed her to the nearest port, Southampton, on the south coast of England.

Everyone was given the choice of staying in Southampton or in Bremen, Germany, while the ship was repaired. Father chose Bremen. It was six weeks before they sailed again, this time without mishap. On their return to Java, Father was transferred from Pandji to Lestari Sugar Factory, a wonderful place, where both Father and Mother took up Scout-leading again.

HEALTH PROBLEMS

Mother's exciting experiences in foreign countries thrilled me. They made me daydream of cultures I, too, hoped to experience. But with Mother so ill, I decided never to desert her, and kept my dreams to myself.

One of those dreams almost became a reality after Juliana and Rob's emigration. Juliana tried to arrange for Mother, Penny, and me also to immigrate to New Zealand. Mother's long wished-for dream to live in a warmer climate, watching her grandchildren growing up, would finally come true. But the New Zealand Government turned her down. Mother failed the physical examination and her dreams turned to ashes.

Then *my* health deteriorated. Recurring cystitis spread to the kidneys, making me listless and bedbound. Mother worried. Thinking Juliana and Rob's departure was the cause, she must have written about it to Juliana. Mother was also concerned about *Juliana*, who was homesick, having had another miscarriage, and struggling with New Zealand's then basic environment and isolation.

I, however, wasn't prepared for what transpired next.

"Ad," Mother asked. "Would you like to go to New Zealand?"

"Yeees! But… I thought we couldn't…"

"Not all of us. Just you."

"Alone?"

"Yes."

"No!" I answered, shocked. I loved Juliana and Rob, and wanted them home.

What will life be like without Mother and Penny? I thought. And if Mother only has a little longer to live, how can I leave her? Two of her children have already departed. One more will break her heart.

"No," I repeated. "I'm *not* going!"

My health, however, continued to decline. Spending months in bed, I missed playing outside with my neighbourhood friends. One morning after a fresh snowfall, I again lay on the divan listening to their shrieks of laughter. Regardless of Mother having already said "no", when the doctor made a house call I repeated my plea.

"Can I go and play in the snow? Pleeease …"

"Hmmm," the doctor hummed. "All right. For a short while… if you wrap up warmly…"

"Yippee!" I called, surprised that he'd agreed. I quickly changed into warm clothes, and met my friends outside. We played for hours.

That night, another fever set in. Bronchitis, and later whooping cough, made me gasp for air, a frightening and painful experience.

This must be how Mother feels when she can't breathe, I thought, coughing my heart out.

While I was still confined to bed, Mother attended an evening chiropody course in Utrecht. Being summer and warm, she coped with the evening air. A colleague collected and returned her. Mother loved the work. Practising on Penny and me, she made plaster casts, and had us walk on our toes and heels to strengthen our arches.

While Mother attended classes, Rob's niece, Hanneke Berends, looked after Penny and me. I liked Hanneke. She showed us how to avoid blackheads and pimples.

"Always wash your face with clean hands," she said. "Don't use facecloths, they harbour bacteria, especially 'used' facecloths." Then she patted on olive oil.

Aunt Tine, Mother's sister, also helped. Too frightened to enter the bedroom in case she caught my germs, she sent Penny in. She and her daughter, Annelies (14), had returned from Indonesia, living with us until they found other accommodation.

Mother passed her chiropody exam with flying colours. Sadly, following her graduation, when she and her colleague had prepared to go into partnership and start a business, Mother became very ill, never totally recovering. This put a damper on all her plans.

She and I now both lay sick in bed in her bedroom. Having missed so much school, I still couldn't read. I felt sick, bored, and miserable. I longed for someone to read to me.

Staring through the window much of the day, a tall beech tree with most of its branches clearly visible, attracted my attention. In the evening, many birds gathered, their joyful chatter cheering me up. Watching the tree day in and day out throughout the months, I observed an unusual spectacle.

The tree's tiny winter buds began to bulge, and, almost in slow motion, gradually burst open to reveal pale pink blossoms, which I'd never noticed before. I called the blossom the tree's *pyjamas*. For it was a magnificent spectacle against the clear blue sky. Slowly, pale green leaves poked through the blossom, creating another spectacular sight. Although I didn't know much about God, this was when I first pondered His beautiful workmanship. Lying in bed constantly also gave me time to observe Mother's loving side, and to realise that she never tired of looking after me. Nor was she angry at me for not eating the meals she'd specially prepared for me, and which I was unable to eat, feeling so nauseous. Although the doctor said nothing more could be done for me medically, she never gave up.

I felt miserable and despondent. Then I thought of Bobby, who, in 1946, had prayed with Uncle Jel for Juliana and Mother's recovery. *Maybe Bobby can pray for me too,* I thought.

"I wish Bobby would come and see me," I said to Mother.

However, because Uncle Jel had died in 1949, I suspected that Bobby might be too sad to visit, but to my surprise she came within days and prayed. I slipped in and out of sleep on the divan in the living/dining room near the fire, while Bobby sat on the edge of the divan all day, her gentle voice murmuring to me like background music. Before leaving, she prayed again, and encouraged me.

"You'll get better after your tenth birthday," she said, reassuringly. "That usually happens." Bobby's words gave me hope.

Later, however, my temperature spiked, and with our doctor away, Mother became concerned. I woke from a deep sleep to see her standing next to my bed with a stranger beside her.

"Hello," he said. 'I'm Dr Steal, the on-call doctor."

After examining me, he straightened up and rubbed his chin.

"I can help your daughter," he said as he and Mother left the room. "But it'll take commitment from the whole family."

This doctor practised homeopathy.

"From now on, we're all going to eat healthy food," Mother announced that same day. Next morning, she brought me a plate of Bircher Brenner fresh-fruit muesli. My heart sank. It looked like something I'd vomited up! But because Mother had painstakingly prepared it under doctor's orders, I kept quiet.

"Thank you, Mother," I said pulling myself up.

When I heard her walking down the stairs, and felt sure nobody would creep up on me, I emptied my plateful into my locker drawer, quickly pushing clothes in front of the sticky mess. I did this for a week. When there was no more room, I used the flue access next to my bed.

One day, Mother sat on the bed, beside my locker.

"What's that musty smell?" she asked. On opening the locker drawer, she discovered my muesli, now crusted. I was very surprised that she wasn't angry!

Next morning, Penny brought my muesli, and stayed to watch me eat. Strangely, after forcing it down every day, I began to enjoy it. Gradually, the raw fruit and vegetable diet, chamomile tea, and homeopathic medicines began to work. I regained strength, and soon was up preparing the muesli myself, and making Mother's and Penny's too, with extra condensed milk improving the flavour. Grated raw cauliflower, carrots, and cabbage with lashings of mayonnaise became a favourite side salad for dinner.

Following my recovery in 1952, Dr Steal became our doctor. Homeopathic medicines, together with raw fruit and vegetables, heavy whole-grain bread, oats, and chamomile tea, were now essential to my diet. As I had to drink lots, and chamomile tea wasn't yet available in shops, the doctor drove me to secluded country areas to pick bunches of wild chamomile flowers. He then suggested to Mother that I attend a Rudolf Steiner Primary school in Zeist. He knew they had small classes. Pupils there received more individual attention, and that would give me extra tuition to help me catch up on three years' lost schooling. Mother decided that Penny should attend the same school. I was so excited to hear that the old house the school used for lessons had been Father's home when he was a small boy!

But life was stressful at home for Penny and me, minus Juliana and Rob and John. We were left to deal with Mother's moods and shouting matches we didn't know how to handle.

Francois Brandt, Roelof Klein and their French coxswain after their victory

During the final race on the river Seine between Courbevoie and Asnières as they crossed the finish line ahead of two other French teams

Grandfather Brandt's bronze statue, his 1st prize at the 1st Olypmic Games Rowing Regatta in Paris, 1900

Addy and Mother (Willy) in the front garden, 1950s

Kroostweg, Zeist, 1920s then Father's (Andrew) old family home, and Penny and Addy's primary school in the 1950s

Dido, 1945-46

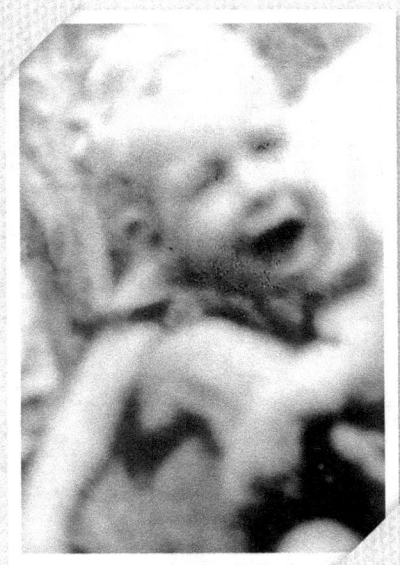

Juliana and Dido, 1930

Willy, Juliana and John, 1930s, on the front steps at Pandji Sugar Estate

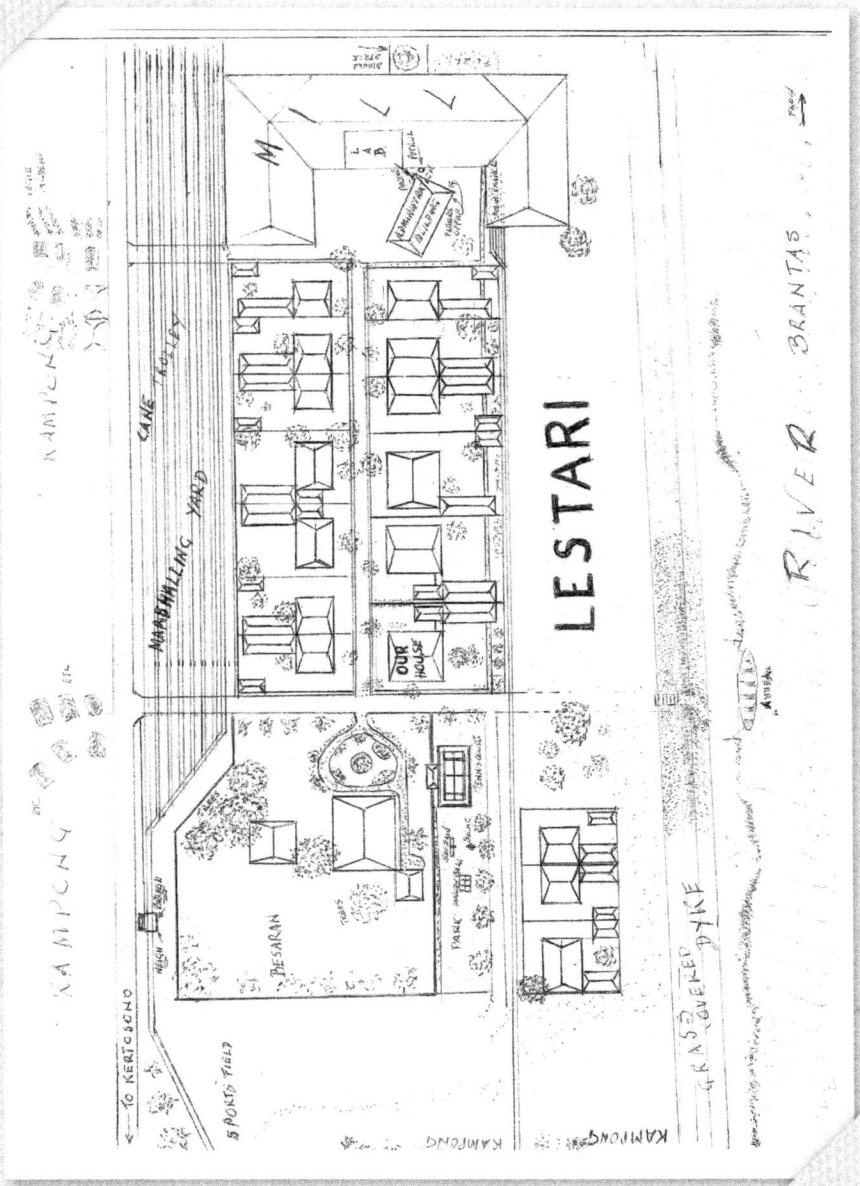

No 1 Sketch / map of Lestari Sugar Estate by John Brandt

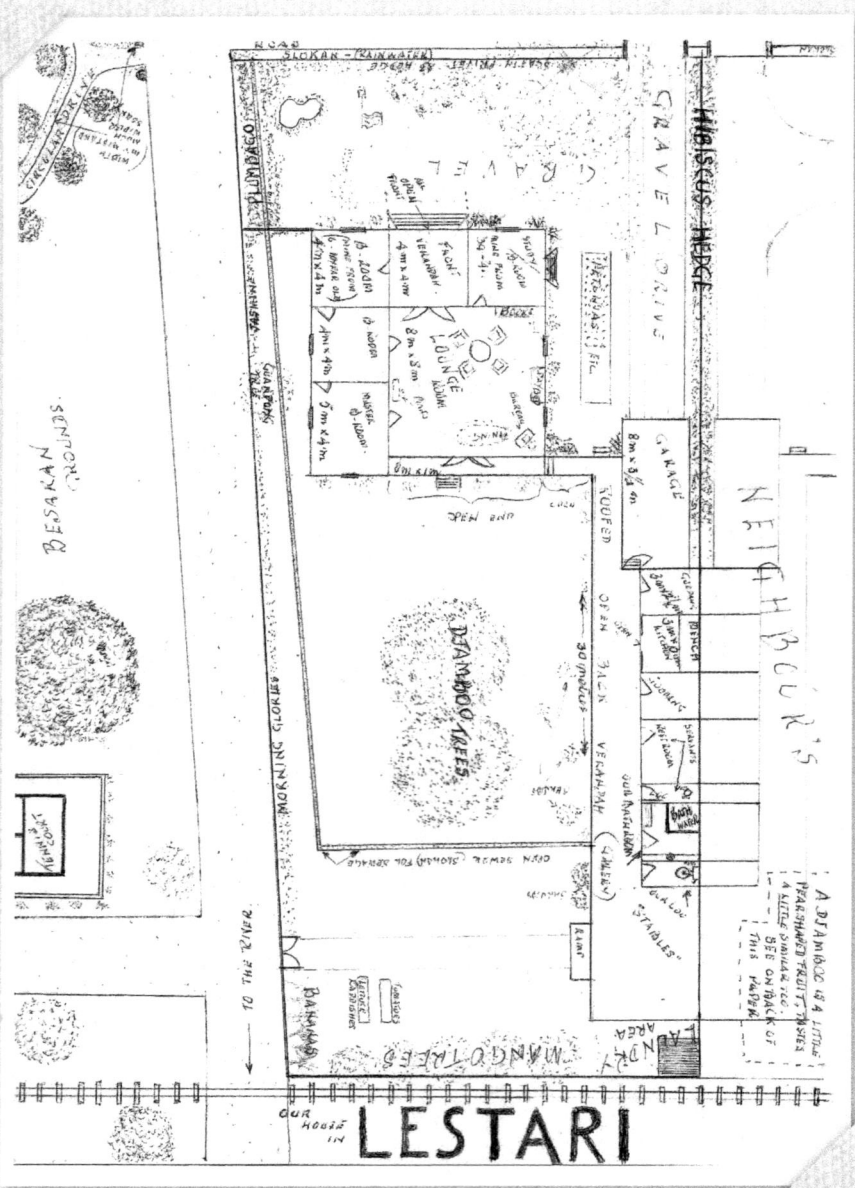

Lestari, map of the Brandt family house, sketched by John Brandt

A NEW PRIMARY SCHOOL

CHAPTER 15

Race you to the Toll house!" Penny called, as we cycled through de Bilt to our new school on the Kroostweg, in Zeist.

It was September, 1952; I was nine years old. I liked my new teacher, Mrs von Gleich, a grandmotherly-type, of German-Jewish descent. Before her escape to Holland, she and her family had experienced much sadness during the war in Germany.

"This is Eengreet," she introduced me to my classmates, pronouncing my name the German way.

She believed changing names would make a spiritual break from my sad past.

"Eengreet is a beautiful name," she added.

Nobody had called me Ingrid before. In the playground that first day, my eighteen classmates surrounded me.

"Where are you from? What was your last school like?" they asked, wanting to know about me.

They called me Ingrid but Penny forgot about the name change.

"Addy!" she called in the playground, loud enough for everyone to hear.

The children looked up, astonished.

"What did your sister call you?" they asked.

"Addy," I said.

From then on, all the children called me Addy.

Wow! I thought. *Everyone is so friendly... boys and girls play together like in our street.* We skipped, played hide-and-seek, ball-games, even leapfrog—my favourite game.

Our gym teacher taught us rounders, casti, handball, and hockey.

"Who wants to play hockey?" one of the older children often called at playtime, the more the merrier being the motto. Because few children then owned expensive hockey sticks, we used broken branches, and someone always had a tennis ball handy.

The playground consisted of a large, dusty area. If there had been grass once, it had completely worn down. In summer, the dust permeated our socks, sandals, and toes, leaving our feet sticky and black. Always hot and thirsty when the bell rang, we all lined up at the school front door for a drink of water. Standing by the basin, the caretaker turned on the tap for short bursts while we hung our mouths just below the stream of water and gulped down as much as possible before he turned off the tap and then on again for the next child.

Mrs von Gleich taught us many things, including how to relate to others. If boys fought in the playground, she marched over to the scene, surrounded by children looking on. As small as she was, she stepped in, took them by their collar, and marched them back to class.

"I'll wait here until you apologise to each other," she said.

Sometimes it took ages but that didn't bother Mrs. von Gleich. She remained at her desk reading. The culprits often still sat there when we arrived back in class! They always gave in, and apologised.

"Say sorry and make up," was Mrs von Gleich's motto. The amazing thing was that, soon after apologising, the boys played together as though nothing had ever happened!

Mother and Mrs. von Gleich also became friends, visiting each other. They talked and talked while I skipped outside. Mrs von Gleich even asked me to call her Aunt Magdalene, although I found that difficult at school.

At lunch time, Mrs von Gleich ate her sandwiches, while we ate ours. Before starting, she always led us in prayer:

In Dutch:
Velen hebben honger,
maar geen brood,
Velen heben brood,
maar geen honger,
Wij hebben honger,
wij hebben te eten,
Laten we't danken niet vergeten.

In English:
Many are hungry,
but have no bread,
Many have bread,
but aren't hungry,
We are hungry,
we have bread,
Let's not forget to give thanks.

THE ARDENNES

My first school trip came as a big surprise. Mrs von Gleich, with a team of parents, took my whole class to the Ardennes. It was my first trip out of Holland. Parents drove us in cars through Noord Brabant and Limburg, with its rolling hills. We stopped in a village to buy freshly-baked, *round* wholemeal bread, unheard of then, and cheese. The locals were friendly, and their Dutch sounded so strange—like another language! After Limburg, we entered Luxemburg. We didn't need passports there, because Holland belonged to the Benelux—a pact between Holland, Belgium, and Luxemburg.

As we crossed the Dutch border into the Ardennes, the scenery became more mountainous.

"See those black layers of slate?" Mrs von Gleich explained, "Thousands of years ago, these hills were like Switzerland's mountains. They've compacted and eroded through the ages."

We stopped at a youth hostel where, following Mrs von Gleich's prayer, we had more fresh bread and cheese with milk. Strolling through the village later, we came across a quaint brook rushing over boulders, the water looking clean enough to drink!

I loved that trip. Maybe Mrs von Gleich exerted her influence regarding holidays for Penny and me, because from then on, we went somewhere each year. She may also have helped provide funding.

TERSCHELLING

"Holidays!" Penny and I shouted. "The beach!"

Having settled into the Rudolf Steiner School, Mother took Penny and me on our first vacation to Terschelling, a small island north of Holland.

We stayed in a *pension* and hired bikes, hoping to explore the island with Mother. The strong North Sea wind, however, took her breath away. Thankfully, we met a couple and their small son at the dining table.

"Why don't your girls come to the beach with us?" the woman suggested.

"Yes, yes!" Tommy echoed.

"Can we, Mother, please...?" Penny pleaded.

"Why not?" Mother replied.

Mother remained indoors while Penny and I, Tommy, and his parents, explored the island's rough and wild south coast covered with mussel shells and millions of tiny crabs to nibble at our toes. No swimming there for me!

By contrast, the north coast had sand dunes, and gentle waves to dive into. It reminded me of another time when Mother took us to Scheveningen; and Penny and I jumped dunes while waiting for Mother to announce when it was safe to swim.

"Can we go in now?" we asked, hot and bothered.

"Okay," Mother finally called.

"Yeah!" we shouted, running off.

"Wait!" Mother called, pulling a thick rope from a basket. "First tie this round your waist—one at a time!"

"What?" I argued.

"I don't want you drowning," Mother reasoned.

Mother only had one rope, and tied one end round Penny's waist, the other round her own light frame.

Someone might see me! I thought, when it was my turn, and jumped dunes instead, although admiring Mother's effort at keeping us safe.

About that time, Mother taught me the Lord's Prayer, perhaps also at Mrs von Gleich's suggestion, to calm my nerves, as I continued having nightmares.

In those dreams, I always ran from someone who was trying to catch me. I'd wake up in a sweat with my head at the foot of the bed—*under* the blankets. It was a frightening experience, as it took ages to get back through the tightly tucked-in bedding to my pillow! A light-switch cord hung on the wall by my bed, but I couldn't find it, and wandered, disorientated, around the room in the pitch dark, feeling for the door and the elusive light switch.

Penny and I rode our bikes to school when few other pupils did, and because my friends still looked on bikes as a novelty, they lined up to be given a lift on the back mudguard during lunch break. One day, Mrs von Gleich marched towards us.

Oh no! Looks like I'm in trouble… I thought. Instead, I received a big surprise.

"Go to the bike shop and get a carrier attached," she instructed.

"But … I don't have …" I tried to reason.

"Payment is taken care of."

What? I thought. *A gift for me, without it being my birthday or Christmas? That only happened one other time, when Aunt Tine took me shopping for my new doll—on doctors' orders.*

From then on, everyone was given a lift in comfort, and my school bag was carried properly, instead of dangling from my handlebar.

Another day I grumbled to Mrs von Gleich.

"I haven't been able to finish my homework; Mother is sick again, and she gives us so many chores to do! I wish I had another mother…"

"Don't you complain about your mother," Mrs von Gleich defended. "She's wonderful. She loves you dearly, and does her best, even though she's so ill. She suffered much during the war and lost many loved ones…"

Her comment made me think.

"Your Mother needs your love and understanding," she continued. "She sacrificed herself for you, now it's your turn to help her. If it gets difficult, remember, we must all carry our cross in life, just as Jesus did."

I couldn't imagine myself carrying a cross, but I hadn't thought about Mother that way before, though I had heard some hair-raising stories about the war in Java.

Mrs von Gleich's lecture showed Mother in a different light, making me more sensitive to her needs, and swallowing my pride when she, seemingly, to me, acted so unreasonably.

My new friend, Urthe, sat next to me in class. I liked Urthe. I didn't have to put on a false front with her, as I felt I had to with others. She lived in Groenekan, close to Bilthoven. Their large rambling house and garden with a barn and hayloft seemed like paradise to me, a haven to run to when Mother was in one of her moods. Urthe's mother and father welcomed me kindly, in sharp contrast to the friction pervading our home! Although I realised that Mother had inexplicable fears, and I felt sorry for her for that, her lack of self-control and explosive temper worried me.

Coby, another classmate, was also serious and sensible. Children like her attracted me, perhaps because I so longed for peace. In winter, the school allocated children living further away to a classmate's warm home for lunch. I was designated to Coby's home and family.

As strict Christians, they prayed both before and after meals. Following lunch, Coby's grandfather then read aloud from a huge Bible written in hard-to-understand old-fashioned Dutch. Although the meaning of the stories went over my head, the solemn ritual birthed in me a deepening awareness of God. Despite the family's strict rules, I liked Coby, and I liked the atmosphere. I longed to talk with Coby about the Bible stories, but the right moment never came.

Then there was Tom. Older boys teased him, while he passively retreated. But I liked Tom. I was now almost 'top-notch' in my class because of my athletic ability. My previous experience at the hands of bullies, however, helped me understand what it felt like to be the underdog, and I hated seeing Tom treated that way. One day, the school bully teased Tom again, and in a surge of indignation, I stepped in. The boy thought I wanted to fight, and before long, we lay on the ground surrounded by a group of children.

"What are you doing fighting a girl?" they all sneered. "Shame on you!"

Then Mrs von Gleich arrived. She also gave the boy an earful, and put an end to Tom being bullied. However, it opened another vista for me. The bully admired my courage, and treated me to sweets. I lapped that up!

As we attended school half-days on Saturdays, we always sang Christmas carols at each consecutive Advent, after Mrs von Gleich had lit one candle on a wreath hanging from the class ceiling. We also brought our own candles in holders, and sat them on our desks. Singing while the flames flickered and danced, made for a magical experience especially when we received mandarins and we squirted the liquid from the skin into the flame.

Each week brought more excitement, but lighting all four candles on the wreath meant something extra special. After Mrs von Gleich had lit the four candles, she led us into the darkened school hall with our own candles in hand. Here we joined the rest of the school who'd gathered around a huge Christmas tree, also lit up with real candles. Together we sang carols.

The most exciting part of Christmas to me, however, was a play the teachers produced and acted in at another venue. The music played softly as we entered; the lights went out, and the stage curtains parted, revealing a scene with shepherds sleeping against hay bales. The musty smell of hay and sack-cloth tunics transported me back to Biblical times; the singing of 'Gloria in Excelsis Deo' seeming like angels' voices. As I listened to the Dutch version, the angels' message about the God of life and death bringing peace on earth touched me deep inside my soul… and brought another miracle—this time to me—as God's peace flooded my soul.

Dutch:	English:
	(almost exact translation)
Engelkens door 't luchtruim zwevend,	Angels through the air a' gliding,
Zongen zo blij, zo wonderschoon,	Sang so gladly, so wonderfully,
Van de Heer van dood en leven,	Of the Lord of death and life,
Die er vrede op aarde bracht,	He who brought peace on earth,
Gloria in excelsis Deo,	Gloria in excelsis Deo,
Gloria in excelsis Deo.	Gloria in excelsis Deo.

Birthdays were also days to celebrate. First thing in the morning I found my dining chair decorated with fresh flowers and crepe-paper streamers. On the table lay gifts, one from Mother, and one from Penny. After breakfast, Mother handed me a big bag of toffees to pass round in class. That made me feel like a queen!

The celebration continued at the weekend when my *whole* class of about 16 children arrived for a party. Mother had baked a turban cake, and drizzled water-icing on top like snow, something other mothers didn't do then. She led us in exciting games, which everyone loved.

Sadly, after two or three birthday parties, Mother became too ill, and from then on, we celebrated with best friends only, at the cinema, or at Indonesian restaurants in Utrecht.

Two close friends, Maria, and Kattelijn Boon, also came from Indonesia. Their father had died in a POW camp, as ours had. Maria was Penny's age, and Kattelijn mine, but we all played together. They lived next to Bithoven's City Council building. I liked their mother, Netty Boon, and sometimes wished she was my mother.

For Maria and Kattelijn's birthday parties, Mrs Boon always cooked a huge pot of *nasi goreng* (fried rice) served with shrimp crackers and *shroendeng* (fried coconut and peanuts), and allowed us two or three helpings! I looked forward to playing the game 'Night Watch' after dark. While the 'night-watch' waited outside the door with a gong, we each chose an animal to represent, and received a number. Then we hid in the pitch-dark room. Mrs Boon had turned off the light and ushered the night-watch in with her gong. If she struck our number, we made the sound of our animal. The night-watch then had to guess who had made the sound.

Meanwhile, back at school, Mrs von Gleich helped me catch up on three years' lost schooling, and with regained confidence, I soon read and wrote fluently. Apart from teaching hand-sewing, arithmetic, and music, Mrs von Gleich also taught us German during normal lessons, as she unconsciously mixed German with Dutch.

Penny and I rode our bikes to school most seasons, except during heavy frosts after snowfalls, when bike paths and some roads became death traps. Roads became totally inaccessible, with tyre tracks frozen rock-hard, and dangerous for us to negotiate.

One winter, a thick blanket of snow covered the landscape, and after many heavy frosts, the snow froze solid again, so we caught the bus.

"Let's see if the pond down the lane is frozen over," one of a group of children called during lunch period at school. We all ran down the lane, climbed a barbed-wire fence, and raced to the pond.

"It's solid!" someone called.

"Thick enough to hold us?"

"Sure to..."

We all ventured onto the ice, until we heard a strange creaking sound. Everyone ran to the edge again, but I was too slow. The ice broke, and I slid into the icy water. Each time I grabbed at ice-floes for support, they slipped away.

I must get out of here, and fast! I thought.

Remembering a news clip at the *Cinemac* about the dangers of slipping under ice and not finding your way back to the point of entry, kept me alert.

"Do something!" I yelled to my classmates, standing near a fallen tree. "Get that branch!" They took ages, but finally dragged a huge branch to the pond.

Please God, let this work, I prayed, while they held the branch out towards me and I grabbed hold of the end. I was really thankful when they pulled me over the ice to safety. I was ecstatic to set foot on solid ground!

"Thanks!" I puffed.

We ran back to school, me dripping wet, and upstairs to the principal. To my surprise, I didn't feel cold. Nearly everything I wore that day was made of wool, which insulated me. The teacher, to my embarrassment, made me undress, wash, and change into her outsized dry clothes. Then she handed me a spoonful of vile medicine.

"This will prevent you getting pneumonia," she said.

Unbeknown to the teacher, I spat most of it into my hand. It tasted ghastly! That afternoon I was the centre of attention. I must have looked weird, but only half as weird as I felt going home on the bus wearing the teacher's clothes and covered by her long overcoat. People stared at me! Thankfully I didn't catch pneumonia.

Practising Mrs von Gleich's wisdom, and asking myself what Jesus would have done in tricky situations at home, changed my life for the better, to a certain extent. Choosing quiet friends didn't mean having no fun. I got as excited as anyone, especially while playing sport. It helped me take my frustrations out on the ball instead of on people.

FAMILY FRIENDS

CHAPTER 16

As I grew older, I became more aware of others' feelings, but also of my own. I felt ashamed if the neighbours heard shouting coming from inside our home, and I cringed when I heard it while playing on the street with other children, or on my return home from school. To avoid the commotion, I quickly turned around and cycled off again—to nowhere in particular.

However, as the sun went down, and the temperature dropped, I had nowhere else to go but home. By then, Mother worried about me, and may have realised why I stayed away. I kept my thoughts to myself, and quickly did my chores, those chores serving more than one purpose.

Swimming at *Brandenburg's* pool with our neighbouring friends enabled Penny and me to forget our problems, temporarily far from Mother's reach and demanding calls. Yet we always stuck to our time limits.

In our street games, the noise we made seemed like an illusionary shield of protection from any outside interference, Mother's calls included. We mostly played team games in which children of all ages joined in, and so we made allowance for the younger ones by choosing games they also enjoyed.

When roller-skating became popular, we held speed races. Our first skates, made by *Hudora*, were for straight skating—no brakes! To stop, we pointed our toes inwards. Later, Mother bought us fancier skates which we could adjust and loosen with a spanner to skate straight or make turns. All our skates were tied on. They were adaptable to different-sized shoes as we grew, and they therefore lasted for many years.

Our only problem was the street surface. Although we all became clever at avoiding bumps, hollows, and tiny stones, we ended up with many scrapes and grazes. No sooner had the street surface become smooth and just right for skating, than the city council resealed it with tar and rough stone chips, dynamite on our knees and hands if we tripped! To our embarrassment, Mother bandaged our grazes with salt-water compresses for everyone to see! She feared tetanus. Tetanus was known to be carried by horses, which were still used to pull vegetable and milk carts, and their droppings became embedded in the rough road chips.

The baker used an Alsatian dog, strapped underneath his small cart. The cart only had two big wheels at the front and two handles for the baker to hold. When working-dogs were finally outlawed, he used a baker's *bakfiets* (carrier tricycle) with a big wooden bin at the front.

The milkman continued making deliveries. Later, he and the ragman used open, flat-decked *bakfietsen*.

Penny and I developed a fascination for bikes, and learnt to ride on Juliana's old bicycle, which she left behind, stored in our garage. Too short to sit on the seat, we pedalled standing up. A push got us started, then we went full speed to keep upright. But we couldn't stop! To do that, we either steered into a soft hedge, falling into it, or hung onto a tree branch, leaving the bike to continue wobbling on alone.

By now, Mother had lots of friends. I don't know where they came from or how they met one another. They appeared out of nowhere. Many had Indonesian connections. Others were family friends or relations; and still others, were friends of Juliana and John's in New Zealand and Australia.

Mother later joined a craft group *'Adelheid'*. She loved sewing. The group usually gathered in our home. One of the group was Noordewiertje. She was also widowed and had lived in Indonesia. She had three children: Wouter, Koen, and Adeel. Penny and I adored their company. While we played Monopoly, Mother and Noordewiertje talked about their Indonesian pre-war escapades. The visits did wonders for Mother! We children listened as they recalled amusing episodes of the past in Java, and roared with laughter. Mother could be very funny, recounting amusing stories when she 'held the floor'. Noordewiertje stimulated her.

Always short of money, Noordewiertje kept a look-out for bargains at railway lost-property-sales, reselling them. That's how we acquired our bikes; and from then on we cycled everywhere, including to school, regardless of rain, hail, and sometimes snow.

'Aunt' Tini and 'Uncle' Frits Klay, friends who also brought normality to our lives, had returned from Dutch New Guinea after the war, and spoke Malay with Mother, especially when they didn't want us to know what was said. We loved going to their cosy home for meals of *nasi goreng*. Although I liked Mother's rice with sajoor (Indonesian soup), Aunt Tini's *nasi goreng*, with all the trimmings, tasted exceptionally good.

The Klays hosted one of my birthday parties in their back garden, and made me feel very proud. Their garden was a forest that lent itself perfectly to a treasure hunt. We also gathered bark, pine branches, and pine cones to make Christmas decorations.

A Quaker friend provided us with food parcels at Christmas time. These contained jam, spicy Frisian loaves, biscuits, and tinned food. Her kindness meant a lot to us. I recall attending her house-church on the Soestdijkseweg when I was so small that I couldn't see over what seemed a sea of adults standing while we sang "Ere Zij God" (Honour God). I still remember the words and melody. They impressed me. I often wondered why Mother didn't continue attending that church. It felt so good to be there.

I also wondered why, when Mother took us to a healing service in Zeist, we left before the meeting finished. I was so looking forward to her being healed of her breathing problems! Perhaps it had something to do with the collection. I didn't ask. I'd learnt from experience, when something bothered Mother, you didn't question her.

When I was about eleven years old, we met two spinsters, 'Aunt' Frida Dolby-Peters, and 'Aunt' Jet van Marle. They became Mother's nicest friends, who also lived in Bilthoven. Mother came to know them through Juliana, when they'd visited their nephew in Hastings, New Zealand. I loved their surprise visits. They dressed and looked like real ladies in their fur coats, fox stoles, and wide-brimmed hats with feather plumes—while riding their bikes! On the inside, however, they were jubilant and so much fun. Mother could have been in the foulest mood before their arrival, but their presence suddenly dissolved all traces of negativity the moment they set foot in the house. What a breath of fresh air! Just looking at them gracefully jumping from their high-handlebar bikes made me smile.

Other times, they often walked into our kitchen unannounced.

"Yoo-hoo!" Aunt Frida's melodious voice echoed through the house, and I knew instantly who'd arrived! Mother's mood immediately lifted. She then urged us to make tea and bring out the biscuits. The visitors always included Penny and me in their conversations; and when they left our home, they invited Penny and me to visit them. With Mother's spirit suddenly renewed, she became light-hearted, and the heavy atmosphere in the house lifted like a cloud on a sunny afternoon. Amazingly, Mother remained peaceful the rest of the day.

Do they suspect what our home-life is like? I sometimes wondered. I'll never tell anyone about Mother's problems. If I ever do, it will only be someone who won't cause trouble for her.

I believed what Mother said about our family. Her inference was that if we told anyone about our way of life, we might be sent to an orphanage. That was the last thing I wanted! But there were many times when the stress became too much. I then took to my bike, aimlessly riding around Bilthoven, past my friends' homes, and Aunt Jet and Aunt Frida's.

Their invitation still echoed in my ears; although I was not bold enough to enter their gate: I usually rode on. One time I plucked up the courage, and they welcomed me in like a long-lost friend, serving me tea, cakes, and sweets. Their happy outlook on life eased my worries, enabling me to return home refreshed—and I hadn't even shared my problems!

Mother also had many good friends in the Scout movement. Similar interests glued them together, even well after the war. As their relationships flourished and they reminisced about scouting events in Indonesia, Mother also looked on her past years as *happy years.*

Aunt Marietje, Grandmother Brandt's younger half-sister, was another visitor Penny and I loved to see. Although she was related, she was also a good friend to Mother. From my observations, just talking with Aunt Marietje eased Mother's worries. She had an air of grace about her, yet she was fun-loving.

At first, she visited with a lady friend, Mrs Pikaard, who at the time shared her house in Doorn. They also dressed in fur coats, fox-stoles, and brimmed hats, with the then fashionable short, black nets draped over their faces.

After Mrs Pikaard died, Penny and I visited Aunt Marietje unaccompanied. There was a relaxed atmosphere in her home, enhanced by her continual humming of melodies. Sometimes she also invited our cousin, Tanja Brandt, and another friend Francine. Then out came the cards—one pack each—to play Battalion, a fast, unpredictable game.

Aunt Marietje lived close to Castle Doorn, where Kaiser Wilhelm II, after his abdication as Germany's monarch in 1918, had lived in exile until his death in 1941. When we saw it, the castle had been turned into a museum with everything in place as though the emperor might return any moment.

"What would you like for lunch?" Aunt Marietje always asked.

"Curried eggs," we answered every time, as any form of rice was our favourite dish.

She, too, spoiled us with chocolate letters at Sinterklaas on 5 December, and chocolate eggs at Easter.

CHURCH

In summer, when Mother was well enough, we occasionally attended St. Michael's Church in Huizen, where we caught up with Bobby after she'd played the organ. Uncle Marijn, Father's brother, preached—in English, which made church boring because I didn't understand English yet, nor the sermon. But following the service we could count on having fun when we met up with our cousins Joris, Myra, Tanja, Sita, and Coen. Their father, Uncle Marijn, usually invited us for lunch at their home in Bussum. While Mother, Uncle Marijn and Aunt Jettie talked, we played.

I liked seeing Bobby and our cousins. When Penny and I were younger, however, we dreaded Sundays and going to church, because out came two prickly woollen dresses which we *had* to wear! Penny's was blue, mine red. We were so glad when we finally outgrew those dresses!

We didn't own many clothes. At first Mother bought these second-hand. Most served only to keep us warm, no style or fashion. I do recall Penny having one favourite vest, and I a pretty, matching summer skirt and blouse. By contrast, it was like a feast to open parcels from Mother's youngest sister, Aunt Jeanne Traill, in England. I especially treasured our cousin Robbie's Fair Isle jerseys.

In summer, when Mother felt a little better, we sometimes cycled to Bussum. Other times, we took similar routes through forests and picturesque fields of heather.

Mother learnt to ride a bike much later in life, and wobbled all over the place. We often steadied her by holding her arm. She was more confident then, and enjoyed the outing. On long trips and very quiet roads, we pushed her along, one of us on each side, especially when she became tired or breathless. This allowed her to stop pedalling, take in the scenery, and relax. This was a peaceful and therapeutic pastime for us all.

I loved bike rides to Loosdrechtse Plassen, a lake district with narrow roads in between shallow streams. Great for picnics! Penny and I paddled barefoot in the water, swam, or hired a row boat. Mother relaxed, and stoically tried rowing, but quickly tired. However, when it was time to go home, and a cool breeze blew, she soon gasped for air. We then pushed her home as quickly as possible. Although Mother felt and looked exhausted, she enjoyed the breeze blowing through her hair.

When I was a bit older and the sales were on in Utrecht, Mother occasionally took us shopping for dresses at Vroom & Dreesman, and C & A department stores. There she searched for clothes that would last at least three or four summers, with waistlines easily taken in and hems shortened, able to be let down later. The thought of owning a new dress excited me, but Mother wanted the best fit, top quality, and lowest price.

I hated being dragged from one shop to the other—so exhausting and boring! We then tried on dresses in both shops, but didn't buy a thing. Then returning to the previous store, we repeated the process. The selection was superb, but Mother was never happy. Just when we gave up hope of ever owning another dress or skirt, Mother decided, and Penny and I walked out with one or two garments each.

After such a busy shopping spree, Mother, particularly, needed a rest. The *Cineac*, a movie theatre close to the C & A department store, that only played *News of the World,* served a good purpose. We could sit there for as long as we liked, while the news flashed on the big screen in black and white for about half an hour. To me the best came last—Walt Disney cartoons, in colour! If Mother was still breathless, we sat through another session of the news and, to my delight, more cartoon strips—at no extra cost. Sometimes, if we were lucky, and there was time, on our way to the bus terminus, Mother detoured to *van Angeren* restaurant, on the same side of the street as Vroom & Dreesman. It could have been the overwhelming aroma wafting onto the footpath. Their Russian salads and soft ice-cream sundaes decorated with pink wafers, and served in ice-cold stainless-steel dishes, tasted delicious. This made shopping sprees worthwhile. And hot coffee did wonders for Mother's breathlessness—until she remembered the time...

"The bus!" she would suddenly wheeze, almost dragging us down the stairs and onto the footpath. Any good effect the coffee had had, quickly evaporated.

Later, when Penny and I were older, we, with a hand under each elbow, practically heaved Mother along the crowded footpath—to the bus-terminus. Later, one of us ran ahead.

"Please wait for my Mother."

The bus driver always did.

If we missed the bus, we waited half-an-hour for the next one. A bus usually stood there waiting, and it was warm inside. If we hadn't been to *van Angeren*, Mother sometimes handed us a few coins.

"Go buy us a snack," she'd say, and without hesitation, we ran down the aisle, past the driver's empty seat and out the door to a potato-chip stand nearby. With our prized chips in a cone-shaped paper bag, we ran back to share them with Mother. Those treats rounded off a tiring day, and made for a pleasant trip home.

TURNING POINT

CHAPTER 17

"Yahoo! Free from the tyrant!" Penny exclaimed, on our ride home from school.

It was June 1954. Penny had finished at Rudolf Steiner Primary, and was about to attend Bilthoven's Lyceum in September. Throughout her two years at Rudolf Steiner Primary, she'd had the same teacher, Mr Blok. She didn't like him, and was pleased to leave his class. He acted strangely, demoralising her and her classmates, especially girls. Years later he was expelled, having been caught red-handed—as a paedophile!

Because Mrs von Gleich retired that year, I inherited Mr Blok as my class teacher from September 1954. During my time in her class, Mrs von Gleich had staged yearly historical productions. I loved history, and as a result, acting became my favourite subject. I lived for those plays, pouring my heart and soul into all my roles, large or small. Mrs von Gleich encouraged me in lead roles, even suggesting acting as a career.

Her encouragement meant a lot to me because, so far, my life had not contained much affirmation or praise.

Our first play was about William of Orange, in which I played William's mother, Juliana van Stolberg. To ensure that I came in smoothly, I learnt everybody's lines, also William's. When Grandmother Brandt's half-sister, Aunt Marietje, informed me we had family links with Juliana van Stolberg, my enthusiasm soared. Later, we also performed other plays: Saint Christopher, George and the Dragon, William Tell, and Romeo and Juliet.

But when Mrs von Gleich retired and Mr Blok took over the productions, everything changed. I sensed that Mr Blok didn't like me, and purposely cast me in minor roles. In class, he made derogatory comments, such as, "You'll never amount to anything."

Undeterred, I kept putting everything into my assigned small roles, and, as always, learnt everybody's lines, so I knew when my turn came to speak. Close to production time Mr Blok often, without notice, asked me to play lead roles. Already knowing the lines enabled me to adapt easily but it made no difference to Mr Blok's view of me. His negative attitude continued.

His destructive remarks during the two years he was my teacher would have lasted a lifetime had I not firmly stood against them. Thankfully, Penny and Mother became my allies and encouraged me. Although Mrs von Gleich came to every production, I missed her input in class and rehearsals. I sometimes visited her at home but didn't tell her what happened at school. She hated gossip, and I presumed talking about Mr Blok was gossip. Although confiding in Mrs von Gleich would have been wise, the way things worked out I used acting and sport as a way of 'letting off steam' about the injustice I felt rising inside.

TRIUMPH

Prior to Easter 1956, Mr Blok taught our class about the 80-year Spanish War between 1568 and 1648. One day he gave us a surprise test and was annoyed that most of us didn't do well. He singled me out, belittling me in front of the whole class. Then he promised to give us another test after the holidays.

When I told Penny what he'd said, mentioning the repeat test, she immediately worked out a plan.

"You're going to pass that test," she said. "When we go to Uncle Ko and Aunt Daisy's for Easter, we'll take your history book and study together. I'll test you right through the holidays. If I have anything to do with this, you're going to gain top marks."

I doubted her words. My self-esteem was low. But I appreciated her belief in me.

We went to Uncle Ko and Aunt Daisy's as planned, and Penny ensured that I brought my history book. Aunt Daisy was my favourite great-aunt. I was a bit frightened of Uncle Ko. He could be gruff, but I fathomed if Aunt Daisy, who was gentle and loving, had married him, he must be all right. Their home, *Klein Gelresteyn*, was far from small (*klein* meaning small)—an extensive, three-story manor house, surrounded by about two acres of landscaped gardens.

After a train trip, a trolleybus ride and a short walk, we arrived at their large front door in Velp. Aunt Leo, the housekeeper, answered the doorbell.

"Penny and Addy!" she exclaimed, as if we were very important people.

"Welcome! We've been expecting you."

I liked Aunt Leo. We knew her well by then, having already stayed other Easters. She hugged and kissed us like a *real* aunt, then took us to see Aunt Daisy in the lounge. Rumour had it that Aunt Daisy had had a compound ankle fracture when she was young. Unable to set the broken bones, doctors planned to amputate her foot. Desperate, Aunt Daisy searched for an alternative cure and met Uncle Ko, a young homeopathic doctor who treated her and saved her foot. Then they must have fallen in love and married. When Aunt Daisy walked into a room with her distinctive limp and high ankle boots, she lifted the whole atmosphere when she spoke. Nobody else had a voice like hers, and in the sweetest, most melodious tone one could imagine, she always put me at ease.

"Penny and Addy, I'm so glad you've come to stay with us for the holidays," she would say, as if she was honoured to have us. "You must be hungry and thirsty." Then she rang a little bell. Aunt Leo promptly entered.

"Leo," Aunt Daisy said. "Could you get Penny and Addy something to eat and drink?"

"Certainly, Madam." Soon Aunt Leo returned with a trolley full of sandwiches and fruit.

"Aunt Daisy, where's Uncle Ko?" Penny, always forthright, asked.

"In his surgery, dear," Aunt Daisy answered.

"Can we see him?"

"I'll get Aunt Leo to check if the patients have left."

Penny was unafraid of Uncle Ko. I, however, had heard a few stories about him. A rumour circulated that he'd expelled one of his own sons from their home because he refused to study medicine.

What might he do to us? I thought. But Aunt Leo eased my fears while leading us to his office.

"Your great-uncle is like a cuddly bear. His growl sounds fierce, but he's really very loving underneath." Then she left us alone.

We knocked on the door.

"Come in!" a deep voice answered.

It was dark in the surgery. There was a strange odour. The shelves were full of stuffed animals which Uncle Ko treasured.

"Hello there..." Uncle Ko said in a gentle voice from behind his desk. "Where did you two come from?"

"Had you forgotten we were coming?" asked Penny.

"How could I forget such an important event?" he said, grinning from ear to ear. He stood up when he saw us looking at his life-like mounted animals and plants in the conservatory.

"Come, I'll show you round." Then he told us what the animals had meant to him, and accompanied us through his warm conservatory. Plants of all shapes and sizes stood in bath-like structures around glassed walls, running water cascading refreshingly, pleasing our senses. I'd never experienced anything like it before.

"I'm famished," he said, suddenly. "It's time for afternoon tea. I'm sure you two can also do with a bite to eat. But first you must hop on the scales."

Uncle Ko worried about our weight. Ever since our arrival in Holland in 1946, he'd hoped to fatten us up. He habitually weighed us on arrival and leaving, but was always disappointed with the outcome. Our weight remained the same. I guess we were too active. Our leanness wasn't the result of unhealthy food. By then we ate healthy food at home, simple fare, without trimmings of cakes and sweets.

During the day, we played and explored their huge home. In the attic we discovered a beautiful old dolls' house that Uncle Ko and Aunt Daisy's children had played with when they were young. It had real electric lights, baths, and basins, a kitchen, many bedrooms with little dolls and four-poster-beds. I could have played there all day! Penny, however, wasn't into dolls, so we compromised.

Although Penny and I were very close, we were different in character. She liked playing with boys, enjoying their rough games. I liked dolls and *girly* play. She was confident, I wasn't. I envied that confidence, which seemed to draw her into people's hearts. It made me feel left out, but there wasn't much I could do about it. As a result, when people asked me questions, Penny often answered for me. I didn't mind her doing that when I was very young, but later I resented it. I was simply slower at working out my answers.

Except for a few bedrooms, of which we used one, a school used the other rooms on the second floor. We slept in high hospital beds with sheets stiff from starch. It made me feel very cosy, especially when Aunt Daisy and Aunt Leo tucked us into bed and kissed us goodnight. I missed that at home. We kissed Mother goodnight and put ourselves to bed. Mother was too ill to come to us.

Meals at Uncle Ko and Aunt Daisy were always fun. Regardless of a nasty-looking two-inch growth on Uncle Ko's face, he always joked. There was a servery between the dining room and kitchen but Uncle Ko had a special way of calling Aunt Leo. Initially we couldn't work out how she appeared so quickly when Uncle Ko mentioned he needed more of something. It was as though they had a secret radio connection between them.

"At your service, sir," she'd say, as she entered.
"We need more cheese sauce for the cauliflower, Leo."
"Yes, sir." Then she darted out, quickly returning with more sauce. When Uncle Ko realised our curiosity, he called Aunt Leo more often. Each time, she entered the dining room, ready to take orders. I think she knew something was up when it happened too often, but always remained gracious. We laughed when Penny and I discovered a bell-button on the floor, *under* the table!

We also loved spending time with Aunt Leo in the kitchen. She was fun to be with, always happy and telling stories. We ran errands and peeled potatoes for her. Licking pots was our reward. She wasn't afraid of Uncle Ko. She even joked with him.

One day when we walked through the herb garden, Uncle Ko motioned for us to come closer to look inside his nearby garage. There stood his black 1926 Packard, the car he would have driven to visit us in 1946 to Huizen and later Eerbeek when we were ill with the measles. The car was so shiny, our faces were reflected in the paint. We could tell it was Uncle Ko's pride and joy by the way he stroked it. Then he showed us three large conifers nearby.

"We planted these trees when your Father, Mother, Juliana, and John came to Holland on furlough in 1936," he said. "One for each person. Strangely, your father's tree died during the war!" I liked climbing one of those trees; it provided a great view over Velp.

Later, Aunt Leo took us down some stairs from the kitchen to the cellar that stretched under the *whole* house and had secret exits.

"Your Uncle Ko treated and hid many Jews during the war," said Aunt Leo. "The exits were hidden by shrubs for emergency escapes."

I could just picture Uncle Ko acting innocently before German soldiers. He seemed a good actor.

After meals, everyone retired to the lounge at the other end of the house, where sunlight streamed through the many glass windows during the day. It was in this lounge that Penny meticulously tested me over and over about the Spanish War, sometimes two to three times a day. As time progressed, I became more familiar with the dates and names involved in the history project.

It didn't mean all work, though. Penny and I explored, played games in the garden and joined an Easter-egg-hunt for coloured, hard-boiled eggs, with poorer, neighbourhood children. Aunt Daisy firmly instructed us to restrict our quota to only three eggs each so there'd be plenty left for others. We understood, recalling a time when even *one* egg had been a treat for us.

Later, Aunt Daisy gave us small wrapped chocolate eggs, which we hid for each other in the garden. We only ate the occasional one, so we could continue our game. Penny, however, never forgot the history lessons, and when it was time for us to go home, I felt quite confident about the 80-year Spanish War.

Aunt Marietje, Grandmother de Wendt's half-sister, had also reminded me that our family was related (through Grandmother de Wendt) to Juliana van Stolberg. Her son, William of Orange I (1533-1584), became the first leader of the Dutch Revolt against the rule of Roman Catholic King Phillip II of Spain during the Spanish 80-year war! His and many Dutch resistance fighters' actions led to the formation of the early independent Dutch Republic, the United Northern Provinces, which rapidly grew into a world power through its merchant shipping, resulting in a period of great economic, scientific, and cultural growth.

I was fired up and ready for the test!

Before our departure, Uncle Ko weighed us again.

"Still not gaining weight..." he muttered.

After farewells, we walked with Aunt Leo to the trolley bus. We caught a train home unaccompanied. We'd become seasoned travellers.

On my first day back at school, Mr Blok handed out our test papers for the Spanish War. I looked at the questions.

I know that, I thought and quickly finished the test. To my surprise, I achieved top marks. Penny was elated, I astounded at my first achievement. Mr Blok's negative comments aimed at me were far from the truth. There was hope for me yet.

By now Mother realised that Penny and I were missing out on much because of her ill health and financial problems. So, as soon as the weather and her health improved a little, the three of us cycled through Bilthoven's tree-lined streets, past picturesque gardens to find the prettiest vacant field with wild flowers, to have a picnic.

On our return home, we sometimes met an ice-cream vendor on his three-wheeler bike.

"Let's have an ice-cream before we go home!" Mother often softened if she'd brought her purse with her. We then licked our ice-creams, sitting on a little brick wall beside the road, treasuring the small luxury.

However, as the day wore on and the air cooled, Mother became breathless; and because her puffers often didn't work, she couldn't breathe *and* pedal. Penny and I, knowing from experience that she needed to get warm and home *fast*, took an elbow each and pushed Mother home, racing like the wind. Although it was a serious matter, to see Mother's child-like facial expression of joy was priceless! Sadly, she usually caught a chill, with complications to follow. Although the outings were fun, they were a huge sacrifice for Mother, resulting in further months in bed.

For Penny's and my second summer vacation in about 1956, we joined a group of girls for an educational experience on a flat barge on IJselmeer, where we witnessed a few dredging-boats and machinery beginning to shape what is now the Flevopolder. Reclaimed below-sea-level-land was pumped dry and protected against flooding by dykes. We understood little of how big that polder would grow—begun in 1956, and finished in 1966—and how much that area would change in the future, with houses and tall trees on it!

We also saw Marken, and Volendam nearby. Marken, then still an isolated island and fishing community, now a peninsula connected by a dyke to North Holland, was originally built around a tiny harbour on mounds and poles to protect it against flooding. It seemed strange seeing little boys with long hair dressed in girls' national costumes—

Marken's custom—until their fifth birthday. Then they received an official haircut and changed into boys' clothes.

Another time, the NBM (Netherlands Bus Company) treated us to a day's outing to the miniature city, Madurodam, in The Hague. The bus was packed with children also orphaned or semi-orphaned by war.

We immediately felt rapport with the other children, and sang and laughed. The miniature village was a child's paradise, full of moving gadgets, tiny buildings, trains, trams, cars, and dolls for little people. Everything worked, and could be viewed at close range. On the way home, we sang to the bus driver.

"De NBM gaat nooit verloren (shall never be lost)."

The bus company still functions today as the Connection.

Another summer, we spent a week at Uncle Ko and Aunt Daisy's holiday cottage, the Driest, in Bennekom, with their son, Uncle Krul, and daughter-in-law, Aunt Ina, and their children. This was where Juliana and Rob had spent their honeymoon in 1949, and where Mother and Father, with Juliana and John, had stayed during their furlough in 1936. Although the original cottage had burned down during the war, a new building had been constructed amongst a pine forest and wild blueberries. The berries grew so bountifully, we ate them to our hearts' content. Aunt Ina even used them to dye clothes!

In Ede, we all swam in popular swimming baths, with walls as high as a house. When the water was calm, the water-level dropped to our thighs. Every half-hour a siren sounded to warn inexperienced swimmers to leave the pool and to draw experienced swimmers in. Then the water would hiss and roar, and suddenly huge waves crashed down for us to dive into, like the sea without an undertow, or—Mother's rope!

INSIGHT

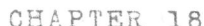

CHAPTER 18

"Hello. I'm your grandfather's brother, Alf," an older, and kind-looking gentleman introduced himself, while standing on our front doorstep. "May I see your mother, please?"

"I'll check," I replied, opening the door, and letting him into our hallway. It was autumn 1954. It was also the first time that Penny and I had seen or even heard from our great-uncle.

Uncle Alf took off his coat, scarf, and hat, and draped them over the coat-hook.

"Mother is ill," I said. "Take a seat, and I'll tell her you're here."

I ran up the stairs to Mother's bedroom door and knocked.

"Come in!" Mother called.

"Uncle Alf is downstairs. He wants to see you," I announced.

"Send him up, please."

I ran downstairs again.

"Mother can see you now," I said. "I'll show you the way."

Again, I knocked on the bedroom door.

"Come in," Mother called. "So nice of you to visit, Alf."

I left them to talk, and darted back downstairs.

When Mother and Uncle Alf had finished talking, he knocked on the family-room door, and, following a brief conversation with Penny and me, departed. Uncle Alf's wife, Aunt Johanna, had died in September that year. He still wore a black armband on his sleeve to signify his grief.

Following that visit, Uncle Alf helped Mother financially. When Mother was confined to bed and unable personally to cash Uncle Alf's cheques at the bank, Penny and I went together to cash them with her signed authority. Each cheque arrived in an envelope sealed and marked with a red plastic blob, which was stamped with his family crest.

Penny and I raced to the bank as fast as we could on one bike; one pedalling, the other on the back, holding the envelope. We then exchanged the cheque for cash and raced back home with it safe in the envelope, not stopping anywhere on the way for fear of being robbed.

Uncle Alf also invited us all to his large home, the *Reehorst*, in Driebergen, for afternoon tea or dinner.

His home stood on a huge property between a deer park and Driebergen's train station. He employed many household staff.

Hendrik was the butler. I liked Hendrik. When Mother was ill, Penny and I visited alone. Realising that we were unfamiliar with Uncle Alf's elaborate table etiquette, Hendrik instructed us on how and when to use the array of cutlery and bowls before the meal. After eating, he filled the small bowls beside our settings with warm water, to wash our sticky fingers. Then he handed us a small towel to dry them.

"Here you are, Miss Addy and Miss Penny," he said, politely.

He wore a butler's uniform with a stiff white collar, tailed suit, and a white serviette draped over his arm. He lived in a cottage on the same property, with his family.

On our arrival, Hendrik often answered the doorbell, and stiffly, yet kindly, welcomed us in. He showed us the washroom adjacent to the front door, because we'd become rather dishevelled and hot after riding fast on our bikes—our usual fashion. He then led us to Uncle Alf's drawing room door and knocked.

"Miss Penny and Miss Addy are here, sir," he announced. Then he left. Before long he returned.

"You rang, sir?"

When Uncle Alf requested afternoon tea, he responded politely. "Yes, sir! Right away, sir!"

Hendrik soon returned with a trolley laden with a tall, three-tiered plate-stand of sandwiches and cakes, a teapot, milk jug, sugar-lumps, and fancy tea set. Uncle Alf liked pouring the tea himself.

With afternoon tea over, it was time for a tune—by Penny and me. As usual, Penny had brought her flute for the occasion. I was meant to play the piano, but was too self-conscious. Not playing as well as Penny, I declined. However, there was more to it than that.

Uncle Alf had bought Penny a flute and me a piano—to become musically orientated. Penny was given a choice, but I wasn't. I secretly longed to play the guitar. However, I didn't have the heart to tell Uncle Alf or Mother. My piano teacher was a composer who taught the old-fashioned Bartok way, a lifeless and boring method with childish tunes.

To make matters worse, when I practised, Mother complained about the noise, and I had to stop playing.

But *Mother* loved playing the piano, and I loved listening to her play. I was afraid that if I mentioned my secret wish to Uncle Alf, he'd take the piano back, and I knew it was Mother's greatest and possibly only joy in life. I just *had* to keep up the charade…

After Penny played the flute for Uncle Alf, I always managed to find an excuse not to play the piano. Uncle Alf didn't seem to mind, possibly accepting my refusal as *nerves*.

"Well then, let's go for a walk through the garden," Uncle Alf said, changing the subject. "Devil needs exercise." He then took us on a guided tour. His little dog, Devil, a Scottish terrier, stood on the lawn. Eager to see us, he spun round and round as if on an axis! Then he followed us, playing *fetch*, while Uncle Alf showed us his colourful flower beds, which inspired me to grow my own garden one day.

As we cycled home down the driveway, Devil 'farewelled' us by running and spinning in circles, yapping noisily on the other side of the fence.

I liked Uncle Alf, not because of his wealth, but his interest in everything we loved and did. He was a true friend, a special great-uncle.

A CLOSE SHAVE

During Penny's last year at primary school, in 1954, when Penny was thirteen and I eleven, Mother required hospitalization for two hernia operations. For the first operation, Penny and I stayed with friends during the day, and our neighbours at night.

For Mother's second operation, about three months later, the friends and neighbour couldn't help her out, and Mother had to find others to care for us. This time a man we called Uncle Boris, whom Mother had befriended several years earlier, offered to have us stay at his home. He'd taken us on outings in his car, first with Mother present; later he'd taken Penny and me only. He often dropped in while we were cleaning our bikes outside.

"If you wash and polish my car, I'll take you for a drive," he'd say.

"Okay," we replied, keen to ride in his new car.

To us, washing and polishing a car was a small job. But after a few times without Mother, he began making unkind remarks about me. I pretended not to hear, although his words stung. Because we didn't go out much as a family, and Mother instructed Penny and me always to stay together, I endured the ridicule. Needless to say, I didn't like the man, but we had nowhere else to go while Mother was in hospital. I didn't tell Mother. We visited his home before the operation to get to know the rest of the family, and I liked his wife, Aunt Anneke, and their three children, so I pushed my fears aside.

Mother was then admitted to hospital, and Penny and I stayed with Uncle Boris and Aunt Anneke. To visit Mother at the hospital, we caught a bus near their home. Because of Mother's existing ill health, she took months to recover. In the meantime, Penny and I slept in Uncle Boris' attic surrounded by old furniture. When the family was out, Uncle Boris' sarcasm to me continued, although I kept a stiff upper lip in front of him.

At first the attic felt like a secret hide-away, where Penny and I could talk without fear of being overheard.

"What do you think of Uncle Boris?" Penny asked.

"I don't like him," I replied.

"It's strange how he always picks on you."

Penny and I were like twins, understanding each other without having to say much. We read books and sometimes played rough and tumble, as most children our age did.

One day, we found a wood-chip on the floor and wondered where it came from. Unable to fathom the mystery, we put it aside and forgot about it. Three or four weeks later, Uncle Boris stormed into the attic with the wood-chip in hand.

"Who broke this off the dresser?" he yelled in a demanding voice.

We'd totally forgotten the previous incident with the wood-chip and wondered what he was so angry about. Then he locked us in and, took us outside one at the time for *interrogation*. This went on for days. Penny was away for long periods of time while I was locked up in the attic. Then Penny was locked in while Uncle Boris interrogated me.

"I know you broke the dresser!" he screamed.

"No, I didn't!" I snapped back in retaliation.

"Yes, you did! I know you did!"

He lashed out at me, but I ducked just in time.

"Why did you duck?" he asked. "I'm not going to hit you."

You could have fooled me, I thought, pleased I did duck!

I was frightened, but tried not to show it. He continued questioning and accusing me. To end our imprisonment, Penny falsely admitted she broke the dresser. Although Uncle Boris didn't believe her, he finally allowed us out of the attic during the day. However, he refused to give us our bus money to visit Mother at the hospital.

Penny, always frugal, worked out a way to outsmart Uncle Boris.

"I still have some sweet money Mother gave me," she whispered. "It's enough for two one-way tickets to the hospital."

"But how can we get away?" I asked.

"We'll tell Aunt Anneke we're going to play with the children across the road. When we reach the high hedge, we'll run to the bus stop."

"Hope it works!"

"Sure to. Follow me. I'll do the talking."

After lunch, we got up from the table.

"What will you two do this afternoon?" Aunt Anneke asked, kindly.

"We're going to play with our friends across the road," Penny answered, as arranged.

"Have fun then," she said. "I'm going to have a rest."

"See you later!" we called, and ran down the driveway, stopping behind the hedge.

"Run!" Penny whispered, as she sprinted with me, following close behind. The bus stop was around the corner, only 100 metres away. Within thirty minutes we stood beside Mother's bed in the hospital and told her everything. Then Mother's physician entered the room.

"Dr Steenmeyer, these are my daughters, Penny and Addy."

"Hello," said the doctor, shaking our hands. "I've heard a lot about you. Your mother is making good progress."

While Penny and I waited in the corridor and the physician examined Mother, she relayed to him everything we'd told her.

"I'll deal with this," he said on our return. "Go back today, and don't say a word about your visit. I'll arrange other accommodation for you."

Mother then handed us more bus money.

"Hide this," she said. "And come and see me every day. If Uncle Boris won't let you go, Dr Steenmeyer will fetch you."

That week we moved to a safe place.

UNCLE JO

On our way to catch the bus after another shopping spree in Utrecht some time later, we saw Mother's physician again.

"Remember Dr Steenmeyer?" Mother asked.

Over time, we became good friends, and also met his wife. We called them Uncle Jo and Aunt Marth.

"Uncle Jo's first wife and two young children were killed by the Germans during the war," Mother told us. "He misses his children terribly. They would have been your age had they survived."

Much later, Mother told us that Uncle Jo and Aunt Marth had agreed to become our guardians in the event of Mother's death, which we knew was imminent.

I didn't like the thought of Mother dying, yet, in another way, after getting to know Uncle Jo and Aunt Marth well, I looked forward to having a secure and peaceful family life with them. I liked their stable way of living, and their unconditional love for us. Uncle Jo practised his Christian values. His continual encouragement aimed at Penny and me after visiting Mother, impressed and strengthened me. He must have guessed that Mother's mood swings were difficult for us to deal with.

"Be strong," he always said, as he left.

There was something very special about Uncle Jo.

Our friendship brought an extremely happy and peaceful period, which overflowed into our home. Penny and I loved Uncle Jo's regular house-calls which gave Mother not only medical but also moral support. If Penny and I missed seeing him, we were very disappointed. We could tell he'd visited, by his distinctive lingering cigar smoke, and Mother's calm and contented disposition.

It was about then that Mother began writing her life story. I don't know how far back she went. I couldn't read her handwriting; her letters flowing into one another made it difficult to decipher. I'm sure Uncle Jo encouraged her, maybe for therapeutic reasons. She, too, responded favourably to Uncle Jo and Aunt Marth's friendship, although this mainly related to her mental health. Uncle Jo's homeopathic treatment and encouragement boosted her confidence. Other doctors had given up on her, but Uncle Jo provided hope and a will for her to live.

When the weather was favourable, Mother occasionally ventured out with us to Uncle Jo and Aunt Marth's home for meals. The adults talked, while Penny and I played board games with another girl Aunt Marth invited to keep us company.

Then Mother's illness confined her to bed again, usually in autumn, winter, and spring. Writing gave her something to do. Keeping her mind occupied, she worried less about things over which she had no control. I remember coming home from school, seeing her with pages and pages of handwritten script all over the bed. She wrote as if her life depended on it. Sometimes she tore up pages to start all over again. I now think her life *did* depend on that expression of all that was within her. Sadly, a publisher looked at her story, but rejected it. His problem may also have been her handwriting. It was sad, because she'd put so much work into it, even illustrating it with her own sketches. It had taken her about three years to write.

Our newfound happiness through Uncle Jo and Aunt Marth, from approximately 1953 to 1958, provided us with emotional strength and a new-found spiritual depth. Although, at first, Aunt Marth appeared stiff and *starchy* to me, I was also attracted to her. She and Uncle Jo, from 1954 onward, became instrumental in providing Penny and me with yearly summer fun at camping/bus holidays with other teenagers.

SMALL DISTRACTIONS

Lack of treats, combined with Mother's limited income, made public transport bus stops an attraction for me. The only times Mother allowed us sweets was at birthdays, *Sinterklaas* (St. Nicholas) and Easter. So, when I found small change on the ground dropped by hurrying people just before entering the bus, I looked for more. Even ten cents bought something nice! But when the pickings were lean, I devised other ways to satisfy my cravings.

While Penny attended Bilthoven's Lyceum between 1954 to 1955, I kept cycling to school in Zeist when the weather permitted. If the roads were too slippery and dangerous, I took the bus. I had to change buses halfway, and Mother sometimes gave me cash for the ride. If the sun shone on the way home, the bus money for the rest of the ride almost burnt a hole in my pocket; and walking became more attractive, especially as I could buy salted *dropjes* (liquorice) at a chemist. One of Mother's proverbs, 'Those who aren't strong must be shrewd' came to mind!

Mother often recited wise sayings to encourage or keep us in line. Some were: "I cannot," says the sluggard, and that's why he can't; The apple doesn't fall far from the tree; More haste and less wisdom is rarely good; Bitter in the mouth makes the heart sound; If someone else jumps off a cliff, would you jump off too?" She spoke each proverb to fit the occasion when wisdom was required.

As Mother also had a sweet tooth, she sometimes craved chocolates, and sent Penny to buy them. Other times she sent me. She liked cherry-liqueur chocolates from Hommes, the chocolate shop. When my turn came, I couldn't resist a nibble on the way home, and of course, I couldn't leave *half* a chocolate in the bag!

Mother won't miss one, I thought, and finished it.

Little did I know she gave us the exact money to buy *ten* chocolates, and counted them later! Consequently, when Penny went, there was always one more! Mother never confronted me about it. Penny told me years later.

When Penny and I were younger, *Kaasboertje* (the grocer) on Vinkenlaan delivered his goods to our door. When we grew older, we, armed with several *tassen* (cloth bags), did the shopping. As Penny had much homework, I did most of it. Shopkeepers served adults first in those days, and, as I was shy about speaking up, shopping took ages: there was only one person serving a shop full of customers! The delay, on the other hand, kept me away from the tense home atmosphere that I dreaded returning to.

Sometimes Penny and I shopped together; one pedalling, the other on the carrier. That was always fun. At the delicatessen, less frequented by other customers, we bought Reform wholegrain bread, loose wholegrain rolled oats, and sometimes, for special treats, *gort* (barley grits) for porridge. Most wares still came loose. The shopkeeper put them straight into paper bags.

Further down Julianalaan was Havecotten, a bookshop, where Mother sent us for book orders. The manageress had a wig to cover her bald head, and sometimes she forgot to wear it. It was hard not to laugh.

I liked buying cheese from the *melkboer* (milkman) on Leyenseweg. He often gave us an extra generous piece to try before buying, and his cheese tasted nice. The smell in the shop was unlike any other. He sold milk the old way, loose for coffee, and poured straight into our containers. Milk for drinking still came in litre glass bottles. The milkman also delivered (before the sun came up) butter, cream, yoghurt, buttermilk, and later, chocolate milk and custard. In winter, to combat heavy frosts and keep him warm without a coat, yet to enable him in his work while still handling money, he wore fingerless gloves. To keep his chest warm, he crossed his arms over to his back and hit himself all over as far as he could reach. His breath wafted up like smoke.

To delay my after-school shopping chores and please myself for a change, I sometimes took the long way home from school, past den Dolder and Soesterberg airfield. But we had to eat, and the shops closed soon after school, so I had to be careful not to be too late home. Having no fridge, we shopped daily. Mother worried if I was late, and was usually pleased when I reappeared, but I hated arriving to shouting matches.

When Mother was given attention, she could be witty and fun, but the most unlikely things triggered conflict. One such occasion was when Mother sat outside in our front garden, and Penny and I were doing handstands on the little patch of lawn.

"I feel like an omelette," Mother said.

"Okay, I'll make some," I answered, and darted to the kitchen to make one for all three of us. Having finished, Mother asked for another, and yet another. I couldn't believe my ears! But I made the most of it. Afterwards, Mother must have realised how many eggs we had used, and suddenly stormed inside. Nothing was right. Her outbursts may have been directed at herself, but Penny and I were made to feel guilty. We never knew when such explosions would erupt, and as a result, we always remained on guard.

I was at an age where I didn't yet understand Mother's struggles and her anxious behaviour. Although I realised the truth later, when I was young, I gained the impression that Mother's love for us was conditional upon our good behaviour or doing things the way she expected. It was hard to please her. Untidy drawers, forgetting to bring the phone up or downstairs, leaving a light on, using too much bathwater, not wiping our feet properly, forgetting to take our snow boots off on the kitchen mat, burning the potatoes, rice, or porridge, or letting the milk boil over, were all triggers for trouble. It was no use defending ourselves. Penny tried to reason with Mother, but often ended up in more strife.

Early on, there wasn't much home help available. Later, Mother employed a cleaning girl twice a week, and when she was very sick, a nurse came to give her a bed-bath. I liked one of the cleaning girls, Rietje. She was like an older sister. When I was home with a sore throat or tummy ache, I followed her round the house as she cleaned. Then we often sang duets together. The song *'De Uil zat in de Olme'* sounded really nice.

Mother, by then, had good friends, some with Indonesian connections, others Dutch, who supported and encouraged her. Some, however, only lasted short periods, taking advantage of her generosity, which in turn frustrated her.

To overcome the stress and receive some love, I turned to kittens. Their unconditional love filled the void. Although I enjoyed feeding and playing with them outside and in the kitchen, I longed for them to grow so they would sit quietly on my lap at the family-room fire.

That, to me, was a picture of perfect peace which I read about in stories. I also realised that Mother could easily have refused to let me have a kitten at all. Their moulting fur worsened her asthma. And yet every time a kitten was run over, it was Mother who urged me to get another one.

In winter, Mother's breathlessness worsened, and summer didn't guarantee respite, especially when the sun went down. The slightest whiff of smoke, a draught, or small exertion had her gasping for air. Her chronic asthma and bronchitis quickly turned into a cold, then pneumonia, confining her to bed for months.

Like most other children at that time, we thought, *What Mother doesn't know won't hurt her.* Preferring play above chores, we often left the dishes stacked on the bench for days before washing them, thinking, *Mother is too sick to come downstairs and find out.* But, sensing mischief, she sometimes surprised us.

Her unscheduled appearances turned into lightning flashes, soon to be followed by thunderbolts. After the first plates smashed amid screaming, I ran to my room, locked the door, and fantasised about replacement mothers and adoptive fathers. When the noise ceased, I came out and picked up broken plates and other debris. These outbursts frightened me, but we couldn't fix the problem. To survive, I wisely put up an invisible wall of silence. Other times, however, I blurted out how I felt, saying hurtful things which I soon regretted.

Although I was very clever at hiding my anxiety, the war had left a deep, inexplicable fear, and Mother's ill health and unreasonable outbursts, combined with many other frightening external experiences, had increased that fear. Apprehension escalated when I heard that teenage girls were being molested in our neighbourhood. I didn't understand the full meaning, and was too embarrassed to ask, in case I was supposed to have known. From people's reaction, I knew it was frightening.

Uncle Jo reassured me to a certain extent. But my fear was difficult to eradicate, especially after my experience with Uncle Boris. *What*

TWO SLICES OF BREAD

if someone is lurking outside, ready to break down the door? I worried, scared of the pitch dark outside. There was no outside light at the kitchen, and the curtains could only partly close. With Mother lying ill in bed, unable to defend me, that anxiety increased.

So, when Mother needed relief from her breathless bouts, and her puffers proved useless in the middle of the night, I pretended to be brave.

"Ad!" Mother called, waking me from a deep sleep.

"Please," she begged. "Make me some coffee. Hot coffee loosens the phlegm... You make such nice coffee."

One look at Mother was enough to gauge her need.

Get it over and done with, I thought, although shivers ran down my spine.

In the hope of scaring away prowlers outside the kitchen window, I sang the Dutch national anthem *Wilhelmus*, in a deep and *loud* voice, trying to imitate a man (without thinking I might disturb the neighbours!).

Dutch:

Wilhelmus van Nassauen,
Ben ik van Dietse bloed,
Den Vaderland getrouwe,
Blijf ik tot in den Dood.
Een Prinse van Oranje,
Ben ik, vrij, onverveerd,
Den Koning van Hispanje,
Heb ik altijd geeerd.

Mijn Schild en de Betrouwen,
Zijt Gij o God mijn Heer,
Op U zo wil ik bouwen,
Verlaat mij nimmer meer.
Dat ik toch vroom mag leven,

English:

William of Nassau,
Am I, of Dutch descent,
To Fatherland faithful,
I'll remain until the end.
A Prince of Orange,
Am I, free, and fearless,
The king of Spain
I have always honoured.

My Shield and Trust,
Are you, oh God, my Lord,
On you will I build,
Leave me never more,
That I may surely live devoutly,

Uw dienaar 't aller stond,	Your servant at all times,
De tir-a-nnie verdrijven,	The tyranny to banish,
Die mij mijn hart verwondt.	That breaks my heart.
Oorloft mijn arme schapen,	Listen, my poor sheep,
Die Zijt in grote nood,	Who are in great need,
Uw Herder zal niet slapen,	Your Shepherd shall not sleep,
Al zijt gij noch verstrooid.	Although you are now scattered.
Die vroom begeerd te leven,	Whoever desires to live devoutly,
Bidt God nacht en de dag,	Pray to God night and day,
Dat Hij mij kracht wil geven,	For Him to strengthen me,
Dat ik U helpen mag.	So that I may help you.

Although Mother was brought up in the Lutheran faith, and Father came from a Liberal Catholic background, we didn't practise Christianity at home. We only started giving thanks before meals after meeting Mrs von Gleich. So, when I learnt the Dutch National Anthem at school, and later sang it repeatedly in our kitchen, I was encouraged. I felt like one of those sheep which God was watching over like a Shepherd! That knowledge gave me strength, not only there in the night, but also later when I struggled to make sense of our way of life at home.

Earlier, a violent man had tried breaking down our front door, so I was wary.

"Only open the tiny window within the front door," Mother warned repeatedly, as extra bolts secured the top and bottom of the front door, and the kitchen and terrace doors.

I remember shutting the little window and racing to the other outside doors to check that the bolts were secure, especially at night. The kitchen and terrace doors were only a stone's-throw from the front-door, and shady characters often roamed our neighbourhood.

An experience when I was about four years old, when a stranger had tried to kidnap me, accentuated my fear.

"Do you want an ice-cream?" a man asked Penny and me, as we stood on the footpath.

"Yeees!" we answered excitedly.

"Then come for a ride on my bike."

"No!" said Penny. "That's not allowed."

I loved ice-cream, and, ignoring Penny's arguments, allowed the man to lift me onto his bike-carrier.

Despite Penny's loud objections, the man rode off with me. Penny immediately ran inside, calling John, who still lived at home. Quickly hopping on his bike, he chased the man, caught up, and rescued me. Once home, I received a stern lecture on *stranger danger*.

HUNEBEDDEN

"Mother!" Penny called, as she ran inside after school, "Tineke's dad says there are good youth hostels and camping grounds near cycling tracks, all the way to Drenthe!"

Penny wanted to make a cycling tour with her classmate, Tineke. Since they were both 15, they were adamant they'd be safe and able to make the round trip through the provinces Utrecht, Gelderland, Overijsel, and Drenthe. Tineke's father, a camping enthusiast, had inspired them. He made enquiries regarding camp-ground safety, and had many camping gadgets. To Penny and Tineke it was irresistible, but not to Mother.

"If there were more of you, I'd feel happier about it," she said, after a long debate.

A camping holiday sounded exciting, and I realised that Penny and Tineke needed help. They struggled to pack all their gear onto two bikes for a start! A third person to share the load made sense, and I felt confident, having camped at school before.

"I'll go," I said.

Penny and Tineke jumped up. "Can she?"

"All right," Mother gave in.

Penny and Tineke embraced Mother.

"I'll bring another saddle-bag for your bike tomorrow," Tineke called to me on her way out. "Then we'll practise fitting the gear on *three* bikes."

I couldn't sleep that night.

The next day after school, Penny and Tineke arrived with the camping gear and saddle bags. They were waterproof, and had big pockets on either side of the carrier and flaps. To spread the weight, we also carried gear over our *handlebars*, but even *that* wasn't enough. The bikes tipped easily. Only when we sat on the saddles with our fully-laden backpacks on our backs, did the bikes' stability return.

It was summer when we departed, and rode over bike paths and back roads, traversing forests and meadows. To avoid carrying extra weight, we bought milk-drinks directly from the milkman on his rounds, and drank there and then, gulping the cool liquid down in his presence, handing him the empties.

Tineke's map directed us through a maze of cycle lanes and back roads. Halfway we stopped to eat pancakes, then resumed our expedition. It was essential to arrive at the camping ground before nightfall.

Tired, but excited, we pitched Tineke's two pup tents, one for our gear, the other for sleeping. Dinner consisted of wild chanterellen, yellow mushrooms with an upward growth, found growing in the forest nearby. We easily distinguished them from poisonous types. Fried with apples in our one-and-only pot, they tasted delicious. After washing our faces and brushing our teeth in the communal bathroom, we squeezed into our pup tent side by side. Regardless of the hard ground and makeshift pillows made with clean clothes stuffed into pillow-cases, we fell asleep instantly, feeling safe with other campers nearby.

At daybreak, we ate porridge with milk straight from the cow. Then we packed everything up and rode off again. One day we found no milkman, and cycling was thirsty work. I became so thirsty that I walked onto a farm, knocked on the farmhouse door, and asked for a drink of water.

The farmer's wife was exceptionally friendly, and gave us not only water, but also freshly baked black rye bread, the nicest I'd ever tasted! After chatting while we ate, she directed us to the camping ground in Emmen, the capital of Drenthe.

Unfortunately, we lost our way. A car filled with yahooing boys pursued us just as darkness fell, and we became concerned for our safety. Then a police station loomed ahead, and without hesitation, we stopped and walked in. Penny explained our situation.

An officer had a word with the boys. Then he escorted us to the camping ground. We breathed a sigh of relief, and remembered Mother at home, who might have been worried. We phoned, telling her we were safe.

After another quick one-pot dinner, we joined other youths for a games evening before going to sleep. Next morning, we cycled to the famous Hunebedden megalithic tombs, huge boulders twice our height, located on the outskirts of Emmen.

The trip proved that we could survive independently from adults and gave us more confidence. It also reawakened my awareness of danger, and helped me appreciate home and Mother, who was always there for us. She welcomed us in with a meal of stuffed capsicums and tomatoes, more upmarket than the one-pot meals we'd been cooking.

Hunebedden (Megalithic Tombs) Drenthe, 1955
Addy (left), Tineke (right)

HIGH SCHOOL DAYS

CHAPTER 19

A NEW EXPERIENCE

In September 1956, I was to start high school. I couldn't wait for my year with Mr Blok to end. One day, he asked our whole class which school we would attend. Some were going to *MMS* (Girls Secondary School), others *HBS*, but most were going to Kees Boeke Mulo (Higher Elementary Education) in Bilthoven.

"I'm going to Montessori Lyceum," I said.

"What?" Mr Blok gasped. "You'll never make it. You won't even pass the entry exam!"

My face felt hot, but I remained silent. My thoughts returned to the time he intimidated me after that first test on the 80-year Spanish War.

Mother was especially annoyed about his comment. Determined I should attend Montessori Lyceum, she consulted Mr Jansen, a teacher friend, and father of three of our neighbourhood playmates. A test revealed that I was behind in schoolwork, but Mr Jansen offered extra tuition to help me pass the entry exam.

During the holidays and weekends, Mother's younger sister, Aunt Tine, a teacher by profession, took over. She soon discovered where I'd been left behind in arithmetic and used *picture-forms* and *stairs* to help me understand. Lessons became fun. I even looked forward to them!

Towards the end of my last year at Rudolf Steiner, Mother and I visited Montessori Lyceum to register for the entry examination. The headmaster, Mr Jordaan, familiarised me with the school's layout and its system. Everything sounded exciting, very different from primary school. On the day of the exam, I joined a line of waiting students to be ushered into a classroom, where a friendly teacher, Mr Loohuis, explained the procedure of the test. Starting with modern art and colouring in our own design, I relaxed.

I tackled the questions with ease, enjoying the experience until morning break. Then I noticed the two bullies from my past Montessori Primary School. They tried their old tricks on me again, but, older and wiser, I turned away. Though calm on the outside, I worried that the girls would ruin my new school experience, and prayed:

"God help me! Let those girls fail their exam, so they won't bother me ever again."

Then I hurried to the busy sportsfield for protection amongst other boys and girls, and watched a game of handball. The ball bounced outside the line. I caught it and threw it back. This happened several times.

"Do you want to play?" asked the boy I threw the ball back to.

"Yes!" I answered. "Where?"

"What about in goal," another boy suggested. "You catch the ball really well."

Joining the game helped me forget the bullies and relax at the next test. After lunch-break, handball continued, and the same boys asked me to play again. I had so much fun it didn't feel like an exam day. The afternoon flew by.

The bullies, however, remained on my mind. With the exam over, I hurried to the bike stand, then raced home in case they planned something nasty. I repeated my earlier prayer, taking it for granted I'd pass.

TYROL

Late June 1956, summer holidays began with a bus trip for Penny and me to Reutte, Tyrol, in Austria. Excitedly, we packed our rucksacks and sleeping bags, and laid out our shorts, tops, and Norsewear socks, ready to slip into the next day. We'd waterproofed our heavy

TWO SLICES OF BREAD

tramping boots with grease. Rather than carry them, we'd been advised to wear them. Next day, Mother accompanied us to Utrecht, where a chartered bus waited near the train station.

Many boys and girls our age from all areas of Holland already filled the bus. A leader greeted us and took our rucksacks. We kissed Mother goodbye, boarded the bus, and joined the happy teenagers who greeted us as we chose our seats. We could tell that this trip was going to be fun, and it didn't take long before Penny and I were included.

Someone played a guitar, and everyone sang silly songs about cows and bulls, holes in buckets, and more. We enjoyed ourselves so much, we hardly noticed dusk falling as we arrived at the German border.

The happy atmosphere changed instantly when a German customs officer, dressed in a long green coat and knee-high boots, entered the bus.

"Pass! Pass!" (Passports) he shouted gruffly.

Regardless of the faint smile on his way out, I was pleased to see him leave. My reaction may have come through my empathy with Mrs von Gleich, whom I heard had suffered at the hands of German soldiers during the war. For anyone to do that to such a gentle person and her family made me angry, but also afraid. Hadn't I, too, experienced cruel soldiers in Indonesia?

A break in our long journey in Bavaria, Germany, at Neuschwanstein Castle enabled us to stretch our legs and explore the castle. All castles fascinated me. Using hand signals and school-German, we found our way round, and bought postcards to send home.

The journey continued through the night, as we slept in our bus seats. Coming to the next border, I expected another gruff customs officer, but was pleasantly surprised. An Austrian officer smiled broadly while moving through the bus, checking and stamping our passports. Our inept school-German broadened his smile.

"Have a pleasant holiday in Tyrol," he said, on his way out.

Sleep overcame us as the bus traversed narrow passes and tunnels.

The next day we reached the beautiful valley and village of Reutte, Tyrol. We offloaded our luggage and entered a hostel. Having found our sleeping quarters, we discovered the dining hall, where there were delicious freshly-baked bread rolls, rose-hip jam, cheese, and milk for us.

During our free time, most of us went shopping in the tiny village. Penny, our new friend Franny, and I, listened to yodelling records. I bought a 45 rpm record. With our limited cash we had to budget, but after phoning Mother and explaining what was available, she sent us extra money to buy a cow bell and a chalet-music-box.

Many expeditions up the mountains followed. I loved seeing cows walking loose, wearing huge bells around their necks. This enabled easy tracking. Wherever they went, their bells tinkled. They were so tame we could pat them.

Excursions began early. After breakfast, we packed our rucksacks and collected our cut lunches, prepared by the kitchen staff.

"Fill your water-bottles," our leaders encouraged. "Mountain climbing is thirsty work." Penny and I had felt-covered army flasks, which kept our water cool. We clipped them onto our second-hand Girl-Guide belts, for easy reach. As it was cool in the morning, and the weather could turn nasty without warning, we always dressed for the cold when climbing, and stripped off as needed, carrying our extra clothes in our rucksacks, or draping wind-jackets round our waist.

We tramped until noon. At first, I got a stitch, and needed to rest halfway up the mountain. Others didn't seem to have that problem, which annoyed me. However, as I stopped and recovered, I was amazed by the beautiful meadows and sparkling clean lakes, shallow at the edge, but deep in the middle. The sun shone, and the temperature was pleasant at midday. In need of refreshing after our climb, some braved the inviting, but freezing water for a short dip. There we often ate our bread rolls and refilled our bottles from the crystal-clear lake or brooks while our leader lectured us.

"These mountains are young," he said, explaining their geology. Sometimes we went further up the mountain, other times we descended again. Descending was fun, especially running down the wider tracks. We had to watch ourselves, though. It was difficult slowing down. We nearly collided with ascending climbers!

High up the mountain we saw many crucifixes with inscriptions, under small roofs. Austria was a Catholic country. The crosses were placed there to remind climbers of God—they did that for me! At home, Uncle Jo had often spoken about Jesus, and because I was slower than the others at climbing, I rested and read the inscriptions under the crosses. Seeing Jesus hanging on the cross, yet surrounded by the magnificent scenery, caused me to think. It happened every time I saw a cross. I couldn't forget God on the mountains. Fellow climbers also reminded me.

"Gruss Gott" (Greet God), they called.

Like a local, I copied them, and greeted everyone I met the same way.

After a few climbs, my endurance increased. Once we had a meal at a chalet-restaurant up the mountain. Penny had Wiener schnitzel, and I, a vegetarian then, tucked into an omelette.

Each day, there was something different to see and do. Austria's milkshakes also featured among Mother's many stories about Austria.

"Milkshakes originated in Tyrol," she told us. Having never tasted them before, we patronised the local milk bar every day after our excursions.

I loved Tyrol so much I wished we could live there for good. The scenery was so beautiful, and the people friendly and relaxed. Nobody hurried. Cowboys herded their cows ahead of them, the cows leading the way as they grazed. High up the mountains they roamed seemingly unattended, without fences. People trusted one another. Wooden chalets lined the main street. Rocks discreetly placed on roofs to weigh them down for heavy winter snow—which could be up to two metres thick—looked so quaint.

Our group did everything together, and friendships soon developed. After ten days of this delightful holiday, we were sad to leave. However, an enjoyable ride home was still to come, when we shared our hopes and plans for the new school year ahead. Franny Prins and Penny, having become firm friends, exchanged addresses and phone numbers. Franny already attended Montessori Lyceum.

"That's where we're going," Penny exclaimed, pleased to have a friend at our new high school.

On arrival in Utrecht, Mother met us. She'd prepared a tasty meal to welcome us home. Penny and I told her all about Tyrol, and our experiences. That night, snuggling into my own bed, I appreciated being home, and having a loving mother, who always organised great summer holidays for us. I suddenly understood why she loved the Alps so much. When looking at the cowbell I'd bought, I dreamed of taking her to Tyrol one day.

MONTESSORI LYCEUM

On our first day at Montessori Lyceum in September 1956, Penny and I secured our bikes behind the school and walked to the old *Berkenhoven* building near the road—still in use then. We parted in search of our allocated classes.

Penny was thrilled to find Franny in her class.

"Hello, Addy," Mr Loohuis, my class teacher, greeted. "Your desk is between Joke and Jan's."

Most girls in my class had only one girlfriend. I felt like an intruder when two were already pals. So, after failing to make friends with some, I decided to get to know everyone. It didn't worry me, as Penny had a circle of friends from her class and they included me too.

Of the boys in class, Jan was my favourite. He was the tallest boy in class and I the tallest girl. He didn't like dancing with short girls, so he always asked me to be his partner at school balls. I was happy with that arrangement.

Penny, her friend, Loekie, and I cycled to and from school together. Loekie also lived in Bilthoven. We met up at Soestdijkseweg, at our turn-off, and returning home, parted there. Loekie didn't play sport like we did, but we still liked her. Both Penny and I played in the school hockey team, with boys and girls. There were six girls in the team: African American sisters, Jannie and Renee, Franny, Yvonne, and us. I felt honoured to be chosen, but when the boys hit that ball, I had to jump high! Their shots whizzed past at knee height, often directly in my path.

Handball was my favourite sport. We played fun games during lunch hour with Mr Loohuis. I played goalie. Having watched the boys play soccer, I tried to dive like their goalie did. Although I couldn't match his capabilities, I excelled sufficiently to be later selected for the provincial team. But the thought of being responsible for goal in *that* team was too nerve-racking, so I played for school only.

During the first year at Montessori Lyceum, we had to take all subjects: Latin, French, English, Dutch, and German, Science, Math, Algebra, Biology, Geography, History, Mythology, Art, and Sport. I liked most subjects, and managed algebra and math to start with.

When I didn't see the two Montessori primary bullies at school, I realised that they must have failed the entry exam. God answered my prayer! I was so happy.

The second year we chose the direction in which we wanted to go: Gymnasium, *HBS* or *MMS* (girls only). I chose the latter, and continued with most of the subjects already on the list, but dropped Latin. In my third year, I swapped mathematics and algebra for Esperanto. Esperanto contained a sprinkling of many of the world's languages, and was then set to become the universal world language. Sadly, it died a slow death.

I loved German, Dutch, Science, Biology, Mythology, History, Geography, Art, and Sport. Having almost grown up with German through Mrs von Gleich's teaching and Mother's love of it, it was like a second language to me. I read book after book and practically *chased* Penza—a marking system whereby teachers tested pupils on satisfactory completion of given subjects, then signing our 'penza booklet'—like a cheque book. I also liked my German teacher, Mrs de Boer. One of my friends, Marjolein, encouraged me with French taught by Mrs Rottier. Most of our foreign language books were children's literature, but with French we read basic *Little Golden Books!* I survived the embarrassment, which was merely my own. Everyone learning languages at school endured it.

I liked English, but found communicating with the teacher difficult. Having helpful teachers like Mrs de Boer, Mrs Rottier, Mrs Kuitenbrouwer for Dutch, and Mr Hishemöller for Geography, who went out of their way to encourage me, made a big difference to my progress. Sometimes I wished Mrs de Boer and Mrs Rottier could be my mother, and Mr Loohuis my father.

Mr Loohuis was sporty and fun. He lived in Bilthoven North, and drove me and other boys and girls living in Bilthoven to school balls or dances in his Volkswagen. At one fancy-dress ball, I disguised myself as an Arab, with a sheet draped round me from head to toe, and round sunglasses on my nose. But Jan couldn't be fooled.

"That's a good costume, Addy," he greeted. We danced together all night, having much fun.

Juliana had left some of her clothes behind when she and Rob emigrated. Her wardrobe was like a treasure-trove to me, where I found many outfits for plays, even everyday wear for school. They made me feel grown up.

Meanwhile, my schoolwork at Montessori Lyceum progressed, and after a year, I received a glowing report. That's when Mother told me my entry-exam result. I'd been given a probation pass. The headmaster had said that if I did my work well during my first year, continuation at school would be guaranteed. I was elated with the outcome.

All was not well at home, however. The strain was quite unbearable at times. Mother's health always worsened in winter, confining her to bed and making life for Penny and me quite miserable. After school, we had chores to finish, shopping as usual, with the addition of stationary, as Mother was still writing her life story by hand. Penny and I took turns at cooking. Having finished my homework at school, and Penny having more than me, I enjoyed the distraction.

Penny always helped with the dishes. To unwind from the stressful atmosphere around Mother, we fooled around and raced to see who could dry or wash the dishes fastest. Nobody won, but we finished the dishes quickly.

Mother's mood swings alternated from high to low, with no in-betweens. Visitors, however, continued having a positive effect on her, lifting her negative disposition. So, when friends visited we welcomed them with open arms. Mother's improved high spirits continued well after they'd gone, making us relish those times.

Although our home atmosphere could be very depressing, the air almost able to be *cut with a knife*, the real lows came unexpectedly, like thunder bolts, usually when Mother gasped for breath, seemingly with an unrelenting tight band around her neck. Realising that her breathing problems were the cause, I hated watching her struggle that way. Her medicine, a *bronchisan* puffer, was practically useless. The only relief was adrenaline, for which we had to call the emergency doctor, Dr Hellares-Larmbars. Sometimes he also injected an antibiotic. That worked miracles! Mother became a changed woman in a matter of minutes.

I realised those times were extremely stressful for Mother, but they also were for Penny and me. Mother could suddenly gasp for breath, needing her puffers, a cup of coffee, steam, or the doctor. She was often so breathless, she couldn't even speak and express herself, and that made it even more difficult, for her, *and* us. We didn't always know what to do. We were frightened and worried Mother would die, but to her it would have been terrifying.

So, when we could, it was a relief to get away from all that stress and focus on something relaxing, like playing games with our friends, Maria, and Kattelijn Boon, in peaceful surroundings. We didn't forget Mother; we simply recharged ourselves through play, often hockey on their lawn. It was our way of coping.

Although I enjoyed Mother's rice with *sajoor* (spicy soup), I loved Mrs Boon's *nasi goreng* (fried rice). Served with *kroepoek* (shrimp crackers) and *shroendeng* (fried coconut, onions, peanuts and ketjap) sprinkled over the rice, it tasted even better. The aroma drew me to her tiny kitchen during birthday parties.

I liked Mother's cooking too, and tried to copy it when she was ill.

We kept her guitar in the bedroom wardrobe, and she played well. We only needed to bring it out, and she'd play, sing, or yodel in bed. That brought the best out of her, lifting her negative thoughts.

Perhaps she reminisced about her youth and her favourite grandfather, the sea-captain, for she often sang her heart out about the sea.

Dutch:	**English:**
Daar kwam laatst een meisje,	There once came a young girl,
Uit Scheveningen aan,	From Scheveningen's shore,
Zij had haar mandje vol zee banket,	She had her basket full of sea banquet,
En prachtige haring belaan.	And a glorious herring catch.
Mijn hart ging open,	My heart opened,
Toen'k haar zag,	When her I saw,
En juichte met haar mee:	And I shouted with her:
Nieuwe haring! Nieuwe haring!	Fresh herring! Fresh herring!
The beste van heel de zee!	The best of the whole sea!

But Doctor Steenmeyer's house calls did the most amazing things for Mother.

THE FRIGHT OF MY LIFE

CHAPTER 20

"Cigar smoke!" Penny called as we ran up the stairs to greet Mother after school, hoping Uncle Jo Steenmeyer, Mother's doctor and specialist, was still with her.

Our home atmosphere had improved considerably since Uncle Jo began his regular house calls to Mother. His visits did wonders for us all.

I was happy. Uncle Jo and Aunt Marth had become our legal guardians in case Mother should die suddenly. The thought of Mother's death and how I'd miss her hadn't really sunk in. Instead of grieving, I looked forward to living with Uncle Jo and Aunt Marth in their stable environment.

ARDENNES

In the summer of 1957, Mother arranged another summer camping holiday for Penny and me. This time we went with a Christian organisation taking a group of teenage girls to the Ardennes. Maria and Kattelijn Boon also came.

I liked camping. About seven girls slept in our tent, and every morning the leaders inspected it for tidiness. We often won. We all had chores to do: peeling potatoes and washing dishes and big pots in a brook running through camp. The weather was exceptionally good, giving us plenty of free time for sight-seeing with leaders. They taught us about God but didn't tell us everything. On the last day, they held a mysterious quest. Each of us was blindfolded and guided through a narrow path. Then someone asked a question. Hardly anyone answered correctly, and they made us feel guilty for not knowing. Sadly, none of the leaders told us what the answer was. I was disappointed because I wanted to know about God.

Now, as I look back, I see God himself ministering to me through what I thought was an ordinary tune but was really the hymn: *Thine be the glory*. We'd learned the melody and words in French, which I didn't understand well. I sang the hymn all the way back to Holland on the train—at the top of my voice! Singing it lifted my spirits while I took in the amazing views.

My only explanation for the lifting effect was that the tune, as well as the words had been written under God's inspiration:

Thine be the glory, risen, conquering Son,
Endless is the victory, thou o'er death hast won,
Angels in bright raiment rolled the stone away,
Kept the folded grave clothes where thy body lay.
Refrain:
Thine be the glory, risen conquering Son,
Endless is the victory thou o'er death hast won.

Lo! Jesus meets us, risen from the tomb;
Lovingly He greets us, scatters fear and gloom;
Let the church with gladness, hymns of triumph sing;
For the Lord now liveth, death has lost its sting.
Refrain:
Thine be the glory, risen conquering Son...
No more we doubt thee, glorious Prince of life;
Life is naught without thee; aid us in our strife;
Make us more than conquerors, through thy deathless love;
Bring us safe to Jordan to thy home above.

Refrain:
Thine be the glory, risen conquering Son,
Endless is the victory thou o'er death hast won.

Time flew by too fast between 1957 and 1958 while we enjoyed our time with Uncle Jo and Aunt Marth. But when the 1958 summer vacation loomed, with another camping trip for Penny and me, I realised that Mother never took holidays, nor had any fun. She always ensured that Penny and I had interesting things to do, but apart from the occasional bike ride in summer, she'd had no special outings or holidays since our Terschelling vacation in 1952. It didn't seem fair.

It was bad enough Mother catching colds so easily, we had to watch those frightening asthma episodes, which I now know were pneumonia and emphysema complications. Mother pretended not to care about the lack of holidays, but I saw through her masquerade.

I also suspected that Mother's time on earth could soon be cut short.

"I'm not going," I said to Mother when registrations for my camping trip arrived. "I'm staying home with you."

In return for all Mother had done for me over the years, keeping her company was the least I could do. So, Penny left for youth camp in Wanneperveen (a Dutch lake district).

"Let's visit my Indonesian friend in Haarlem," Mother suggested, after Penny had left. "Nel and her husband, Jeroen, have offered to have us stay."

It took us only a day's train trip to get there.

From the outside, Mother's friend's house looked huge. When we rang the bell, the door opened almost immediately. Instead of someone standing by the door greeting us, an empty stairway stood before us and a voice at the top called,

"Yoo hoo! Willy! Come up!"

After we'd rung an old-fashioned bell and heard it tinkle, we'd been spotted from the upstairs window through a two-way *spy* mirror. Having ascertained we were friends and not foes, Mother's friends had pulled a long rope from upstairs to release the door-latch, which opened the door for us without them having to come down.

"This is Aunty Nel," Mother introduced us. And this is Ad, my youngest daughter." *Aunty* Nel introduced me to her husband, *Uncle* Jeroen, and their daughter. From then on, Mother and her friends talked about Indonesia, where they too had lived before and during the war. They often spoke Malay if a subject wasn't suitable for my ears, but I didn't mind. Mother was happy, and that was all that mattered.

It was a quiet but enjoyable holiday. Mother's friends were kind, and I liked Indonesian food. Aunty Nel cooked the best Indonesian *rice table* (an assortment of Indonesian dishes).

Uncle Jeroen was Dutch, and had travelled through Africa, where he befriended a *Pygmy* tribe (very small people 122–142cm tall) who, when he visited them, inhabited tropical rain forests (today in Burundi, Cameroon, Congo, Gabon, Rwanda, and Zaire). Uncle Jeroen told many stories about them. Gifts of spears, daggers, bows, arrows, and grass skirts decorated their walls. Indonesian replicas also adorned the house. The relics scared me, and Uncle Jeroen's stories sounded so lifelike, it seemed that a warpaint-covered warrior would jump out, grab a poison spear, and throw it! I preferred spending time in the kitchen with Aunty Nel, or with their daughter and her new baby.

My most precious possession was still my baby doll. Seeing a real baby close up, even holding him, seemed to fulfil a deep longing. Maybe it made up for the love I wished for. I would have liked to have stayed longer, but Penny was due home at the weekend.

UNCLE JO

By then our friendship with Uncle Jo and Aunt Marth had blossomed into something really special. Sadly, Uncle Jo suddenly became unwell. On our return from Haarlem, Aunt Marth phoned Mother.

"Jo's been admitted to hospital in Amsterdam," she said. "It's bad news. He's been diagnosed with cancer. They started radiotherapy treatment today."

TWO SLICES OF BREAD

After Penny's return from camp, we visited Uncle Jo with Aunt Marth. Having recently learnt to drive, she bravely drove us to the hospital in Amsterdam. I was shocked! Uncle Jo looked washed out and so thin. The last time I'd seen him he'd been sturdy and rotund. Now his body had suddenly shrunk and his skin had turned grey. It made me sad and afraid.

Once home, I spent hours in the attic, praying. I feared Uncle Jo's death, but also worried about Mother's. I was afraid that if he died, Mother would lose hope, and give up on life. With a strong faith in God, Uncle Jo had been the only physician who had given Mother hope and helped her change for the better.

About a month later, we heard that Uncle Jo had returned home to Utrecht. Jubilant, Penny and I rushed into the garden to pick flowers for him. Expecting his recovery, we mounted our bikes and raced to their home. I rang the bell, excited about seeing Uncle Jo well again. There was no response. We waited and waited, but no one came to the door. I knew Aunt Marth wouldn't have gone out, so I pulled the bell handle again. Finally, Aunt Marth peered through the slightly opened door. She looked sad.

"Shhh…" she whispered sternly at our happy chatter.

"Here… flowers for Uncle Jo," I whispered back, thinking he was asleep. "For when he wakes up."

"No…" she said sadly. "Uncle Jo is dying. He won't need those."

"Dying?" I asked, deeply shocked, compassion for Aunt Marth now overwhelming me.

"For you then…" I said, handing her the flowers.

"No, I don't want them," she answered, almost angrily, and she closed the door. Stunned, Penny and I stood on the doorstep. Neither of us understood. *Uncle Jo… dying? How could he?* I thought. *He's home from hospital!* I didn't understand death. I'd seen the situation and had assumed the outcome before knowing all the facts.

What are we going to do with these flowers now, I thought, and angrily threw them in some bushes in the garden. *I don't want them either!* It was as though they were to blame for Uncle Jo's death. Deeply grieved, Penny and I cycled home without saying a word. Mother greeted us, expecting good news, but noticed our downcast expressions.

"What's wrong?"

"Uncle Jo's dying!" I blurted out that horrible word I hadn't wanted to say, and ran to the attic, where I cried the rest of the afternoon.

First, I grieved for my own loss, having looked forward to Uncle Jo becoming like a real *father* in the event of Mother's death. Worse still, now without Uncle Jo to encourage Mother through her illness, I was certain she'd miss him more than me, and go downhill.

Sure enough, in the weeks ahead, Mother's bouts of breathlessness and grief increased, fear gripping her once again. She seemed consumed with death.

"My papers are in the black dresser," she said repeatedly. "You know where the key is." It was not *if,* but *when* she died.

"Call my lawyer when it happens."

Mother must have been experiencing frightening symptoms that she hadn't shared with us but I didn't like the subject, so ignored her instructions as best I could. Up until then she'd survived by sheer willpower, always concerned for us. Uncle Jo had increased her determination, possibly through sharing his faith in God.

Hating to see Mother struggle to breathe, I prayed:

"Please God, take Mother so she doesn't have to suffer any longer, but... take me too."

The prospect of living without Mother was too hard to bear. Her fast-approaching demise reminded me of Father and other loved ones I'd lost in my life. Uncle Jo's, and now Mother's imminent death left me bewildered. What was life all about?

Then the sound of the dinner gong echoed through the house, and reminded me that I was hungry. Mother had cooked dinner. I bounded down the stairs and took my seat at the table. That evening, Aunt Marth phoned. Uncle Jo had died. From that day on, I spent all my spare time in the attic, grieving.

On the day of Uncle Jo's funeral, Mother, Penny, and I arrived at Aunt Marth's home, next door to Utrecht's Homeopathic Hospital. Together with Aunt Marth and her close friends, we walked into the hospital foyer for the service. A mass of uniformed nurses had gathered and surrounded us. There was standing room only, no seats, not even one for Aunt Marth! So we squeezed in at the back in a small alcove.

This was the first funeral I'd ever attended. As the service began, I was deep in thought, recalling Uncle Jo's frequent words about heaven and Jesus. I hadn't known anyone like Uncle Jo before. He'd reached out to us in love and wisdom, and seemed to understand everything about us and our situation. I felt safe with him. Now he had died, I was convinced he'd be going to heaven.

While we stood in the foyer, I looked up at the ceiling, wondering what heaven would be like. Suddenly the roof of the chapel seemed to open up and I saw Jesus, sitting on a high-backed throne-like chair. Jesus' clothes were different from ours today, although he didn't wear a crown or kingly robes in my vision. Then I saw Uncle Jo walking towards him, to his feet. The rest was a blur. After what seemed only a moment, I opened my eyes and saw a sea of concerned nurses staring down at me while I lay on the floor. Aunt Marth, Mother, and Penny, also looked worried.

"What happened?" I asked.

"You fainted, dear," Aunt Marth whispered.

"Oh no! I wanted to see more…"

"Of what?"

"Jesus…"

"You saw Jesus?" Aunt Marth gasped. "You're so privileged, my dear. But we must leave for the cemetery now."

Why does Aunt Marth think I'm privileged? I thought, but didn't ask. Outside, a shiny black car awaited us. Still dazed, I sat in the back seat with Aunt Marth, Mother, and Penny. In a world of my own, I still thought of the *picture* I'd seen earlier. Then the car slowly followed the hearse to the cemetery in Zeist.

"It hurt Aunt Marth that Uncle Jo requested to be buried in a plot with his first wife and two children," Mother told me later. We all grieved in our own way. It was September, 1958.

I've never forgotten that vision. It's encouraged me throughout life. I don't know how I would have coped without God. I was so glad Uncle Jo came into our lives and shared Jesus' love with us. It was priceless, although at the time I didn't realise just how priceless.

Mother (Willy), 1957

Addy, 1958

THE SILVER LINING

CHAPTER 21

"Willy, bring the girls for afternoon tea this Saturday," Aunt Marth invited over the phone.

Uncle Jo's death had drawn us closer to Aunt Marth. Although she also grieved, she seemed to understand our grief, and made an effort to reach out to us. Forced to make room for another homoeopathic superintendent to replace Uncle Jo, she relocated to a flat on Stadionplein, near Diaconessen Hospital, also in Utrecht. Despite her fear of fast traffic, she'd purchased a new car, having bravely learnt to drive when Uncle Jo became ill. Although now more confident during daylight hours, she still avoided night driving.

Her new home, a nice little flat with expansive views, was on the second floor of a large apartment building. At first, we all visited for afternoon tea or lunch, but as Mother's health deteriorated, Penny and I went alone.

Sensing her time was near, Mother continued telling us over and over where to find her papers, and which people to phone in the event of her death. I hated her talking that way, and tried to change the subject.

Without Uncle Jo's calming influence, Mother's condition worsened, and her breathlessness increased. Combined with her old unreasonable and explosive behaviour, life resembled a *tightrope walk* again.

Although Mother didn't share her feelings with me about Uncle Jo's death, I understood how she must have suffered. The lead-up to Christmas 1958 was extra stressful. We argued and exchanged hurtful words. Mother's comments grieved me and my response must have hurt her.

Just as if nothing bad had ever happened, we made up, and exchanged gifts on Christmas Eve. The next day, Christmas morning, Mother dressed, came downstairs and played the piano—unusual when she'd been sick in bed so long. When she played music, we knew she was in a good mood. The sound of Beethoven's Fur Elise, as well as Remembrance, and other classical pieces spread calm through our home. It put a spring in my step. I savoured every moment, as it meant that Mother was happy. Moments like that didn't happen often.

Music had a soothing effect on me, and maybe on Mother too. It made me feel as if strife was a faraway stranger. So, with the serverydoors between the kitchen and living room open, I pottered happily in the kitchen while Mother played the piano in the living room. I was baking Orange Madeira cakes, one for our friends, 'Aunt' Tini and 'Uncle' Frits Klay, the other for ourselves. Earlier, I'd deep-fried several batches of *oliebollen* (doughnuts) which now stood ready to eat on the dining table.

Later in the evening, we sang Christmas carols, while Mother played the piano, and Penny the flute. The Christmas tree, lit up with real little candles, shone brightly in the darkened room. Two candles on the piano lit up the music sheets.

There was something peaceful and mystical about the candle flames and the cosy glow they spread. It made me think of the night Jesus was born. The crude nativity scene, which I'd made from clay at school years earlier, enhanced those thoughts. Then my eyes turned to our gifts, now unwrapped under the tree.

We always started making gifts months before Christmas. Mother encouraged us to sew, whittle wood, and use our varied skills. This Christmas I'd bought Mother a baking book, sewing the cover, and embroidering it. She loved baking as well as crafts.

While Mother and Penny played, I sang along with them. I became hungry, so went to the table to eat. As I ate, I watched the Christmas tree. Suddenly the candles flickered wildly.

How can this be? I thought. *The windows and doors are shut...* As the flickering continued, an eerie sensation crept over me. I stopped singing, but the words of the song echoed in my mind:

Dutch:	**English:**
Stil nu, stil nu, Maakt nu geen gerucht. Stil nu, stil nu, t'Ruist al door de lucht.	Quiet now, quiet now, Don't make a sound. Quiet now, quiet now, It rushes all around.
'T wonder komt heel zachtjes aan, 't Kerstkind wil naar binnen gaan. Stil nu, stil nu, Maakt nu geen gerucht. Stil nu, stil nu, t'Ruist al door de lucht.	The miracle comes so gently, The Christ-child wants to enter. Quiet now, quiet now, Don't make a sound. Quiet now, quiet now, He rushes all around.

What is this? I thought, feeling a tight knot clamping my stomach. *Something strange is happening.*

Unaware of my feelings, Mother and Penny kept playing. A lump lodged in my throat and made me nauseous. Hoping to escape the strange sensation, I decided to deliver one of my cakes to Aunt Tini and Uncle Frits in Bilthoven North, half-an-hour's bike ride there and back.

"I'm going to deliver my cake," I announced, not waiting for an answer. I got my bike out of the garage and rode off into the night.

On my return, I stopped in our driveway and looked at the night sky. The full moon spread a strange light. Many more stars than usual seemed to adorn it.

There's something different about everything, I thought, and waited outside to search the sky intently.

What does it all mean? Why do I feel so strange?

Going back inside, I saw the food on the table still untouched, plates piled high with *oliebollen*, but I'd lost my appetite. I watched Mother and Penny from behind the table as they continued playing music. They played a different tune now, but I couldn't get the words of the previous song out of my mind and the strange lump remained in my throat. Something scared me. Something... but what?

Suddenly, Mother jumped up and ran from the piano.

"Turn on the light! Snuff out the candles! Find my Bronchisan puffer!" She yelled instructions to Penny and me as she rushed into the passage. "Get the phone! Ring the doctor! I'm... d-y-i-n-g!" Her screams, laced with fear and panic, echoed through the house.

Penny and I froze. The word *dying* glued us to the floor, unable to respond. As always during Mother's breathless bouts, it was good to have Penny by my side.

I felt she understood me, and I was terrified. Mother's orders became increasingly urgent. Tension and terror flooded over us but we were incapable of responding. Mother's continued calling, more tense and fearful, came from the bathroom now. Finally we stirred into action.

Penny grabbed the plug-in phone from Mother's bedroom upstairs, and handed her the puffer. Seemingly useless, Mother threw it on the floor, and stormed into the living room while I, affected by the anxiety-laced atmosphere, struggled to plug the phone into its socket. Finally, I managed and dialled Doctor Hille Ris Lambers' number. I opened my mouth to tell him about Mother's condition, but no words came out.

Mother snatched the receiver from my hand and yelled: "Quick! I'm dying!" But it was a recorded message. It was Christmas!

Thank God the doctor lived nearby on Leyenseweg, for Penny to get him in person!

"*My mother is choking!*" she cried to a woman, opening the door.

The compassionate doctor heard Penny, and instantly came. He rang our doorbell almost immediately. His presence gave me hope, and I relaxed. *He'll take care of Mother now,* I thought, as Penny and I left him to examine her. Uncle Jo had arranged for another doctor, Dr Albrecht, to care for Mother in emergencies. Since Uncle Jo's death, he'd also administered adrenaline and antibiotic injections when needed. Previously the drugs had worked like a dream, quickly turning Mother into a different person.

We'd only climbed up the first landing when a loud thump stopped us in our tracks.

"What was *that?*" I gasped.

"Addy!" called the doctor almost immediately.

Penny and I ran back into the room.

"Mother…! Mother…!" I called, seeing her slumped on the floor.

"She's gone," said the doctor softly.

Shocked, I hugged and kissed Mother. Not wanting to let her go, I began artificial respiration the old-fashioned way, lifting her arms up and down, one after the other, over her head then beside her chest.

"Don't leave us," I pleaded with her lifeless body.

Why doesn't Dr Lambers do this? I wondered, looking at him, hoping he'd carry on bringing Mother back to life. *Surely, he can do this better than I can.*

"Nothing more can be done," the doctor tried his best to comfort me. "Your mother is at peace now."

But I wasn't comforted.

With the doctor's help, we moved Mother's lifeless body onto the divan. My mind was in turmoil. The doctor then suggested we phone a relative or friends.

I turned to Penny for support. She, too, looked shocked, so I dialled Aunt Marth's number.

"Aunt Marth," I began. "Mother… Mother…is…" I tried to get that dreaded word out for some time, but my voice broke.

"Dead?" Aunt Marth finally finished my sentence.

"Yes," I answered, relieved she'd said the word.

"I'll be there as soon as I can," she reassured. "Phone some friends and your mother's sister, Tine. Ask them to come over immediately."

We followed her instructions. Soon Uncle Frits, and Aunt Tini Klay arrived. Aunt Marth braved the night traffic, arriving in record time. She embraced Penny and me.

Dazed, Penny and I repeated the evening's events. Deep down I wondered whether we could have handled things differently, and perhaps prevented Mother's death.

Those thoughts were futile. Heart attacks strike when least expected, and God only knows what state Mother's heart was in. No autopsy was carried out.

"Have a cup of tea and a biscuit," Aunt Marth urged. I managed a drink, but couldn't eat. The lump in my throat now felt double the size.

Then Mother's sister, Aunt Tine Roukens, arrived. She, too, urged me to eat. In due course our friends, Aunt Tini, and Uncle Frits Klay, left. Mother's sister, Tine, stayed.

"Tine, help me carry Willy upstairs to her bedroom," said Aunt Marth. "We can't leave her here." But Mother was too heavy.

"We'll help," Penny and I offered. The four of us struggled up the stairs with her. There wasn't much of Mother, but now lifeless, she seemed to weigh a ton!

Once upstairs, Aunt Marth and Aunt Tine set to work.

"What shall we dress your mother in?" Aunt Marth asked.

I searched the drawers and cupboard.

"Will these new pyjamas do?" I asked.

"They'll be perfect," said Aunt Marth.

Penny and I left the room, relieved we didn't have to help. I'd become fearful of Mother's dead body; her lifeless form seemed like a stranger's. It was so eerie. Aunt Marth and Aunt Tine took a good hour to prepare Mother, to make her look peaceful. They took care of all the practical details, which funeral directors do nowadays. I was enormously relieved when Aunt Marth offered to stay the night.

She slept in my room. Penny and I huddled together in Penny's bed. There was a spare bed in Mother's room, but I wasn't sleeping in there! It was comforting to embrace Penny all night anyway.

Next morning, Aunt Marth prepared breakfast. I still couldn't eat. Thankfully, she stayed until the funeral, a week later. After a few days, a funeral director transferred Mother's body to a coffin, and placed it in the 'good' lounge for those who wished to see her before the burial. It was eerie and icy in that room, not only temperature-wise. Regardless of my fear, Aunt Marth urged me to look at Mother's face in the coffin. Seeing her finally at rest gave me some comfort; and the expression on her face was in sharp contrast to her frequently tense countenance during her long years of suffering.

Death, however, still stared me in the face; and many more fears, which I didn't understand, remained. Believing people either went to heaven or hell, I was certain that Mother would go to heaven. Her stiff and still body with all the life removed, upset me. I'd grown to love and appreciate her, regardless of the negatives. After all she was my mother, the only parent I'd ever known. Although she was now released from her suffering, her death—for me—was too final and difficult to accept. Somehow, I'd expected her to live forever.

I missed Mother, but also Uncle Jo. He'd been so supportive, someone we could truly trust. By faithfully looking after Mother as well as being a good friend to Penny and me, he had gone beyond his responsibilities as Mother's physician. As Penny and my new advocate and father figure, he left a huge gap when he suddenly died. Worse still for me, had been watching Mother's health and confidence deteriorate, following his death. When Mother died three months after Uncle Jo, I hadn't grieved enough for him. Two deaths so close together caused my world to totally fall apart.

MOTHER'S FUNERAL

Family and friends continued visiting and paying Mother their final respects. Penny and I accompanied them into the icy lounge. I put on a steel front on the outside, but on the inside, I ached. One of the visitors was our new guardian, who came to express his condolences and discuss our future. We'd met him briefly at his home when Mother was alive. He was pleasant enough, but nothing like Uncle Jo.

"After your mother's funeral, you'll be staying at our home," he said, before leaving.

A week after Mother's death, Aunt Marth drove Penny and me in her car behind the hearse to the cemetery in Zeist. As we walked in a procession with family and friends behind Mother's coffin, we passed Uncle Jo's headstone. Aunt Marth must have felt devastated. Walking so close to his grave reminded me how much I missed him and his encouraging words.

Mother's plot was a short distance from Uncle Jo's grave. A hole had been dug and her coffin stood next to it. Someone said a few words, then the coffin was lowered into the ground.

Many family members came and stood at the graveside. Suddenly, a wave of resentment welled up in me. *There you are now*, I thought. *But where were you all these years when we really needed you?*

I didn't know that other family members had tried to help Mother financially following our return from Indonesia and that she'd refused their assistance. Perhaps others' attempts to take Penny and me away from Mother caused her to misinterpret their well-meaning actions.

Later, I heard Mother's fears about losing us were not altogether unfounded. To me, such a response would be normal from a caring mother. Now I understand how that fear fueled Mother's determination to remain alive for us children until we grew old enough to speak up for ourselves, and less likely to be taken advantage of. With hindsight, it would have been better, especially for Mother, to have been offered professional counselling and a listening ear, something she desperately needed.

While we stayed with our new guardian and his family, my overwhelming grief for Mother continued. Regardless of our guardian's wife's kindness, I couldn't be consoled, and silently wept each night under the bed covers. Because Penny seemed indifferent to Mother's death, I didn't feel able to share my deeper feelings with her anymore, as I used to. I didn't understand Penny's reaction. During the day, I put on a brave face, but ate far more than usual. After consuming all six sandwiches during morning tea at school, I felt so hungry at lunch-time that I returned to our guardian's home for more. The bike ride there and back to school filled in time, and possibly supplied me with crucial endorphins. The unusual eating habits, however, continued for some time.

I was depressed, but didn't know it. Without Mother, I felt devoid of hope and a future. Unable to concentrate on lessons, my schoolwork suffered, and my teachers worried. I thank God Aunt Marth reached out to me. Just as Mother had struggled to fill her lungs with oxygen, I struggled with a broken heart, but Aunt Marth slowly mended it.

One day, our guardian informed us that our rented home's chattels would soon be auctioned off.

"Gather whatever you treasure," he said. "The rest will be sold."

I didn't want to set foot in the house again. After Mother's death, the place felt really eerie. I ran in and out as quickly as possible. Penny took her flute and music books.

I grabbed a photo album, and the souvenirs from Tyrol, and ran out the door. My mind was so blurred, I didn't think clearly. Much later, I wished I'd taken the Grimms' brothers' and Hans Andersen's Fairytales, Rudyard Kipling's Jungle Book, and especially John's Children's Bible. I thought it wasn't mine to take. It didn't occur to me that it would be auctioned, and probably sold for very little. Leaving my brown-eyed doll and doll's chairs, however, almost broke my heart. The doll had been my dearest possession, in a way acting as a counsellor, consoling me during my childhood griefs. Had there been room in my trunk, I would have packed it. But it felt good to give both the doll and the chairs away. Knowing my friend's younger sister would treasure them, made the parting bearable.

As I write today, I see Jesus had a plan when He showed himself to me at Uncle Jo's funeral. He gave me something precious and encouraging to hang onto after Mother's death (and the years which followed). For I'd lost all hope, and couldn't see the point of living any more. But the vision helped me turn to Jesus, at first through remembering the vision itself, later by a hunger to know Him. But at the time He nudged me towards the right person to confide in.

PREPARATIONS
CHAPTER 22

"Ad, what shall we cook for lunch?" Aunt Marth asked, during one of my visits to her flat.

"Scrambled eggs," I answered. "Yours are the best!"

She laughed.

"Thanks—you're the first person to mention that. It's nice to be commended."

We cracked the eggs and laughed some more. Having once judged Aunt Marth as over-religious and stiff in her outlook on life, she amazed me with her gentle, and yet fun-loving side.

Penny disagreed, and stopped visiting. I wanted to give Aunt Marth the benefit of doubt, and kept popping in, alone. I knew she loved God by the way she spoke, and that meant a lot to me. She impressed me, not only by what she *said*, but how she *acted*.

After we'd prepared lunch, we sat at the table, ready to eat.

"Let's give thanks," she said, as usual.

She closed her eyes and prayed quietly. Having watched her do this before, I followed suit. Too embarrassed to share my thoughts with people, yet with plenty on my mind, I opened myself up to God.

"God, I feel so miserable. I miss Mother so much…"

It felt good talking to God, and as my prayer took longer than Aunt Marth's, I found her waiting for me before she started eating. The scrambled eggs tasted extra nice that day.

We spent many weekends and holidays together talking, joking, and preparing lunches; my quiet prayers preceding meals.

At last, having loosened up, I shared my thoughts and feelings with Aunt Marth. She had a practical approach to life, not pushy about her faith. She simply reminded me that Jesus would always be my hope and that helped me take a different outlook on life.

But having stayed at our new guardian's home and then suddenly being moved to Aunt Tine's in de Bilt worried me.

Will we continue shifting from house to house like unwanted strays? I wondered, realising we were now orphans, who, according to world statistics and my juvenile perception, had become *unwanted* individuals. This made me determined to stand on my own two feet as soon as possible. *I'm not going to be pushed around,* I thought. *Family members included.*

Aunt Tine, who looked Indonesian, seemed nervy, but was extremely kind-hearted and jovial towards Penny and me. She tried so hard to please and make us feel comfortable in her home. Unconsciously observing her behaviour and movements—as I'd always been in the habit of doing with people—she emerged as a woman who'd received little credit for being the 'giant-slayer' she truly was. She, too, had overcome many struggles in life.

Why did Mother behave so badly towards Aunt Tine? I pondered. *She's always been kind and generous to Penny and me. Look at her now… she treats us like her own daughters!*

Staying with Aunt Tine became a change for the better, yet, strangely, I still missed Mother.

Perceptive Aunt Tine must have read my thoughts, and worried.

"You aren't getting enough iron by not eating meat," she said. "You need extra nourishment on a vegetarian diet."

"I'm all right," I replied. "We always ate this way at home."

"No, you're a teenager now. You need more iron. I'll make an appointment for you to see my doctor for a blood test."

"Okay, then."

I saw the doctor and, true enough, my iron levels had decreased. As a result, a course of iron tablets and regular check-ups followed. Aunt Tine then allowed me to prepare whatever food I fancied, even between meals! I only had to mention my favourites, and she'd buy or cook them for me.

For our birthdays, she ensured that we invited friends to celebrate and eat nasi goreng or bahmi goreng (Indonesian noodles) followed by a then-popular ice-cream cake, delivered after the meal to keep it frozen. Aunt Tine's little fridge didn't have a freezer...

NEW EXPERIENCES

"I've bought a TV", Aunt Tine's neighbour announced excitedly at her front door one day. "Bring Penny and Addy to watch Wuthering Heights tomorrow evening."

"Television!" Penny and I called, jubilantly.

"Sounds like we'll be there," Aunt Tine laughed. "I'll bring some biscuits for supper."

The next evening, we walked into the neighbour's flat. She'd set up her small lounge like a miniature picture theatre! Other neighbours arrived to fill the seats. Together, we watched the movie in black and white on the tiny screen. That was the beginning of modern technology for me.

"Why don't you both come to New Zealand?" Juliana wrote to Penny and me in spring 1959. "You can stay with Rob and me until you decide on the career you wish to follow. Nursing studies are attractive here. Girls begin training at 17½ years and the qualification required is three years' high school."

Wow! I thought, excitedly. *I'll be seventeen in November, and, if all goes well, at the end of this school year, in July, I could have the equivalent of a three-year high school qualification for nursing in New Zealand!*

Nursing had been a childhood dream ever since Mother spent those long months in hospital, and nurses seemed like angels to me. The dream now extended to New Zealand.

Fancy riding to school on a horse! I thought, after reading a New Zealand magazine Juliana had sent. *No skyscrapers there! I'd be mad not to consider an offer like this.*

The thought of nursing and living near Juliana and Rob after eight years apart, instantly drove my depression away, replacing it with hope and excitement. Nothing could keep me from New Zealand now!

Penny, however, wanted to stay in Holland, and attend university.

I'll miss Penny, I thought. *But New Zealand and a nursing career are for me.*

Mixed emotions whirled through my head, while I weighed up the pros and cons of leaving against staying.

Penny has protected me as long as I can remember and has spoken up for me over the years, I thought. *But now I want to speak for myself. It's my chance to grow up and stand on my own feet...* so, I stuck to my plans.

Penny didn't show any obvious emotion about my leaving, but then we were two of a kind, and she probably thought the worst thing to do was to cry. Crying, to us, was like giving another person licence to touch our hearts, perhaps a strange way of thinking, but one we had long adopted to protect ourselves and remain sane.

However, this prevented Penny and me from communicating when it was so important to do so. To me, emigrating made sense. I also yearned for adventure and unusual places.

What's the point of remaining in Holland now Mother has died? I asked myself, and with my mind made up, I concentrated on learning as much English as possible.

Everything required for emigration and nursing training in New Zealand fell into place. My teachers agreed to prepare a report with the required qualifications for New Zealand's nursing school, provided I studied hard the rest of the year. As hope returned, I concentrated on study again, and my appetite returned to normal.

Our new guardian bought me a one-way ticket to New Zealand for the steamship *MS Oranje,* using half the proceeds from the auction of our house contents. The other half went to Penny for her studies.

TORQUAY

"Please teach me English!" I'd pleaded with my Scottish cousin, Elisabeth Traill, who was visiting with her mother, Aunt Jeanne, Mother's youngest sister, during the 1958 summer holidays.

"If you teach me Dutch," she said. 'I want to learn."

"Okay, it's a deal."

"You write letters to me in English and I'll correct you," Elisabeth suggested.

"Then I'll correct your Dutch," I added.

Impressed with Elisabeth's perfect English, I began writing to her. I think I received the better deal. She wrote back, mostly in English, correcting me, and giving hints. We continued corresponding weekly.

Elisabeth lived in Torquay, England, with her mother and brother, Robbie. She attended college, and Robbie boarding school. After Mother's death in December 1958, Aunt Jeanne invited Penny and me over for Easter, 1959.

Aunt Tine escorted us to Rotterdam's wharf where, after customs checked our passports, we boarded the overnight ferry to cross the English Channel to Dover. We explored and familiarised ourselves with the ship's layout, then settled into our cabin bunks and slept. It was our first trip alone.

At 5 a.m. the next morning a young steward poked his head round the door.

"The ship's landing in Dover in an hour!" he called, waking us from a deep sleep. "And you must catch the train to London!"

Rubbing the sleep from our eyes, we discovered two cups of hot, already sugared, milky tea, with several dry biscuits, on our lockers. This gave us energy to pack quickly, disembark, and find our connecting train to Charing Cross, London, where we'd planned to meet Aunt Jeanne and Elisabeth.

"Look at the lush green of the grass and leaves!" I called to Penny over the noise of the train whistle, as the railcar sped through the English countryside. The dirt and smoke-smudged station walls of

London were a sharp contrast. They were unlike Holland's spotless surroundings, where electric trains had long since replaced steam trains. A tinge of pride came over me. Dutch cities were so much cleaner!

Suddenly the train stopped, and everyone rushed to the exits.

"Is this Charing Cross?" Penny asked a man wearing a bowler hat.

"Yes, Miss!" he answered. Someone also shouted it from the platform and the wall sign confirmed this.

Aunt Jeanne had asked us to wear something red so she and Elisabeth could recognise us. They would wear red too. It worked!

"Aunt Jeanne! Elisabeth!" we shouted, waving our arms above our heads as we stepped off the train.

"Wait there! We'll come to you!" Elisabeth called as she led Aunt Jeanne through the crowd.

"Penny and Addy!" Aunt Jeanne puffed when they reached us. "Let's sit on this bench. You have grown since we saw you last! Did you have a good trip?"

"Oh, yes," Penny answered.

"I got a shock to see a steward in our doorway this morning!" I shared, reliving our morning's excitement. "Then seeing a cup of tea on our locker, and we'd locked the door! It was so embarrassing…"

"That's usual practice on the ferry," Elisabeth soothed. "It's to wake you, so you'll catch the train."

"Here, sit down. You must be hungry," said Aunt Jeanne, as she brought out the thinnest cucumber and tomato sandwiches I'd ever seen.

Food! Penny and I thought. We hadn't eaten since our early cup of tea. Hungry, and being used to doorstep sandwiches, we finished them instantly!

"I'll get more," Aunt Jeanne said, aghast, and rushed to the cafeteria.

Having had our fill, the four of us caught another train to Torquay, Aunt Jeanne and Elisabeth's home town. Aunt Jeanne smoked, thankfully not in our home near Mother, who couldn't breathe near smoke. She appeared easier going than Mother, but could she talk! She spoke Dutch with us; Elisabeth spoke a mixture of Dutch and English. I loved Elisabeth's hands-on English teaching, especially the pronunciation. That helped enormously.

Torquay was nice, different from Dutch seaside cities.

"Taxi!" Aunt Jeanne called, waving her arm. The driver stopped and took our luggage.

"Please take us through the city," Aunt Jeanne said. "My nieces are new to Torquay."

He then drove us all around the fascinating central city, much bigger than Bilthoven, with shops I'd heard so much about, like Marks and Spencer.

"We'll go there later," Elisabeth said. "You can pick up real bargains, from lamb's wool cardigans to souvenirs."

I was excited. The spending-money Aunt Tine had given me for the trip almost burnt a hole in my pocket!

Suddenly the taxi stopped in front of Aunt Jeanne's home, one of many in a row. Hers had a small front and a long back garden, with enough lawn to hit a hockey ball around with Robbie.

As promised, Elisabeth often escorted Penny and me on the bus to town. We found lovely and cheap woollens, famous *Clarks* shoes at amazingly low prices, and cute Walt Disney's 'Lady and the Tramp' animal figurines.

At breakfast, we talked so much that we forgot the time and remained seated until the next round of food came out at lunch time! I relished the cornflakes with creamy top milk. We didn't have that kind of cereal at home.

Before returning home again, Aunt Jeanne took us on a bus tour through Devon where we saw amazing herds of wild Shetland ponies running free on the moors, and centuries-old roads built by the Romans could still be seen. Devon's quaint old thatched-roofed houses impressed me too. I enjoyed our stay, especially speaking English with shop assistants and bus drivers, feeling proud that they understood me, and I them. Most English people pronounced their words clearly and listened patiently.

After a sad farewell, we returned to Rotterdam, again by ferry. Elizabeth and I continued our correspondence in English.

Learning English in preparation for emigrating remained exciting. However, there was more to emigrating than expected. Just when I became confident about it, some relations and friends sowed seeds of doubt in my mind.

"What's wrong with nursing in Holland?" some asked.

Plenty, I thought, I want to go nursing now. I don't want to wait and attend school for another two years...

"There are no fees for nursing In New Zealand," I said. "Board and lodging is free and I'll even get paid! If I nursed in Holland, who would pay for it? I don't have the money and I'm not asking the family for handouts..."

I couldn't think of a better way to start a career than the one on offer in New Zealand. Starting two years earlier than in Holland was an extra bonus. Even though I already had my ticket and I'd weighed up the pros and cons, the negative talk continued. Thankfully, Aunt Marth encouraged me to take the comments with a grain of salt. Having been a nurse herself, she understood my reason for wanting to nurse, and the sooner the better. It wasn't glamour that attracted me—I wanted to help people.

I also wanted to forget the heartache of Uncle Jo and Mother's deaths, and everything in Holland reminded me of these loved ones. Neither did I want to be a burden on the family by accepting their money for study or training. Rightly or wrongly, Mother's experiences with some of the family made me suspicious. Becoming independent seemed the better option.

GLORIA

In June 1959, John's wife, Gloria, arrived in Holland from Australia for a holiday. She'd booked her fare before Mother's death and decided to come to Holland anyway. Uncle Alf offered her accommodation at his home in Driebergen. Penny and I only caught up with her twice. With Gloria being twenty-four and me sixteen, our interests contrasted greatly. Eight years' age difference mattered a lot to me then. None of my friends wore make-up, but Gloria did. This created an invisible barrier on my part, as I'd formed unusual teenage ideas about make-up.

Later, however, I discovered that underneath that layer of make-up, Gloria was much like me, only a little older. Uncle Alf's daughter, Nancy, and her husband, John de Jong van Schouwenburg, showed her the Dutch countryside and around Switzerland, introducing the rest of the Brandt family in Geneva.

I, busy with preparations for what seemed a once-in-a-lifetime trip, was shopping for gifts and clothes for New Zealand's semi-tropical climate, taking care of inoculations, immigration papers, and farewells. I didn't think I'd ever see Holland again. New Zealand, to me, was far away, and the passage expensive. I presumed saving for a return fare would take me years!

MORE EXCITEMENT

I completed my three years' high school at Montessori Lyceum and, as arranged with the headmaster, Mr Jordaan, and teachers, was awarded a certificate with glowing grades, qualifying me for nursing in New Zealand. My chest swelled with pride. I was ready to face the world!

Then, as an extra, to gain knowledge for nursing in New Zealand, I secured a two-week voluntary job at Utrecht's Diaconessen Hospital's X-ray department. My head buzzed with excitement.

Aunt Marth's friend, *Aunt* Martien, the X-ray charge sister, arranged the job for me, and as Aunt Marth's flat was only five minutes' walk from the hospital, I stayed with her. Working each day from 8am until 5pm, I befriended all the staff and doctors, who went out of their way to teach me, and answer my questions about human biology.

At the end of the fortnight, I was sad to leave. Everyone had treated me kindly, like a grown-up. If Aunt Martien had offered me a permanent position, I may have accepted. I was glad she hadn't, or I'd have missed out on the fantastic experiences which followed. On my last day at the X-ray department, I served afternoon tea with my favourite Limburgse vlaaien (fruit flans), a delicacy from Limburg.

Aunt Martien had a surprise for me too.

"We've appreciated your help so much," she said. "We want to reward you with some pocket money for your trip."

I couldn't believe it! My first pay-packet!

Aunt Marth helped me spend the money: a lipstick, a pair of dainty sandals, and Polaroid sunglasses. As most Dutch nurses carried wicker baskets to work, I bought one for New Zealand. I also had my long hair cut short.

Dressed in my new gear, I heard wolf whistles from a train full of soldiers. Although ignoring them, I inwardly felt delighted to be noticed as an adult.

KANDERSTEG

Late July, Penny and I joined Father's brother, Uncle Marijn, his wife Aunt Jettie, three of their five children, Tanja, Sita, and Coen, and Aunt Jettie's sister, Aunt Adee, for a holiday in Switzerland.

Clothed in mountain-climbing gear, and carrying a full-to-the-brim backpack each, we met at Utrecht's train-station. The platforms buzzed with foreign tourists.

We travelled through Holland's provinces, Utrecht, Noord Brabant, and Limburg. Then we crossed Germany, Austria, and finally reached Switzerland. As the train sped along the Rhine, an announcement over the loudspeaker told us of the Rhine's famous Lorelei cliff. I instantly hummed the sad song my teacher, Mrs von Gleich, had taught our class.

The Lorelei cliff towered about 130 metres above the Rhine, between Mainz and Koblenz, where the river flowed swiftly and dangerously. Legend says that the echo heard at the cliff is the voice of a beautiful, but sly siren, luring boatmen to destruction.

After many valleys and tunnels, we stopped in Kandersteg, a quaint Swiss village, tucked in a valley between high mountain peaks.

We related well with Uncle Marijn and his family. Coen (9) was small for his age. When he wore his big climbing boots, he reminded me of Tom Thumb!

With our gear on our backs, we walked from the train to a furnished wooden chalet, with rocks on the roof. All beds had feather duvets about 60cm thick! I'd never seen duvets that size before, probably for extreme winter chills, though I was glad it was summer. With only a bottom sheet to straighten, bed-making was a dream.

Making excursions up the mountains nearly every day, we always had something new to see and do. One afternoon Uncle Marijn, Aunt Jettie, and Aunt Adee had an afternoon sleep so Tanja, Sita, Coen, Penny, and I decided to go for a walk.

"Don't go far," Uncle Marijn called.

"We won't," Penny and Tanja choroused.

Walking up the road towards what seemed a low hill, we found a narrow path.

"This looks interesting," Sita called. "Let's see where it leads."

We walked the narrow path in single file, on what appeared a gentle slope. Then the track suddenly gave way and we all slid down a steep bank!

"God! Help!" I prayed, while hanging onto a clump of grass and, presuming regular praying was essential for Christians, added, "I'll pray every day!"

Although it was touch and go, most of us recovered our footing and climbed back up. Unfortunately, Coen, couldn't hold on and began sliding down further. Penny, still hanging precariously from a clump of grass nearby, saw him go. As he slid past, she grabbed him with one arm and hauled him up. Surprisingly, they both made it back to the path. Phew!

We quickly descended, and back on level ground, walked round to see the high and narrow path that had given way under our feet. The cliff-face looked even more menacing from below; a steep ravine with jagged edges and rocks. Had we known earlier, fear may have incapacitated us!

When we returned to the chalet and told the adults of our close shave, they hugged and kissed us. From then on, they accompanied us on all walks. The experience made us more aware of danger. But we soon brushed the episode aside, ready for other adventures.

Gondola and chairlift rides enabled us to see everlasting snow and glaciers. One big gondola departed from Kandersteg. With room for at least ten adults, it ascended a steep rock face, and provided a magnificent view. From the top, we tramped to other beautiful valleys, tucked further up the mountain. Gondolas saved time, energy, and longer treks.

Although it rained occasionally, the temperature remained steady and, drying off quickly, we continued tramping. I also enjoyed family times in the chalet where we all pitched-in doing chores, so we could play board or card games together. Aunt Adee hand-sewed and made me a serviette. Before long, the holiday ended, and we arrived back at Aunt Tine's home in de Bilt.

The cliff-face experience reminded me of my prayer promise to God, and that death threatened not only the old and sick, but also the young and healthy. It convinced me even more that nursing was right for me.

THE OPERATION

CHAPTER 23

"Now that you're emigrating in September and going to start nurse-training in New Zealand," Aunt Marth insisted, "we must get your hammer toe seen to. Nursing requires much walking."

That week we saw the orthopaedic surgeon at the Diaconessen Hospital's clinic.

The second toe of my left foot was deformed, and the middle bone stuck out. It had always been troublesome, restricting my choice of shoes.

"It'll be a simple operation," the surgeon said, showing me how he'd remove the small bone to straighten the toe.

"Addy is leaving for New Zealand on 9 September to start a nursing career," Aunt Marth explained. "Can it be done before then?"

"I can do it this month. That will allow the toe to heal considerably before departure."

On the day of admission, Aunt Marth and I walked to Diaconessen Hospital. In the foyer, a strong carbolic antiseptic smell wafted toward us as I checked in at the reception desk and waited. Several doctors and staff from X-ray department greeted me as they passed. I felt famous!

Still day-dreaming, a tap on my shoulder startled me, as a young nurse extended her hand.

"Hello, I'm nurse Jannie. Are you Addy Brandt?"

She looked a likeable girl, a little older than me. Like all Diaconessen Hospital junior student nurses then, she wore a plain white uniform. Senior and registered nurses wore blue uniforms with white pinafores and various coloured epaulettes.

"I'm taking you to the women's orthopaedic ward. Where's your bag?"

"I'll carry it," I argued. But Jannie wouldn't hear of it, and even placed me in a wheelchair!

"You need this more than me," I whispered to Aunt Marth, but she just smiled, knowing hospital regulations inside-out.

It took ages before we arrived at the ward. Talking continuously, however, relaxed me.

"What are you going to do when you leave school?" Jannie asked.

"I've left already," I said. "I'm emigrating to New Zealand in September."

"You're not serious? You're only sixteen!"

"Addy's mother died last December, and her father died during the war in Indonesia," Aunt Marth added.

"How sad… who are you emigrating with then?" Jannie asked.

"No one. I'm going alone."

"Aren't you scared?"

"No… my brother lives in Australia, and my older sister in New Zealand. She and her husband are meeting me in Wellington."

By asking many questions, Jannie put me at ease, and before long she knew all about me.

"But New Zealand?" Jannie asked. "Isn't that at the other end of the world?"

The whole story then tumbled out why and how I was emigrating, and my desire to be a nurse like her.

"Oh! Now I see why you've been watching me so intently!" Jannie said, and then we talked about nurse training in Holland, the required age to start, and qualifications needed.

Just as I expected, Jannie tried to change my mind about emigrating and training far away, when there was a good nursing school on my doorstep.

"You might never return."

"I'm not planning to."

On arrival at the women's ward, Jannie wheeled me into a room occupied by three other ladies.

"This is Addy," Jannie introduced. "She's emigrating to New Zealand and wants to become a nurse. Her mother died last Christmas."

"Oh, you poor child," one older lady soothed. "Fancy losing your mother at such a young age."

Then the others chimed in and asked about Father.

"Are you sure you want to leave?" another lady asked. "Do you know how far New Zealand is? Why don't you train here?"

"I know all about New Zealand," I said confidently. "My elder sister lives there. She's sent me lots of information. Nurses there can train much earlier. Jannie tells me I'd have to wait until I'm nineteen here! I want to nurse *now*."

They all smiled, and over the next few days continued trying to change my mind, but I was immovable. Hadn't my heart's desire always been to see the world like my parents and Juliana and John? Since Mother's death, my inner vow not to leave her no longer counted.

The door had opened for me to help the sick, and my hospital experience gave me an inside glimpse of nursing. Albert Schweitzer had inspired me first, when Mrs von Gleich showed us a film about his work in Africa. Later, kind nurses at the Homeopathic Hospital, in Utrecht, during Mother's long stay, had also provided motivation.

Jannie seemed to enjoy having a younger person in her ward, and answered my many questions.

"Now, time for a bath," she ordered.

"I had a shower this morning..." I remonstrated.

"Hospital rules," she said. "Come with me."

While Aunt Marth waited in the ward, Jannie and I left for the bathroom. She ran the water till the bath was half full. I waited and waited for her to leave before undressing, but she didn't! Again hospital regulations. To my horror she stayed until I finished and even scrubbed my back! When it was over, I breathed a sigh of relief. Back in the ward, I had to climb into my high hospital bed and stay there. It felt stupid. I wasn't sick!

"You're clean now, and we're going to keep you that way," said Jannie.

After Aunt Marth left, I became the centre of attention again. The surgeon breezed in, shook my hand, and undertook a pre-operative examination for anaesthesia. He checked my toe and drew on it.

"I'll take that middle bone out tomorrow," he said. "That'll fix your problem." He explained the procedure again and how a cage would be placed under the blankets to keep my foot comfortable. Then he left.

Penny visited that evening with a friend, in awe of all the fuss I received.

Next morning, I awoke to find a 'nil by mouth' sign over my bed. Then Jannie walked in with a tray full of strange looking implements.

"What's that?" I asked.

"An enema..."

"What's an enema?" I asked.

Jannie tried to explain.

"You'll see," she said. Having to get on with the job, she escorted me to the bathroom yet again.

After that second ordeal, I felt relieved to re-enter the ward and hop back into bed. Then it was time for a bed wash (again hospital rules), a finger prick for a blood test, and an injection by another nurse. Soon sleep overcame me.

"When will I have the operation?" I asked, when I woke.

"It's over," laughed Jannie. I couldn't recall how or when I went to the operating theatre! Before discharge, Jannie bandaged my foot with extra wadding. She enlarged my Scholl sandals with a narrow bandage as a shoe lace, and tied it in a big ribbon above the wadding. Those sandals became my only footwear for months, until the tenderness and swelling settled. Luckily, it was summer in Holland, and spring would be on its way in New Zealand.

I felt sad leaving the ladies and Jannie. Later I visited Jannie in the nurses' home and she showed me around. I also saw one of the elderly women from the ward who'd moved to a rented room. It had no window and was so tiny!

I'm going to become a good nurse, I thought, *and stand up for the underprivileged.*

With my departure date for New Zealand fast approaching, excitement mounted. I was eager to experience the warmer temperatures of tropical and sub-tropical countries en route to New Zealand, especially Indonesia, the country of my birth, the country that reminded me so much of my father and mother who had loved the Indonesian people as their own.

MY JOURNEY

CHAPTER 24

"Hurry, Ad!" Penny called.

It was September 2, 1959. It was also Penny's first day back at school after the summer holidays.

I was so pleased to have finished with school! But wanting to farewell some class mates before leaving Holland, I came along for the ride.

"It'll be strange without you..." Penny mused, as we rode side by side on the bike path.

Exciting for me though... I thought.

Silence followed as we both immersed ourselves into our own worlds, until Montessori Lyceum's school grounds appeared.

"See you soon!" Penny called, riding through the open gates. "Meet you at the little gate..."

Having left school, I felt obligated to stay outside the grounds, a rule for outsiders.

Penny soon arrived, flanked by my friends.

"Hi," I said. "Just wanted to say goodbye before leaving next week..."

"Good luck!" Tineke and Marjolein chorused.

"I'll miss you," said Loekie.

An eerie silence followed. Then the bell rang. They had to go.

"Bye!" we called to each other. "See you after school, Pen!"

While cycling alone to Aunt Tine's apartment, I pondered on my friends' apparent lack of excitement about my trip. Although saying nothing negative, their body language did. I gained the impression they considered me foolish for interrupting my education. Adults had said so, some even considered nursing a demeaning profession! Nothing, however, could dampen my enthusiasm or determination for it.

Emigrating and nursing in New Zealand was a dream come true for me. I almost wanted to pinch myself to check if everything was true. I'd missed Juliana and Rob so much the last eight years; and now they had an eighteen-month-old daughter, Jennifer, an extra little niece for me to love. All my hopes and plans buzzed through my teenage head, many real, some far-fetched.

A trunk packed with extra clothing for a warmer climate, my new bike, and gifts for Juliana, Rob, and Jennifer, had been sent ahead by the then freight ship, *Johan van Olde Barneveldt*. Together with Mother's gramophone and records, my two partially packed suitcases stood in a corner of my room.

A week later, 9 September 1959, I woke early, dressed before Aunt Tine and Penny, and rechecked that I had everything needed for my trip. Twirling round once more in front of the mirror in a new outfit, I imagined myself already in New Zealand, in different surroundings, meeting new friends.

After breakfast, Aunt Marth arrived.

"Well, Ad, I'll say goodbye now, I'm off to work," said Aunt Tine. "Have a good journey. All the best for your nursing studies in New Zealand, and stay safe. Oh, remember to use the talcum powder I gave you for the tropics... and... don't forget to write!"

A tearful farewell followed.

A neighbour carried my luggage, and lifted it into Aunt Marth's car.

"Goodbye! Farewell! Auf Wiedersehn!" they shouted, as Aunt Marth started up the car and drove Penny and me towards the motorway. Nearing Rotterdam, we saw the ship *MS Oranje*, sparkling in the sunlight.

TWO SLICES OF BREAD

"Customs first," said Aunt Marth, while she parked the car. As other ocean-liner passengers had checked in earlier, going through customs was quick and easy. Meeting up with Aunt Marth and Penny again, we walked up the gangplank together. A porter with my luggage in tow, led the way to my cabin. Then I proudly showed Aunt Marth and Penny around the ship as though it were mine.

Having talked on upper deck for some time, we suddenly heard the ship's motors whirr, and saw plumes of smoke billow from its smoke-stacks. A loudspeaker then blared in our ears.

"Visitors must leave ship in thirty minutes!"

My confidence suddenly drained, and butterflies flew around in my stomach. Too proud to admit it, I remained quiet.

Finishing our conversation, another announcement, more urgent than the first, startled us again.

"All visitors must leave the ship, now!"

"We'd better go," said Aunt Marth. "Or we'll be sailing with you."

Whether it was Aunt Marth's words, or the thought of leaving for good, the moment we hugged and kissed, I felt a check in my spirit. Instead of showing my true feelings, however, I put on a brave face. It was a habit of the last thirteen years, birthed through necessity.

"Goodbye, dear," Aunt Marth said, hugging, and kissing me on both cheeks again.

"Do write."

"I will!"

"Bye Ad," Penny said, also keeping a stiff upper lip. "I'll write every week!"

"Me too," I replied deliberately cheerful, but my heart almost breaking in two.

Aunt Marth and Penny then walked down the gangplank, waving continually before sailors pulled in the plank and loosened the heavy ropes. Surrounded by a multitude of passengers, yet feeling desperately alone, I gazed at the crowd on the wharf. To most, it appeared a happy occasion, with passengers throwing streamers to family and friends below. Then I spotted Penny and Aunt Marth again, waving once more. I waved back.

When the boat drifted further and further from shore, and Aunt Marth and Penny had become tiny dots on the horizon, I panicked.

I don't want to go! I thought, almost feeling the weight of the ship descending on me. *I could still jump in the water and swim back...*

The distance dividing us had suddenly become symbolic. The thought of earning a return fare *home* to see Penny and Aunt Marth in the future seemed an impossibility at the time. But not wanting to make a fool of myself and upset Aunt Marth or Penny, I descended to my cabin. There I met my two travel companions, a German girl, Heidi, and an older English woman. Heidi and I quickly became friends, communicating in German. Like Mother, I liked the language.

Rummaging through my suitcase, I found a little Saint Christopher medal.

"Is this yours?" I asked Heidi.

"No," she said.

"Did *you* drop it?" I asked the older woman.

"I've never seen it before."

"Someone must have wished you well," Heidi added. "The name Saint Christopher' means 'Christ carrier'. He's known to have carried people across unfordable streams. He's the patron saint of travellers..."

So, I tucked the medal into a pocket in my suitcase.

But who would have put it in here? I thought. *Perhaps it was Aunt Tine wishing me well. She's like that...*

Heidi and I talked and read on the upper deck. I'd bought the book *Uncle Tom's Cabin* by Harriet Beecher Stowe, from the purser's office. The tale stirred me, and reminded me of Father, who hated racism, and had treated his Indonesian servants well. Reflecting on the story, I wanted even more to be like him.

When the boat had sailed through the warmer Mediterranean Sea, we inched through the narrow Suez Canal, surrounded by miles of desert, bringing with it a pleasant warmth. Arab traders dressed in flowing robes, some in small boats, hoped to sell their wares on ship. Others were already aboard.

At Port Said, *MS Oranje* passengers took camel rides through the desert, later to re-join the ship further along the canal. I would have liked to try, but didn't dare. Mother's admonishing stories about human trafficking and slavery in the Middle East stuck freshly in my mind. Heidi thought like me. Playing safe, we remained on ship, our *home* for another four weeks.

After sailing through the Suez Canal and then the Indian Ocean, we berthed at Colombo, Sri Lanka. This was close to where my brother, Dido, had died on the ship *MS Boissevain* in 1946, during our family's evacuation from troubled Indonesia to Holland.

Heidi invited me to join her and a German family to see Colombo's sights. Before disembarking, the captain sternly warned us against buying and eating fresh fruit, food, or drinks from stalls. Cholera, dysentery, and dengue fever could result and cause serious illness, even death. He urged us to eat and drink on ship only.

On our walks through the filthy streets, we saw local people display their wares on tables and the ground. The fruit looked appealing. I was tempted to disobey the captain's orders as Mother had told me so much about the delicious taste of tree-ripened tropical fruit.

Traders squatted beside their wares urging us to buy their goods. Some even pursued us, always bargaining. A snake charmer played his flute, while a snake swayed in front of him. It sent shivers down my spine! That was my first taste of the tropics. It made me think of Mother and Father and their life in Indonesia before the war. Then, just when nostalgia almost got the better of me, my circumstances changed; I think for the better.

On our return from sightseeing in Colombo, I checked the ship's noticeboard for letters, and found one from John. He reminded me, discreetly, that his wife, Gloria, was also a passenger on the *MS Oranje!*

As a preoccupied teenager, with far too much on my mind, engrossed and distracted by many new experiences, I had completely forgotten my sister-in-law! She was also aboard, on her way back to Sydney, Australia, after spending the summer of 1959 in Holland. Having only met twice, I hadn't caught up with her travel plans. Nor did I know that a *class system* divided us—arranged, without my knowledge, for my safety as a sixteen-year-old travelling alone. Until then, I hadn't been aware that second-class passengers were restricted to their area, while first-class passengers could roam anywhere on board.

Boredom having almost got the better of me by now, I welcomed a change of scenery, and ventured down a few decks into second class, to find Gloria surrounded by a group of friends.

"Ad!" Gloria called, excitedly, when she saw me. "It's so nice to see you!"

She immediately introduced me to her many companions, and from then on, I spent all my time with her and her friends, swimming, playing deck games and cards. We visited Penang, and in Singapore ate *nasi goreng*. To my delight, Indonesian chefs on the *MS Oranje* also treated us to the tasty dish!

Of all our stopovers, I enjoyed Singapore best, pleasantly warm, clean, and safe. Policemen watched for litterbugs and robbers, instantly handing out fines to perpetrators. I felt at home. Tropical palm and coconut trees reminded me of Mother, who often drew palm trees in her sketches. Temples and markets reminded me of her stories about Java, the past I so longed to learn more of, and to experience.

Djakarta was our next stop. Excited at the thought of seeing Java after thirteen years away, I'd dreamed of travelling the 321 km from Djakarta to my birthplace, Pekalongan, although that proved impossible.

"Owing to Indonesian unrest, there'll be no disembarking," the captain announced. "Europeans are in great danger!"

Disappointed, I could only watch Indonesian workers unload and reload goods on the wharf. I so yearned for more than a glimpse of my birth country, wanting to bring Mother's stories to life…

But I did get a small introduction. The ship employed many Indonesian/Dutch nationals who'd also escaped the freedom fighters' violence after the war. So, too, were several young and friendly stewards allocated to our deck. They often sat on the floor near our cabin, smoking cigarettes, and always giggling whenever I walked past them on my way to the bathroom. Despite being first class, our cabin had no en suite.

After a few days, we eventually sailed from Djakarta's Tandjong Priok Harbour, dejection still washing over me like a flood. So much of our family's life of love and loss had been spent in Java—thirty-one years of coming and going, to end like that...

The ship refuelled in Melbourne, cold compared with the tropics, and a disappointment, as I expected all of Australia to be tropical. But by then Gloria and her friends had become the centre of my activities; and as we neared Sydney, Gloria invited me to stay with her and John for a holiday in Australia. I accepted.

Before the ship arrived in Sydney, John had organised my stopover with the Australian authorities and rebooked my passage to New Zealand as an open ticket, to continue my journey later. He also notified Juliana and Rob about the plan change.

Looking much the same as I remembered him when he left Holland nine years earlier, John stood on the wharf, welcoming Gloria and me.

We then picked up their son, Lance, from school. Lance was my 6-year-old nephew, of whom I'd been so proud all those years, but had only known from a distance.

Gloria, John, and Lance lived at 30 Phillip Street, St. Mary's. As with other houses then, theirs had an outside toilet at the back. Thankfully, I didn't know about Australia's dangerous funnel-web, red-back, and white-tail spiders. Gloria merely warned me about spiders in general.

While John worked, Gloria showed me around close to home. On weekends, John drove us to other interesting areas, especially the Three Sisters in the Blue mountains. We stopped for a cup of tea at Gloria's sister, Phyllis, who lived there.

I also met Gloria's mum, Sally Weirick, in Manly. I'd heard so much about Manly's famous beach, that to have a house there seemed the ultimate to me. 'Mum' was very welcoming and loving. Her husband, Leslie Weirick, Gloria's dad, had died in December 1952, six months after John and Gloria's wedding.

I liked the Weirick family. They were down-to-earth people, and spoke clearly so I could understand them. I also liked Gloria's practical English teaching exercises which required me to make solo errands to shops. Sometimes, however, I returned empty-handed because of my pronunciation. Saying *Paul Maul* with a rounded a, instead of *Pell Mell*, the Australian way, confused the shop assistant. I needed to learn as much English as possible, before commencing nursing training in New Zealand. I even watched children's television programmes and advertisements with six-year-old Lance!

Having an open ticket to New Zealand meant that I could stay in Australia almost as long as I liked, so Gloria suggested I nurse in Australia. When I heard how close New Zealand was, however, and in spite of John and Gloria's exceptional hospitality, I suddenly pined for Juliana and Rob again.

John and Gloria understood, and arranged my Tasman Sea crossing on the New Zealand ship *MS Wanganella*, a much smaller boat than the *MS Oranje*. This time, however, the crew spoke English, and my farewell was easier than leaving Holland.

"Come back any time," said Gloria. "Fares between Australia and New Zealand are affordable!"

I promised to write, and to return in a year's time.

THE WANGANELLA

Being smaller, the *Wanganella* only had one accommodation class, and my cabin was on a lower deck than on the *MS Oranje*. I shared the cabin with six Greek women. Not understanding a word they spoke, I wandered around and explored the ship alone. Although still only sixteen years old, I felt quite the experienced traveller.

At breakfast one morning, a waiter passed with another passenger's order.

"What's that?" I asked in my limited English, tapping him on the arm.

"Weetbix, Miss," he answered.

"Can I have some too, please?" I asked, tired of porridge, the only cereal familiar on the menu until then.

I continued to explore the ship between meals and discovered Cadbury chocolate bars at the purser's office/shop. To my amazement, the bars were triple the size of the Dutch variety, and cheap! After one bar, I became addicted, and returned for more each day. Not having used my travellers' cheques much so far, they suddenly became handy!

MS Orange
Addy's departure for New Zealand from Rotterdam

THE CHOSEN COUNTRY

CHAPTER 25

After four days munching on chocolate and searching the horizon for land, New Zealand's coastline came into view. From then on, my thoughts focused on New Zealand, the change probably doing me good.

As the Wanganella entered the harbour, the sun shone brilliantly. It was November 1959, a magnificent, cloudless day. As I looked in the distance, I saw the sun reflect on the skyline as though it were covered with welcoming gold. I instantly felt that I'd come to the right place!

This is the country for me! I thought, remembering how Mother's illness had prevented me from seeing Juliana and Rob; and how her death had finally set me free from my vow never to leave her.

When several tugboats pulled the ship through the bay into Wellington Harbour, I noticed a small group of people on a jetty and, believing I had spotted Juliana and Rob amongst them, I waved wildly. They, in turn, answered with both arms, and their familiar blown-kisses of bygone years.

It wasn't long before I stood on Wellington's quay, with my two suitcases, Mother's portable record player, and her two cardboard cases, containing classical long-playing records (LPs). They were my last link with Mother. Customs checked my luggage, while Juliana and Rob waited behind ropes and smiled. Finally, we embraced!

Rob then drove us towards Hastings. The country scenery was totally different from Holland. I sat in the back seat of their VW, leaning forward to speak and hear everything Juliana and Rob had to say. The radio played staccato classical music as we drove through a town with old wooden verandas and overhanging roofs. I felt we were participating in a *Country and Western* movie! Expecting to see cowboys and Indians on horse-back galloping past, I was disappointed that none appeared. Nor were there Maori people dressed in grass skirts, the typical picture of New Zealand I'd seen on postcards and magazines before my emigration!

Night fell as we drove. With no street lights in rural areas, the surroundings became pitch dark. In Holland, streetlights lit up all roads, even in the countryside.

"Is that Hastings?" I asked, pointing to hundreds of little lights as we drove through farmland.

"No!" laughed Rob. "They're sheep! Their eyes are reflecting our car lights!"

We stopped to pick up Juliana and Rob's 18-month-old daughter, Jennifer, who'd been cared for by a friend, Verna, in Tikokino, Central Hawke's Bay. I couldn't believe the quantity of cakes and party food that was spread on the table just for us. At home, that amount of baking was supplied for birthdays only, and then shared with my whole class.

Our journey continued late into the night. Jennifer, wrapped in a shawl, slept in Juliana's arms in the front seat, while Rob drove on. After about an hour's drive over the still-narrow shingle Maraekakaho Road, we arrived at Rob and Juliana's home in Frederick Street, Hastings. Rob lifted Jennifer from the car, and put her straight into her cot, opposite my bed in the same room.

"Don't worry if you hear loud noises and feel the house shake during the night," Rob whispered. "There's a railway track just two doors from here and they shunt all night…"

I woke the next morning to a chatty little girl, excited to see me. I met many of Juliana and Rob's friends in town on Friday evenings, while we were out *late-night window-shopping*, which was fashionable then. Many people congregated on the footpaths, stopping to talk to friends and neighbours.

I especially liked Truus and Jan Koster. They lived on a farm in Maraekakaho, where I stayed once to baby-sit their two little girls. I also rode my first horse with Jan, around the farm. It was exciting. I fell in love with the countryside and farming. It was so different from anything I'd experienced before. My love for animals almost replaced my desire for nursing…

"We must show Addy Rotorua," Truus said to Juliana. "What if we took our van and the three of us stayed in a cabin?"

"What a good idea," said Juliana.

"It's a thermal wonderland, with many interesting things to see," Truus explained.

A week later, we drove to Rotorua over the old, winding, hot and dusty Taupo Road, much of it still narrow and unsealed. When following other cars, and meeting oncoming traffic, we had to quickly wind up the windows to avoid getting thick dust inside!

On arrival in Taupo, the van was covered in dust, and we were hot, thirsty, and tired. A soak at Taupo's DeBrett's Thermal Hot Springs soon invigorated us. Hungry, we then stopped to buy take-away fish and chips, eating them out of newspaper wrapping, a novelty for me then.

It was late when we neared Rotorua. The sulphur smelled much stronger than in Taupo, and pockets of steam twirled up nearly everywhere. Truus then drove us to the motor camp, and before long, we were asleep in our cabin.

"Let's visit Whakarewarewa, the old Maori village," Truus suggested the next morning. "Addy will like it."

"Oh, good!" I said, eager to see and learn Maori history and culture.

"Little boys dive for coins from a bridge at the entrance," Truus explained. "Part of the village is a thermal wonderland with a steaming geyser, boiling hot water, and mud pools."

We saw Maori women cooking their food in a *keti* (flax basket), in the boiling water outside. I especially enjoyed the old Maori village. Some parts were eerie to begin with, but as we explored, it became very exciting.

"I used to be a nurse," Truus said, on our drive back to Hastings. "I trained in Holland, and soon after Jan and I arrived in New Zealand, I nursed in Waipukurau Hospital, a town 50 kilometres south of Hastings. I loved working there. The staff were friendly. Why don't you nurse-aid there until you begin nursing in Hastings? Accommodation is provided."

What a good idea, I mused. *I want to learn as much as possible before I start training.* That's how, in the end, I began nurse-aiding at Waipukurau Hospital. In November, 1959, aiding started well enough, but I struggled to make myself understood, and to understand the local New Zealand dialect. It wasn't the BBC variety of English I'd learned at school in Holland! After a month of trying, the struggle wore me down, especially as Christmas approached.

Carols echoed around the corridors as the nurses and I walked around the wards in slow procession, singing traditional Christmas carols and hymns.

"Silent night, holy night, all is calm, all is bright," we sang, holding our music sheets and candles, and wearing crisp white uniforms, little white caps, and red capes.

Nursing staff had decked the hospital corridors and wards with colourful streamers and tinsel. There were huge Christmas trees—real pine trees—with shiny baubles and twinkling lights, in the foyer, and in each ward.

It was Christmas Eve, December, 1959, and I had only been in New Zealand a month. Just 17, I was working temporarily as a nurse-aid in Waipukurau until I would be old enough to start training in Hastings. I was so keen to begin my life-long vocation, but had to wait until I was 17½ to begin. However, as the communication struggle wore me down, I succumbed to homesickness and grief. I missed

Penny and Mother on my birthday in November and Saint Nicholas celebrations on 5 December, a fun night in Holland, celebrated with poems, sweet treats, and small gifts. Juliana and Rob didn't celebrate it in New Zealand.

Many of the patients in the children's ward where I worked, had gone home for Christmas. Those too sick to leave had to stay in hospital for specialised medical care.

To lift the morale of these remaining children, the nursing staff had adorned the ward with colourful decorations, and they played Christmas carols through an intercom system so that everyone could hear. Despite this, the little ones still cried out:

"Mummy!" and "I want to go home!"

Yes! I want to go home, and I want my mother too, I thought, as I tried to soothe the little ones' plaintive sobs, only making myself sadder.

"You're homesick," Matron Shaw later observed.

But it wasn't as simple as that. Carol singing had brought back the painful memories of my family's last Christmas together; Mother's illness and her sudden death flashed before my mind's eye with an overwhelming sense of loss. With her death, my familiar world ended so abruptly, that I grieved for some time, unable to cope with life. But I hadn't told anyone. Now it happened again.

After Mother's death, my sister, Penny, and I stayed with our new guardian and his wife. They were kind, but I missed Mother and our previous guardian, Uncle Jo, who had died in September that same year. I think I was depressed: I ate much more than usual, and isolated myself, crying under the bedcovers at night. I kept thinking of the night of Mother's death, wondering whether I could have done anything to stop her dying. Perhaps I shouldn't have asked God to take her, to release her from her suffering, and miserable life on earth...

Matron sent me to Juliana and Rob's to recuperate, and to enjoy their company during Christmas and New Year.

"Let me know how you get on," she said. I did as I was told, and temporarily returned to Juliana and Rob's home in Hastings. They decided we'd all speak English to help me learn the language faster. But I struck another problem. Although I'd never said so, Juliana must have thought I wished to return to Holland.

"How do you like New Zealand?" her friends asked me.

"Addy is homesick," Juliana answered for me, in a disapproving tone of voice. The longer this went on, the worse I felt.

Jennifer helped me forget my troubles while we played games on the lawn. Rob was compassionate, but worked all day. Then I received a nasty letter from my guardian in Holland, telling me there was no money for a return trip to Holland, and that I shouldn't be such a coward.

Well, I thought. *The cheek! I have no intention of going back to Holland! Who does he think he is to write like this? I'll show him what I'm made of!*

The more time I had to think, the more I wanted to return to Waipukurau Hospital. So, I began writing a letter to the Matron without telling Juliana. I wanted to do this on my own. I used my Dutch/English dictionary to search for the right words and finally sent my letter to the matron, Miss Shaw, at Waipukurau Hospital.

I told her that I had liked working at her hospital, and wanted to return, but I really wished to start nurse-training. Then I prayed.

"Please help me, God. May the Matron understand what I wrote."

Life went on, and I almost forgot about the letter. Suddenly, one of Juliana and Rob's neighbours at the back of the house, called out to Juliana over the fence:

"The matron of Waipukurau Hospital wants to speak with Addy!" she called.

I was excited but also afraid.

What might she want? I thought.

"I wrote to the matron!" I called to Juliana, as I ran past her and hurdled the fence, suddenly remembering that I hadn't told her.

"We have a new class starting nurse-training at the end of January," Matron Shaw said, "Would you like to join it?"

"Yeees!" I almost shouted. "I'd love to!"

Thus, in January 1960, I started nurse-training classes at Waipukurau. The matron moved me to the women's ward, where the patients were kind, listening carefully to everything I said, and teaching me new words, even Maori words. The change from nurse-aiding to nursing studies diverted my thoughts and drove my sadness away. I changed my original plan of training at Hastings Memorial Hospital to training at Waipukurau Hospital, because everyone there treated me like family. With their support, I started the new life I so longed for.

Making friends with my eight nursing classmates, many from different nationalities, made me feel less isolated. Ruth Peni from Samoa, Lucy Wong, and Dutch-born Nellie Strooper, became close friends. Nellie grew homesick, and went back to Holland after a year's training, but the rest of us continued. Our kind Scottish tutor sister, Zane Slater, (Truus's friend) also helped us settle in. I understood her better than New Zealanders because she pronounced her words clearly and audibly.

"Read as much as possible," she urged, and so I pored over my text books intently, and committed them to memory. Sister Slater even allowed me to use my Dutch/English dictionary during tests and exams, and said:

"Draw pictures if you're lost for words." I did, and we all passed our exams!

I especially liked working with two Scottish senior nurses, Lena Sutherland, and Renee Taylor. As well as being fun loving, they always pronounced their words clearly, so I could understand them, as I did Sister Slater.

Maori nurses were good to work with too, very patient, taking me under their wing, and always ready to explain what I needed to know, often by *showing* me how to do the work. Gill Grant, a student nurse, was also kind. She was especially patient when my English was far from perfect, and I was afraid to answer the telephone in case I didn't understand important instructions. Some nurses took me to their homes to meet their parents, see the surrounding countryside, and experience their culture and family life.

Now that I had new friends, who understood how I felt, the grief over Mother's death lessened. Nurses even had a hockey and basketball team, the Matron alternating our duties to fit in with our games. I chose hockey, and played first for Central Hawke's Bay and then for Hawke's Bay as goalie. We travelled all over the country for games against other provinces. Consequently, I saw much of New Zealand, and made more friends.

I graduated from nursing at Waipukurau in November 1963, then did a year's staff-nursing there, continuing living at the nurses' home and playing hockey. I then sailed to England in 1964 on the *S.S. Northern Star*, stayed with friends in London, and flew to Amsterdam, where Penny met me at Schiphol Airport. She was now married to Joop Quint, and was studying geography and music at Utrecht University.

Soon after my arrival in Holland in 1964, I staff-nursed at Utrecht's Diaconessen Hospital, on the men's medical ward. I liked the relaxed method of work and the Christian content, although I was at first told I would not be able to work there unless I was Dutch Reformed or agnostic. So, my guardian, who was on the board, put me down as agnostic, and they accepted me! There was one condition: I read from the Bible to my patients at bedtime, and on Sundays chaperone them to church within the hospital complex.

Working there on Sunday was different from other hospitals. We only did what was important—no scrubbing floors that day! We even listened to records like Mahalia Jackson's and other old-time singers. Our team of nurses was like a family, and we did a lot together.

On March 4, 1965, during my time at the hospital in Utrecht, as little children walked to school in the early morning past the Plompetorengracht canal where I was boarding, I heard a loud splash, and children yelling: "Can you swim!?"

Alarmed, I ran outside and saw a boy, aged about seven, in the water on the other side of the canal. The water was filthy, and full of rubbish. A few months earlier, a carload of people had drowned near the bridge, as the car sank quickly, as though into quicksand. That happened only 20 metres from where the boy was. Not knowing that then, I took my shoes off, and, telling a friend what I was going to do, I quickly worked out a way of reaching the boy. I climbed over the railing, lowered myself carefully down the steep, brick wall, and slipped into the water on my side of the canal.

By then, a group of onlookers had gathered, and a friend instructed me to keep my head above water; and, whatever I did, never to stand up in the canal because of broken glass and other sharp rubbish.

So, I swam breaststroke to the crying boy. I grabbed him by the shoulders and swam backstroke, the way I'd been taught lifesaving by an uncle, hoping to make it to some stairs further down the canal, but my friend yelled:

"Don't go there! Come back here!"

Obediently changing direction, I then swam with the boy still in the *life-savers' hold* to the side, where my friend and the crowd stood. There was a little ledge under foot, but nothing to hold onto. The wall went straight up and I couldn't climb up anywhere. My friend now lay on the road, holding both his arms outstretched towards mine.

"Grab hold of me, and don't let go," he urged. "You're not safe yet."

Then he told me about the car accident that had taken the lives of that carload of people.

I grabbed his hand in an iron grip, while, with the other arm I held the boy, and comforted him (in English, without thinking!):

"Don't worry! We'll be out of here soon."

But getting out was harder than it looked. There was a ladder further down the street, but nobody wanted to use it. It took ages for help to arrive. When a rescue team finally did come, they lowered a rope ladder. Getting the exhausted boy up was hard, but lifting me, wet and heavier, was even harder!

Once on solid ground, the boy and I were wrapped in blankets and ushered into my apartment, for a warm shower, to wash off the filth.

Guess who barged in? The press! I was so annoyed, but they made so much noise they didn't hear my complaints. I had to take care of that later.

The boy and I were injected with antibiotics to prevent us catching typhoid from the filth in the canal, but both of us still caught influenza. The boy's mother brought my favourite cake to thank me, but I was too ill to eat it. I received a Carnegie Heldenfonds certificate from the Mayor of Utrecht about five months later.

My remaining four months in Holland was spent staff-nursing in the men's ward, but an invitation to play hockey pulled me back to New Zealand in July 1965. I loved hockey, and still played for the Hawke's Bay women's representative team.

"Please return and play hockey for us at the tournament in Stratford," wrote our captain, Margaret Hiha. "We have no goal-keeper!"

I applied for a nursing position at Royston Hospital in Hastings, on condition that I could have time off to play in the hockey tournament, and Matron Nancy Barron gave her consent. So, I returned to New Zealand in July 1965, in time to play in the 1965 K cup hockey tournament in Taranaki, in August. Having won the previous year's Mills Cup, in a lower grade in Nelson, our team moved up to K-cup level. We had a lot of fun, but didn't win.

In 1962, after our tournament in Auckland, many of our team had played in the North against South game. That was nerve wracking! A huge TV camera pointed directly at us! I think the game ended in a draw. Two months after the tournament, at Labour weekend 1965, I met Mark, a carpenter, at the Top Hat Dance Hall in Napier.

"Come to the dance with me," a nursing friend pleaded. "I have a blind date and I'm scared."

Concerned about being a *wallflower*, having no partner, I nearly refused, but for my friend's sake I agreed to come along.

Almost as soon as we arrived, a quietly spoken young man approached me.

"Hello," he said. "Would you like to dance?"

"Sure," I answered.
We danced and talked all night!
"Can I meet you at the Hastings clock tower?" Mark asked, when the dance ended. "I want to take you home, but I'm on my motor bike and I don't have a helmet for you to wear."

How sweet, I thought. *He's thinking of me!*

Mark wanted to walk me to Royston Hospital Nurses' home. Being from Ongaonga, the only familiar place in Hastings to him was the Clock Tower. I knew my way round Hastings, and we kept the arrangement. Mark parked his motorbike near the Clock Tower and waited for me there. We then walked together to the Royston nurses' home. Afterwards, Mark had to walk back to pick up his motorbike!

After an eighteen months' courtship, we bought a section in Hastings and Mark built our own home. On April 1, 1967, we were married at the Anglican Church of the Good Shepherd in Ongaonga, Hawke's Bay. All Mark's family attended, but Rob, Juliana, and their two little girls, were the only relatives on my side. Mum and Dad Coles then put on a memorable wedding banquet for us at their home in Ongaonga.

A year later, our eldest daughter, Kate, was born in April 1968, followed by Nancy, in 1969, and Shirley, in 1975. A bright and peaceful future lay before us…

I settled into the New Zealand way of life after my marriage to Mark in 1967. We now have ten grandchildren.

I enjoyed motherhood. However, with a busy family life, the past caught up with me in the late 1970s. As I walked through a difficult period of about nine months, I experienced a huge change in the way I perceived many of life's issues, both past and present.

Counselling, Mark's patience, and love, together with the knowledge that God is my Eternal Father, who loves me unconditionally, and accepts me as I am, helped me through. Returning to nursing for two years at Hastings Memorial Hospital re-instilled the confidence I thought I had lost.

My siblings and I all needed counselling at later points in our lives. Sadly, our mother never had that privilege, although she needed it most.

Today, I'm satisfied that, regardless of our hardships, God has enabled each of us to make something good out of our brokenness.

Diaconessen Hospital, men's medical ward with nurses' signatures

POST SCRIPT

Surrender, or meet utter destruction.' This was the ultimatum issued to Japan by the leaders of the Allied Forces.

Germany had finally surrendered on May 8, 1945, and from July 17 to August 2, leaders from the Soviet Union, Great Britain, the United States of America, and China, met in Potsdam, Germany, to decide on Germany's accountability for war crimes.

The Allied leaders also issued the *Potsdam Declaration,* outlining terms of *surrender* for Japan, who was then still engaged in war in South East Asia against the Western Allies.

Japan refused to accept the declaration and continued fighting, torturing, and abusing prisoners of war, and plotting more attacks on unsuspecting Western countries.

To halt Japan's relentless violence in South East Asia, America issued them with an ultimatum:

"Surrender or suffer the consequences."

Japan ignored the ultimatum.

America then dropped the first atomic bomb *(Little Boy)* on Hiroshima, on August 6, 1945.

Japan still refused to surrender, and so America dropped a second bomb, *(Fat Man)* three days later, on August 9, 1945, on Nagasaki.

Finally, Japan surrendered, on August 15, when Emperor Hirohito himself stepped in and forced Japanese leaders to surrender.

Tragically, most prisoners of war remained incarcerated for another one to two weeks <u>after</u> Japanese surrender. My father, Andrew, died on February 5, 1945, five months before liberation in August 1945. My younger brother, Dido, died from starvation and pneumonia on board ship to Holland. I've often wondered whether Father and Dido would have survived had they received medical treatment sooner.

The Japanese continued their use and abuse of prisoners as sex slaves, field workers, and hard labourers—on a starvation diet, and without medical attention!

Sometimes I reflect on this difficult period in my family's past.

Although too young to remember many details of the prison camps, I grew up observing the after-effects on my mother and siblings.

Mother, especially, spent years struggling with the events which began with the bombing of Pearl Harbour in 1941, and continued during the 1942 to 1945 Japanese occupation of Java.

Prone to severe asthma attacks, she contracted bronchitis, pneumonia, and emphysema in POW camps, which increased in severity without treatment. She had to endure the suffering of her five children—including three pre-schoolers, one disabled son—in POW camps. By age 42, she'd lost her beloved husband, her son, and her father, and had eventually become bedridden in Holland. Mother died of a heart attack exacerbated by post-traumatic stress and physical illness.

What had been a tropical paradise, with secure employment and a serene life, turned into a nightmarish, three-year ordeal in POW camps. Those of us who survived have all been affected to varying degrees, both psychologically and physically.

Juliana endured numerous heartaches through suffering many miscarriages. John, on top of the psychological pain he endures, still suffers from severe spinal and circulatory problems. For Penny and me, our overall health was affected by severe malnutrition in our formative years: we have suffered anguish and turmoil. Today, Penny has osteopenia. I have osteoporosis, spinal problems, and a digestive disorder. We suffered additional turmoil through our mother's post-traumatic stress disorder, and frequent outbursts while she was bedridden, and struggling to breathe.

While it's easy to reflect on the negatives, I've come to understand that a greater truth lies behind the horrors and hardships we endured. This truth is that life on earth is not all there is. The Bible promises a secure, eternal future for all who believe. It promises that nothing can separate us from God's love, and that our sins are forgiven when we come to Him who sits on the Throne of Heaven, and to His son, Jesus Christ, who took the punishment for our mistakes; and promises never to leave or forsake us. He has a far greater future for mankind, a future without pride, hate, war, and strife.

It seems hard to do, but for our own good and with God's help, we can rid ourselves of hate and forgive those who treated us badly.

TRANSLATION OF FOREIGN WORDS

Adih	sister
Arang	charcoal fire
Autoped	children's scooter
Babu	Indonesian female servant
Bahasa	Indonesian
Bakfiets	carrier tricycle
Besaran	boss's quarters
Balebale	bamboo slab
Babu anak	nanny
Blachan	a stable
Brandenburg	the cleanest, smaller, swimming pool in Bilthoven in the 1950s
Cineac	movie theatre playing News of the World and Walt Disney cartoons
Chanterellen	wild, edible mushrooms
Djalang Pandjang	long road

Djongos .... Indonesian male servant
Dokar .... horse-drawn cart
Gajung .... special pot used for mandi showering
Gedek .... woven bamboo fence
Gracht .... canal
Gudang .... pantry
Hansop .... bloomer shorts
HBS .... Public High School
Heiho .... Indonesian soldier
Kaasboer(tje) .... grocer
Kali .... river
Kampong .... Indonesian village
Kempetai .... Japanese military police
Kempetai-cho .... head of Japanese military police
Kepiting .... shrimp
Ketan .... sticky coconut rice
Kite .... Maori basket
KNIL .... Royal Netherlands Indonesian Army
Koninginnedag .... Queen's birthday
Kokki .... Indonesian cook
Kusir .... Indonesian coach driver

Mandi	Indonesian shower
Melkboer	milkman
Mevrouw	Mrs
Natuurbad	a park-like swimming pool in the 1950s, with a restaurant and rental canoes
NBM	Nederlandse Bus Maatschappij (Netherland's Bus Company)
NEFIS	Dutch East Indies Forces Intelligence Service
Overbruggings HBS	Bridging High School, to enable POW children to catch up on lost education
Passar	Indonesian market
Pension	boarding house
Polder	low-lying land reclaimed from the sea or river
Rampokkers	troublemakers
Rakoes	greedy
Sajoor	Indonesian soup
Sake	rice wine
Sinterklaas	St. Nicholas celebration on 5 December

Straat	street
Sukerelas	Indonesian volunteer
Tandu	sedan
Tenko	Japanese bowing parade
Tongtong	bush telephone
Tuan	Mister
Wedono	village head/mayor

www.ingramcontent.com/pod-product-compliance
Lightning Source LLC
Chambersburg PA
CBHW051351290426
44108CB00015B/1969